Super Realism!

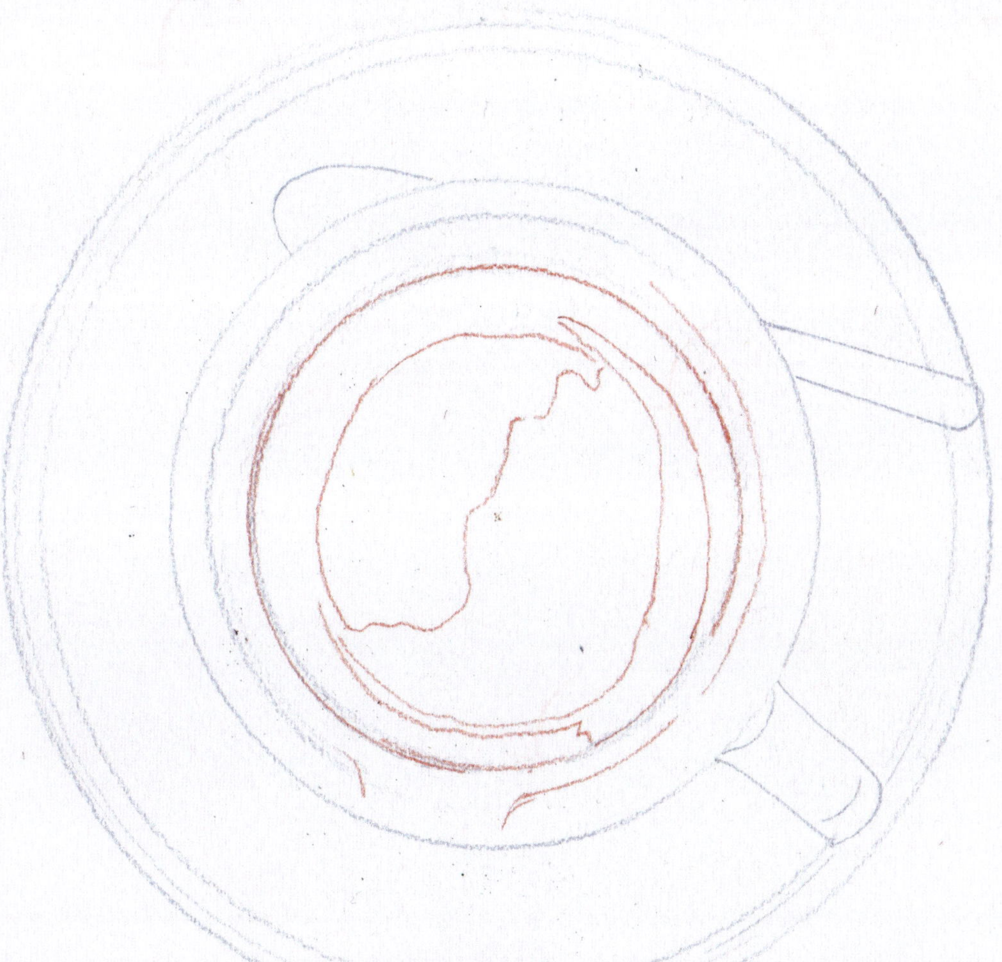

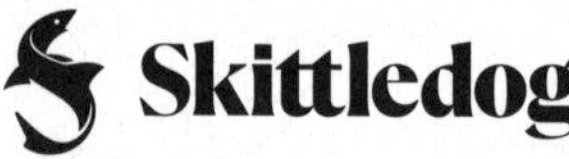

First published in the United Kingdom in 2024
by Skittledog, an imprint of Thames & Hudson Ltd,
181A High Holborn, London WC1V 7QX

Concept and layout © Thames & Hudson 2024
Text and illustrations © Sarah Evans 2024

Image of torn paper, p.8 swavo/Shutterstock

Project editor: Gaynor Sermon
Design: Louise Evans
Production: Felicity Awdry

British Library Cataloguing-in-Publication Data
A catalogue record for this book is available from
the British Library

ISBN 978-1-83776-046-6

Printed and bound in China by C&C Offset Printing Co., Ltd

Be the first to know about our new releases,
exclusive content and author events by visiting
skittledog.com
thamesandhudson.com
thamesandhudsonusa.com
thamesandhudson.com.au

Super Realism!

How to draw amazingly lifelike objects with colored pencils

Sarah Evans

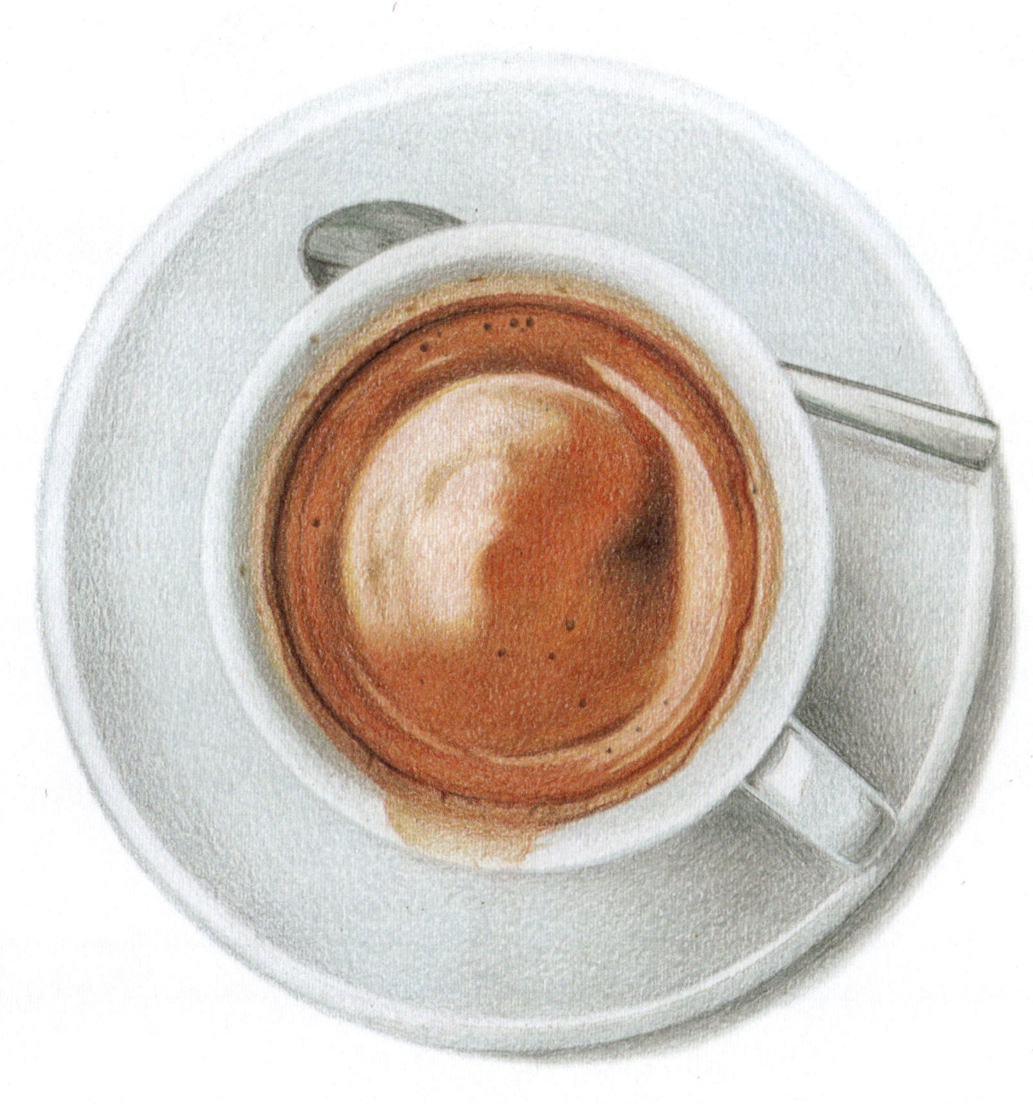

Contents

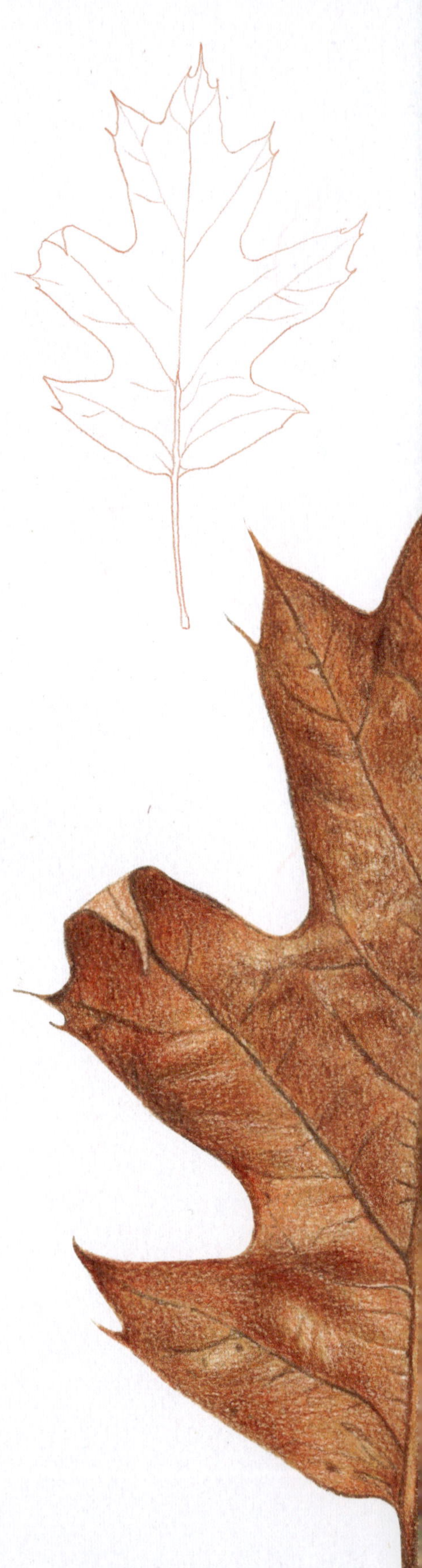

Introduction

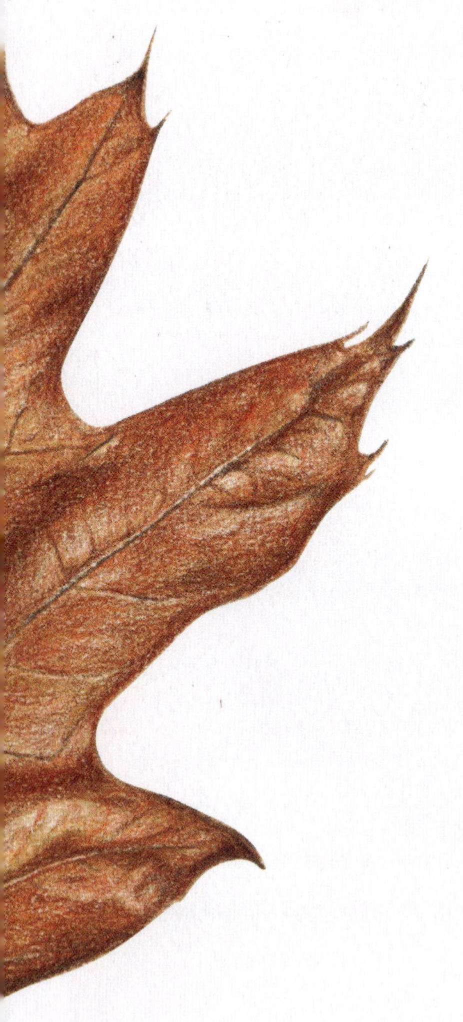

My love of drawing began as a child and developed into a passion in my teenage years when I became interested in still life drawing. During this time I was intently focused on pencil drawing and dedicated most of my free time to it. I would stage scenes with jars, condiments, and fruit in an attempt to emulate the Dutch realist paintings that inspired me. I pored over art books, filled sketch books, and spent hours developing my pencil skills.

Practice is, without a doubt, the single most important thing. To master any skill you must commit to it consistently and with courage. Failing is a necessary part of your progress.

The subjects in this book have been chosen, for the most part, because I enjoy drawing food and ordinary objects. But the practical reason is that these items can usually be found in the average kitchen or garden, so are easily accessible. They were also selected to showcase a variety of textures, shapes, and color progressions. They are broken down layer by layer in order to demonstrate the rendering process.

Before you get started on the projects, you will find a quick guide to some of the most common colored pencil techniques used to create different effects. These are not hard and fast rules, but are among the many possibilities that colored pencil drawing offers. I hope you will use this book as a source of information and inspiration, to be picked up and put down until its pages are worn.

> "As practice makes perfect, I cannot but make progress; each drawing one makes, each study one paints, is a step forward."
>
> VINCENT VAN GOGH (1927)

Tools & Materials

There are no hard and fast rules when it comes to pencil art, but be aware of the properties of different materials and how they interact. For example, you can mix and match pencil types, but if you try to use oil pencil on top of thick layers of wax pencil you will struggle to make it stick, so build up layers slowly. And if you intend to use water-soluble pencils with oil- or wax-based ones, bear in mind that the latter types will not disperse in water in the same way and you'll need to use thicker watercolor paper to absorb the liquid.

Colored pencils

There are lots of different brands available and they can vary wildly in price. Pricier pencils contain a higher pigment content (the natural or synthetic powder that provides the color), so will give a richer result than the more washed-out color you are likely to get with cheaper ones. Cheaper colored pencils have a higher filler content in their core, such as kaolin, talc, or chalk, and less pigment.

Cheap and expensive pencils are usually marketed as Student and Professional Artist respectively. Most established colored pencil brands cater to both ends of this spectrum, and will also have ranges that span the gap in between in order to increase their offer to different budgets. This means that the higher-end Student ranges can be a close comparison to the lower-end Professional Artist ranges, explaining why you will find two same-sized tins of pencils by the same brand with different price tags. Since beginning to sell my work, I have always used Professional ranges in order to create archival-quality artworks that will last a long time.

It is common to use different brands together on the same piece of art, purely because of color choice, as different pencil brands will have variations in their color spectrum.

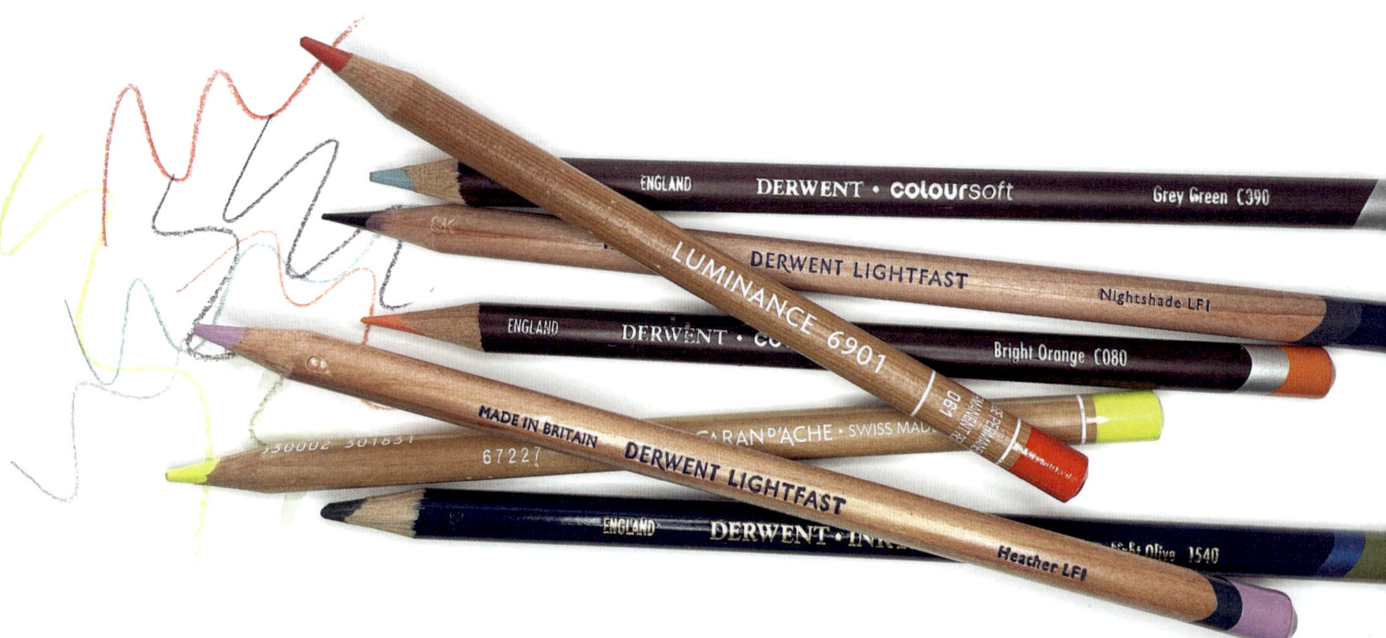

Lightfastness

This is an additional consideration when choosing colored pencils, and is a measure of a pigment's ability to resist fading: a lightfast pigment does not fade over time. Colored pencils that are 100 percent lightfast promise that the core is resistant to color change, ensuring artwork will not fade for up to 100 years under museum conditions. Lightfast pencils generally sit firmly within the Professional Artist ranges. It is also worth noting that certain colors fade more than others, such as pinks and purples. Established brands provide charts that indicate the color fastness of their range.

Oil-based pencils

These are more specialized so can be a little harder to find than wax-based pencils. They are usually made with vegetable oil as a binding agent, and the core is harder than wax-based pencils so they hold a sharp point with less breakage. This is why they are often the go-to for fine detail drawing. They can be easily layered multiple times, but rarely achieve the ultra-smooth finish that layering wax-based pencils can.

Wax-based pencils

These are very popular, with more choice available, and are easier to blend, mix, and erase. Layering and blending with wax-based pencils can produce amazing results, though "wax bloom" is a recognized disadvantage. This occurs when the wax in the core rises to the top of the layers and forms a white haze over artwork. The softer the pencil and the heavier the pressure applied, the more likely wax bloom becomes. You can reduce the risk by using less pressure or using a mix of oil- and wax-based pencils when layering colors.

Water-soluble pencils

On first inspection, these look the same as standard pencils, but there should be a symbol of a water droplet or paint brush stamped on the side to indicate that it is water soluble. These pencils are a hybrid, combining the ability to both draw and paint. You can easily sketch with them, and once you have drawn your artwork you can use a wet brush to create a watercolor wash. These pencils are manufactured with a binder that dissolves in water, allowing the color to disperse quickly.

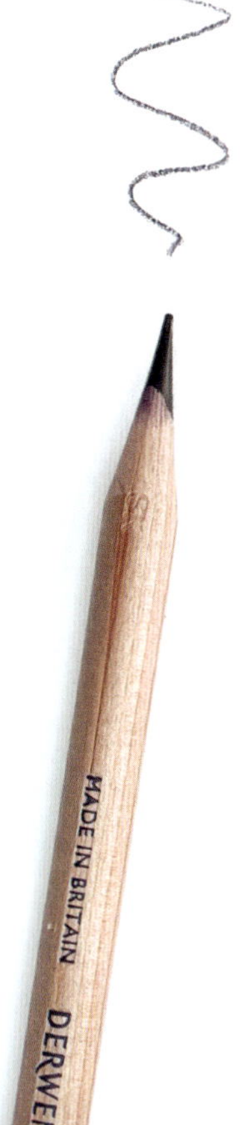

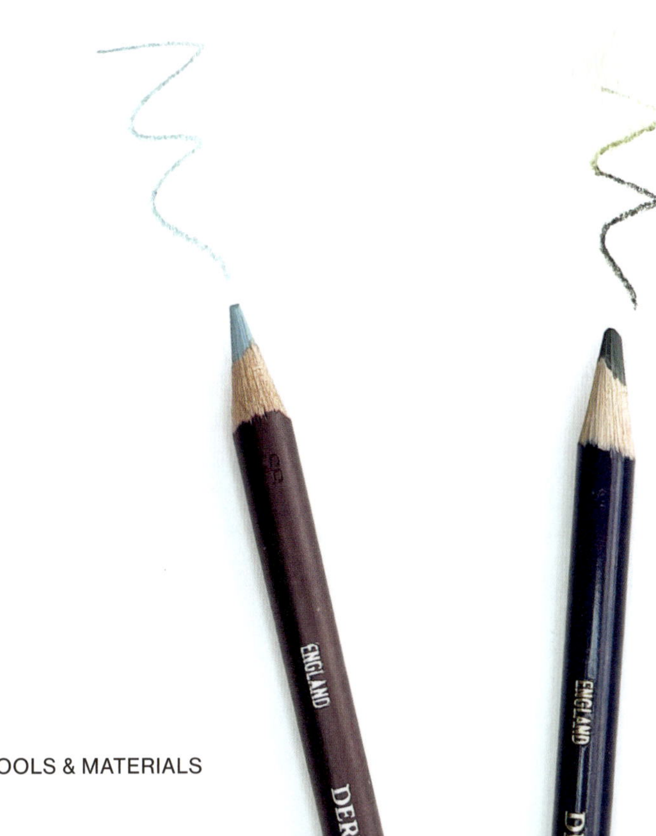

Papers

Artists draw on all types of surfaces – it doesn't *have* to be paper! But paper is the go-to substrate, so here you'll find some of the most popular papers for colored pencil drawing. I recommend visiting an art shop rather than buying online, so you can feel the texture and weight of the paper. When working on the projects in this book I used Daler Rowney Fine Grain Heavyweight 200gsm cartridge paper; this has a smooth surface with a very slight grain and takes detail well, and the thickness ensures that smaller works feel comfortably robust and rigid.

Cartridge paper

This is most commonly used for drawing. It is usually made from wood-free cellulose, and derives its name from its early use in making paper cartridges that held gunpowder and bullets together for loading into firearms. It is available in a variety of weights and shades of white. Decent quality cartridge paper will have a fine texture, often called the "grain" or "tooth." I prefer to use a heavier weight of cartridge paper: for small artworks I choose 200gsm and for larger artworks 300gsm. Thicker paper is less likely to buckle with humidity or the moisture from a hot hand.

Bristol board paper

This comes in a variety of thicknesses, from two- to four-ply: two-ply is a similar weight to card stock, while three-ply and four-ply are more rigid. Bristol board paper is available in two main textures: smooth and vellum. Bristol smooth is best for pencil work, pen drawings, and detailed artwork as the smooth surface takes fine lines very well. If you want an ultra-smooth finish then Bristol plate paper is for you, and is suggested for fine detailed pencil work or technical drawing. Vellum has a more textured finish and is recommended for pastels, charcoal, and graphite. Less detailed pencil drawings also look great on vellum. Semi-smooth Bristol paper is also available, giving a little less texture.

Paper sizes

North American sketchpads and drawing paper generally come in standard US Architectural paper sizes, rather than letter, legal, and tabloid sizes: while there's nothing to stop you from using those, the Arch sizes offer a better aspect ratio for drawing. They also relate more closely to the standard European paper sizes: Arch E is similar in size to A0, D to A1, C to A2, B to A3, and A to A4.

Popular European brands are also readily available, and pads and paper come in standard ISO sizes. There are 11 sizes in the A series, designated A0–A10, but it's rare to use anything smaller than A5 for art. Since A series sizes share the same aspect ratio, they can be scaled to other A series sizes without being distorted, and two sheets can be reduced to fit on exactly one sheets, so the scaling process is very simple. I tend to work on A4, A3, and A2 cartridge paper when drawing.

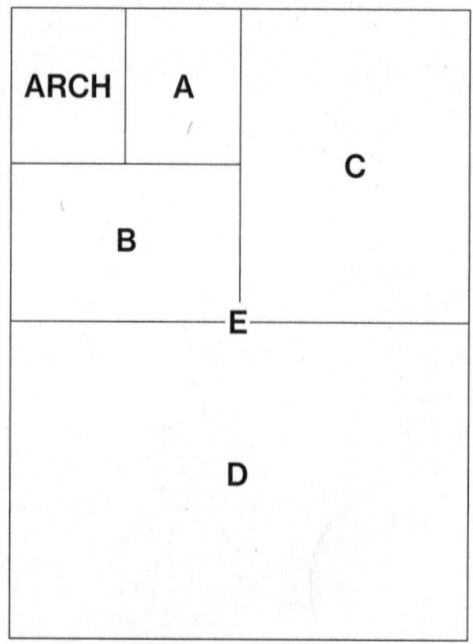

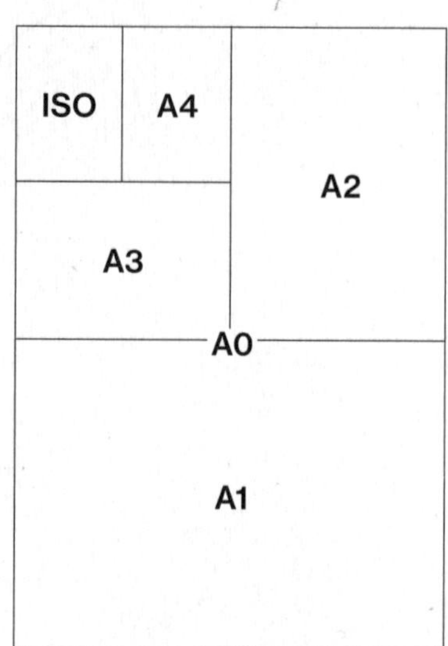

US ARCH
A = 9 x 12 in (229 x 305 mm)
B = 12 x 18 in (305 x 457 mm)
C = 18 x 24 in (457 x 610 mm)
D = 24 x 36 in (610 x 914 mm)
E = 36 x 48 in (914 x 1219 mm)

EU ISO
A4 = 8.3 x 11.7 in (210 x 297 mm)
A3 = 11.7 x 16.5 in (97 x 420 mm)
A2 = 16.5 x 23.4 in (420 x 594 mm)
A1 = 23.4 x 33 in (594 x 841 mm)
A0 = 33.1 x 46.8 in (841 x 1189 mm)

Toned (colored) paper

This is paper that has a value other than white. It is commonly available in earthy tones such as brown, tan, gray, eggshell, and black. Most paper brands will offer a variety of colors. This paper is great for drawing highlights and shadows due to its established mid-tone.

Watercolor paper

This is often used when drawing with water-soluble pencils or using solvents to blend, as the thicker and more absorbent paper can take on liquid without warping. It is available in three textures: hot-pressed, NOT (or cold-pressed), and rough. Hot-pressed is the least textured surface and works well with fine detail. NOT or cold-pressed are essentially the same thing and have a slight texture, making it more absorbent than hot-pressed paper. Rough is exactly how it sounds, the most textured of the three, and is not recommended for fine detail work.

Almost all watercolor papers are made of cotton, acid-free wood pulp, linen, or a mix. Linen and cotton papers are more robust, while acid-free wood pulp papers are less forgiving of rough treatment. The higher the cotton content, the more expensive the paper.

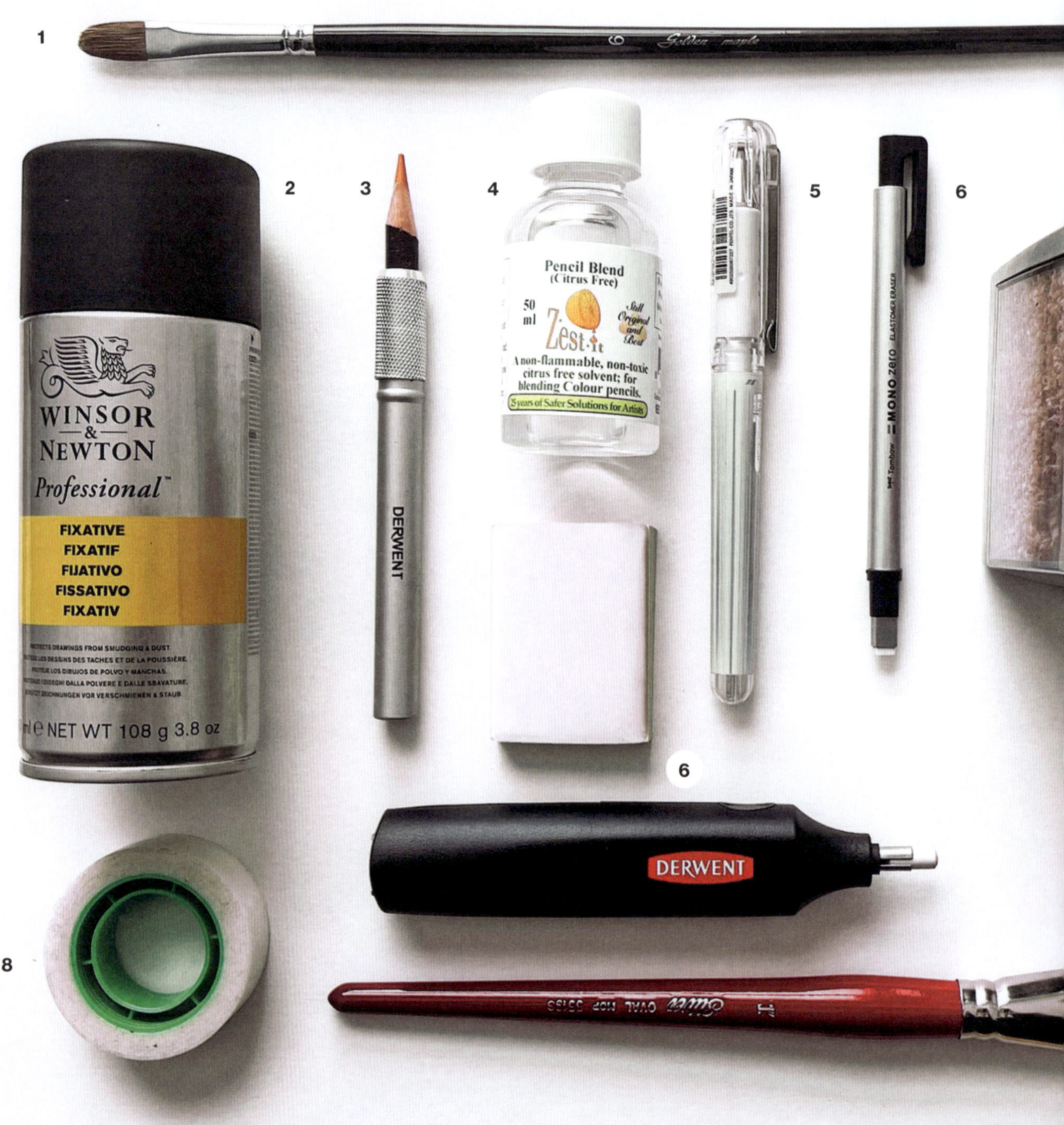

WINSOR
&
NEWTON
Professional™
FIXATIVE
FIXATIF
FIJATIVO
FISSATIVO
FIXATIV
NET WT 108 g 3.8 oz
DERWENT
Pencil Blend
(Citrus Free)
50 ml
Zest-it
A non-flammable, non-toxic citrus free solvent; for blending Colour pencils.
MONO zero
DERWENT

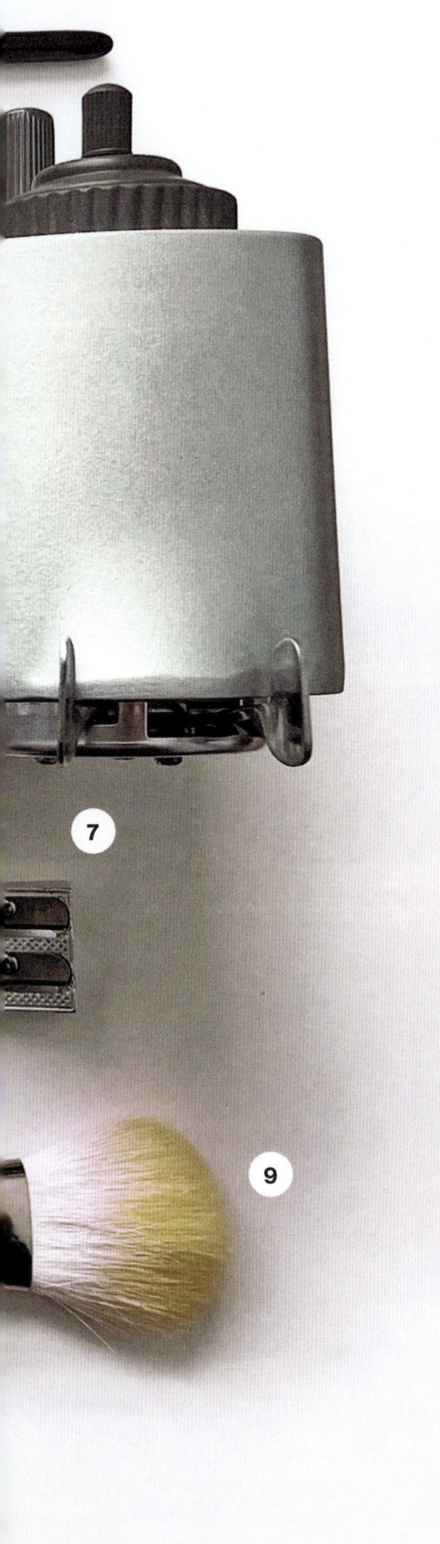

1 **Paint brushes** are often used for the application of solvents to blend colors. Sturdy brushes can also be used for "dry blending," which is exactly as it sounds, using the brush without water or liquid solvent to move and blend the color. This is more effective with soft, wax-based pencils.

2 **Fixative** does exactly that, it "fixes" your artwork. If you have used wax-based pencils, fixing your work will keep the wax binder in place and prevent "wax bloom" from occurring. It also provides added protection against damage or deterioration. You can buy fixative specifically for colored pencil artwork.

3 **Pencil extenders** prolong the life of your pencils. When your pencil is too short to hold but there is still plenty left to use, you can use a pencil extender. They are made in different diameters to fit different-sized pencils. Over the course of a few years of drawing regularly with expensive pencils, this simple little tool will save you money.

4 **Solvents** are often used by pencil artists to help with color blending. Rubbing alcohol, odorless mineral spirits, and turpentine are some of the solvents used for this purpose. Work with solvents in a well-ventilated area and dispose of them in a safe manner.

5 **White gel pens** are used to highlight artwork and create light spots, and work on top of all colored pencils and other media. If you don't want to erase work to create a highlight, then white gel pens are a useful tool. The thin nib makes it easy to create precise shapes and very small light points quickly and without mess. These pens are not archival quality, so if you are selling your work I wouldn't advise using them.

6 **Rubber erasers** come in many shapes and sizes. Plastic erasers are similar, but rubber are slightly firmer and the most effective at removing pencil. Both of these are commonly sold in a block shape. I like to use a mechanical eraser pen for fine points, as it allows me to pinpoint the tiniest marks and remove them without affecting the surrounding artwork. The electric Derwent eraser shown opposite has replaceable tips that allow for precision without applying too much pressure, so less chance of damaging your artwork.

7 **Pencil sharpeners** are essential tools for pencil artists and a good quality sharpener can make all the difference. When shopping for a new one, you should consider whether you want to go electric or manual, and what type of blade you prefer. You also need to take into account the diameter of the colored pencils you use, and the brittleness of their leads.

8 **Magic Tape** (a low-tack "invisible" tape with a matt finish) is a really useful tool. When I am working on a new artwork I like to fix it to my drawing board so that it doesn't move around. Magic Tape allows you to do this without damaging your paper. It can be peeled off and replaced several times and, although you need to take care doing this to avoid unwanted damage, it is pretty reliable.

9 **Soft brushes** are probably the least commonly known tool, but many pencil artists use a large soft brush to clean specks of dirt, pencil lead, or eraser crumbs off their artwork. This avoids using your hands, which risks leaving unwanted marks and smudges.

Subjects & Set-up

When drawing your subject you can either draw from real life or from a reference image. If you decide to draw from real life, find an area with good light where you won't be easily disturbed while you work; if you are drawing over the course of more than a day aim to work at the same time each day to try and get consistent light levels.

Working from a reference

A reference image is a photograph of your chosen subject. I like to stage my own subjects and photograph them to create my own reference images. I prepare the food that I draw, such as fried egg on toast, because I can create the exact image I want by controlling the light, shadows, and composition.

Once I have completed the initial line art, I either work from the image on my computer or I download it onto a tablet. The backlit screen gives me a super-clear image, and I can enlarge areas to see small or complicated sections more easily. My artwork often takes more than one day to complete, so I find it convenient to draw from a reference so I don't have to worry about consistent lighting, or the subject decaying!

I variously use all three of the methods described here to lay down basic linework – I don't use any one method consistently as it depends on the size and complexity of the image as well as the time I have to complete it. You can of course draw your guidelines freehand if you prefer.

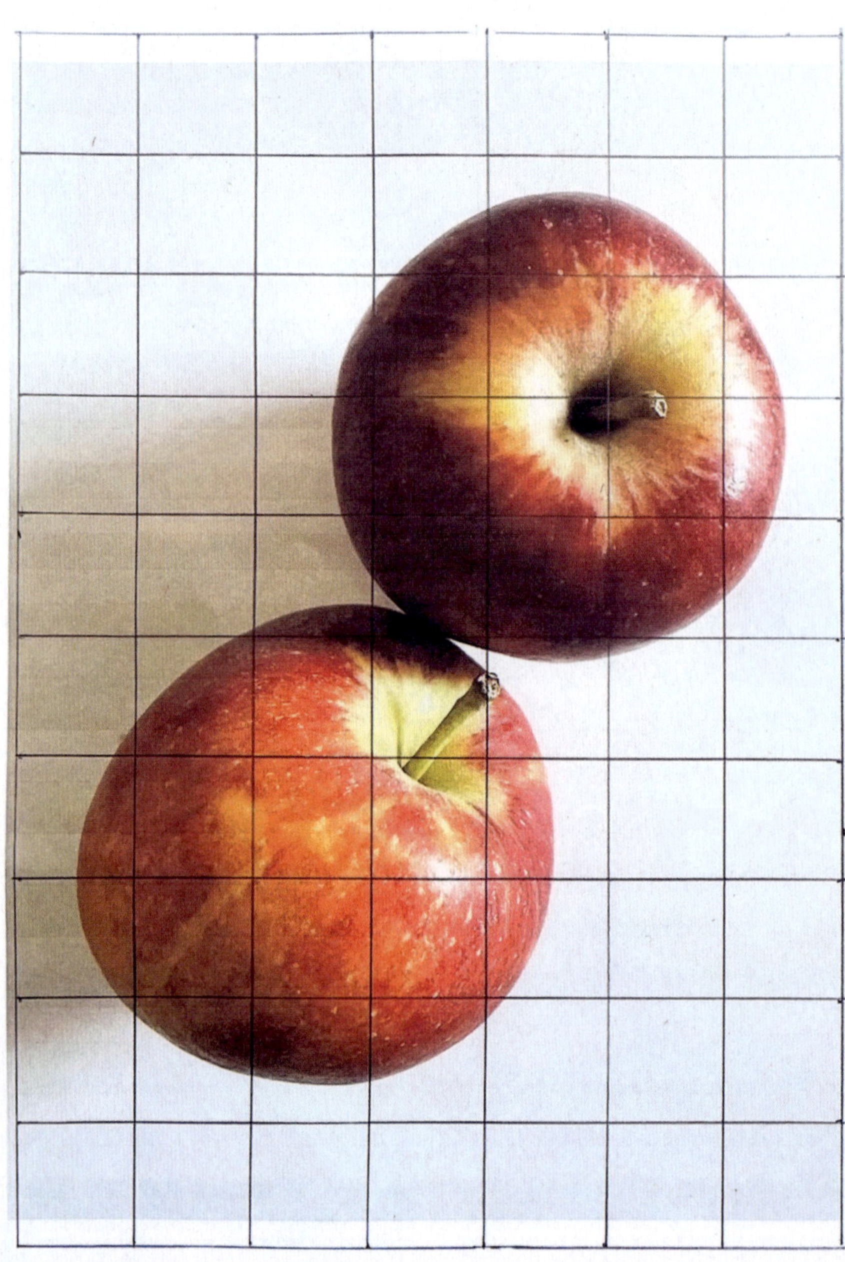

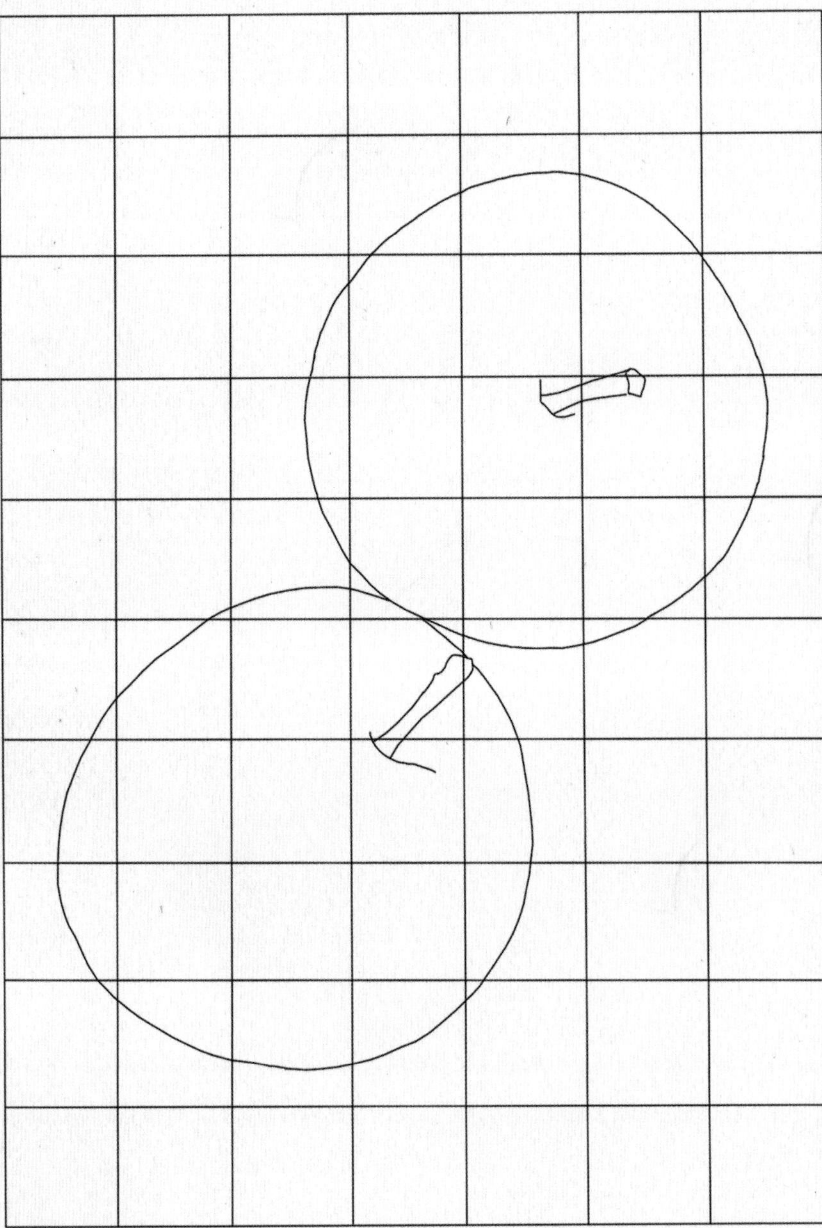

Guidelines

Using a grid
Divide your reference image into a grid of squares and divide your drawing paper into the same grid, with the same number of squares on each. Once you have done this you can sketch your line art in small segments using the reference image squares as your guide.

Transfer
This is something you may have done as a child. Transfer your guidelines by printing the image horizontally back to front, then take a piece of tracing paper and trace over the image once using a soft graphite pencil. Place the tracing paper face down on top of your drawing paper so that the pencil lines are facing down, hold it in place using Magic Tape, and redraw carefully over the lines.

Light box
This is a quick way to lay down guidelines. A light box is essentially a backlit screen where you can adjust the brightness. Place your reference image on top of the light box and fix it in place with Magic Tape. Place your drawing paper on top, fix it in the same way, and sketch out your guidelines. If your drawing paper is very thick you will struggle to see all of the detail, so thinner paper is best. You can buy light boxes in a range of sizes.

Drawing Techniques

There are dozens of techniques for artists drawing with colored pencil, and you can disappear for days researching them and the many views on how to apply each of these curiously named methods: frottage, stippling, scumbling, and burnishing, to name just a few. Here we won't overcomplicate things but will stick to explaining the core techniques used in the projects in this book, and you can explore other ways to experiment as well as develop your own unique methods when you're ready.

Underpainting

Underpainting is the process of laying down a starter layer of color or colors. Complementary colors (those that are opposite each other on the color wheel) are often used when underpainting to enhance the subsequent layers of color.

Here, two base colors that will be featured in the finished image are used.

Yellow and green form the background for the deep reds and burnt oranges that will give these Braeburn apples their characteristic look. Use light pressure when applying these initial colors so that you can build the layers on top. Begin to shade areas by applying a bit more pressure, as a guide for the shadow and light zones on the surface of the apples.

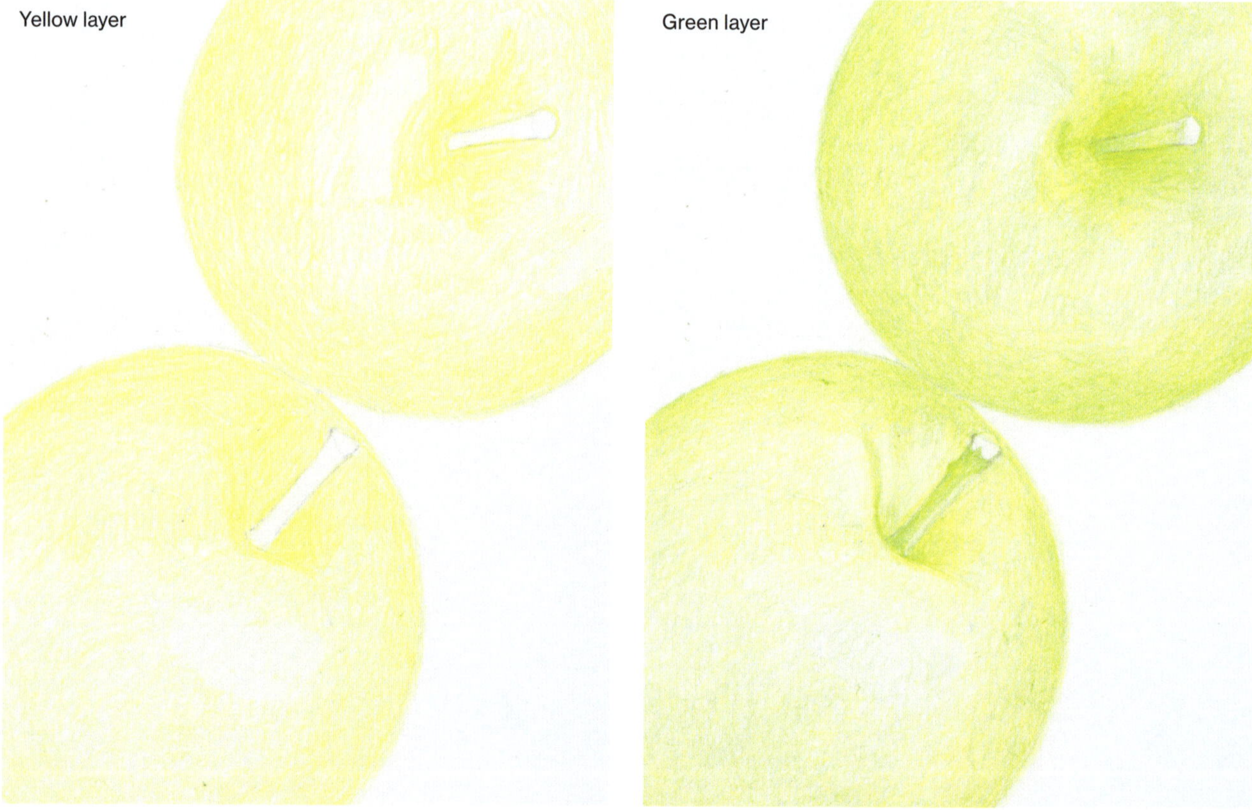

Pressure blending & shading

Pressure blending and shading are simple techniques where more pressure is applied while coloring to create darker tones, and less pressure to produce lighter areas. This is useful for blending different colors into one another and for creating gradients of light to dark within the same hue.

Use terracotta and rusty red tones to lay down and shade in the base for the darker red areas. Keep these light and use them to mark out the edges of the green areas around the stalks. Continue to shade around the darker zones by adding more pressure. Use darker green and dark blue to shade around and pick out the apple stalk.

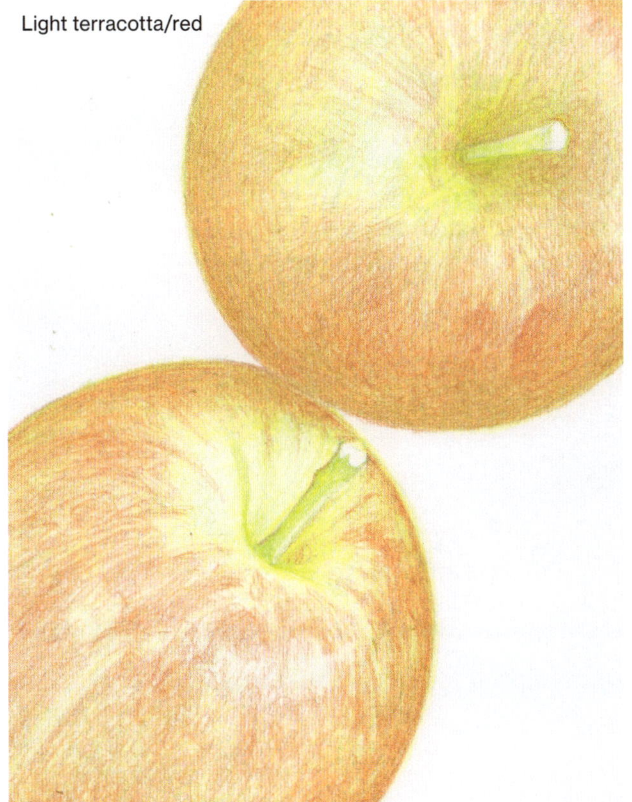

Light terracotta/red

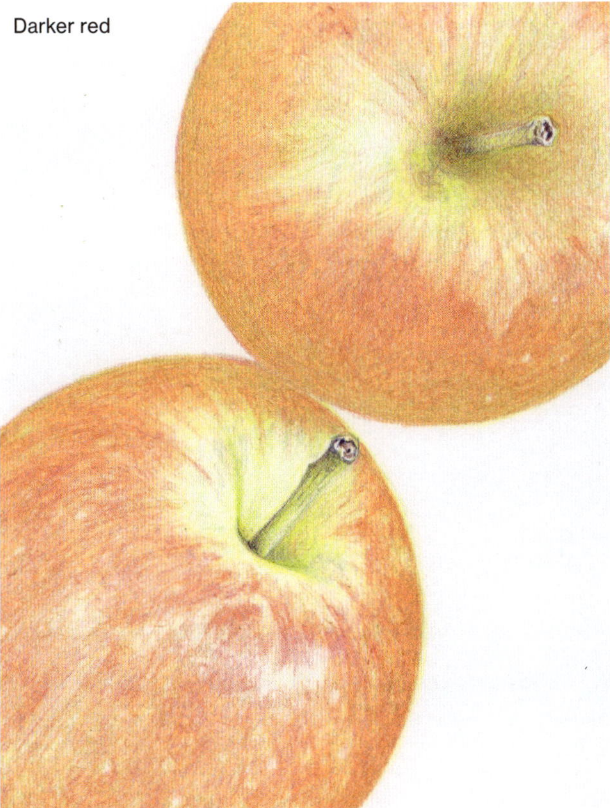

Darker red

Burnishing

This technique is concerned with layering the color with pressure, pushing the color into the grain of the paper until a sheen is created and you cannot see any paper texture underneath. This is used on the final layers of your drawing, and once completed it will be almost impossible to add more color. Here I have used deep reds, berry reds, dark purples, and a dark blue to complete the final layers of the apple's skin. Now I can work on adding the areas of shadow.

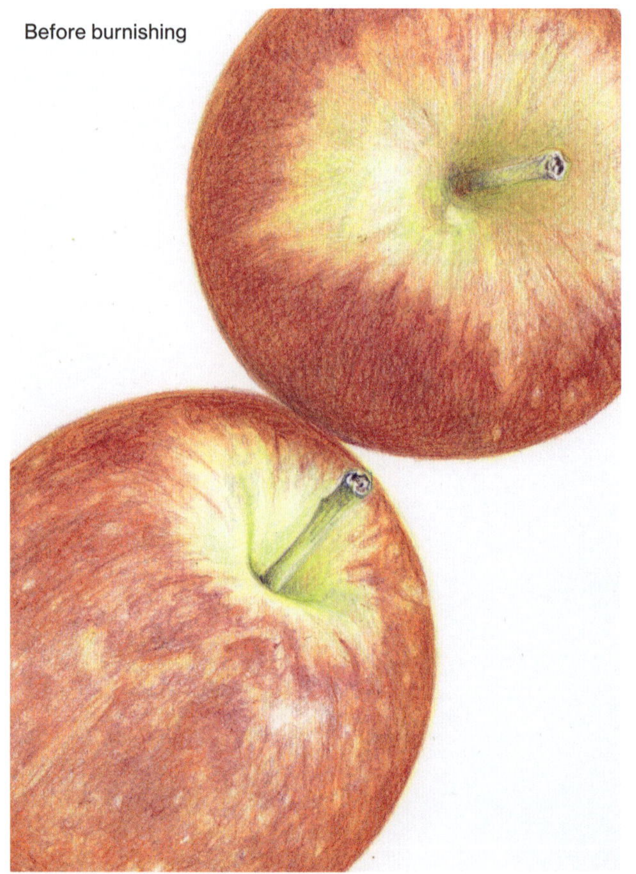

Before burnishing

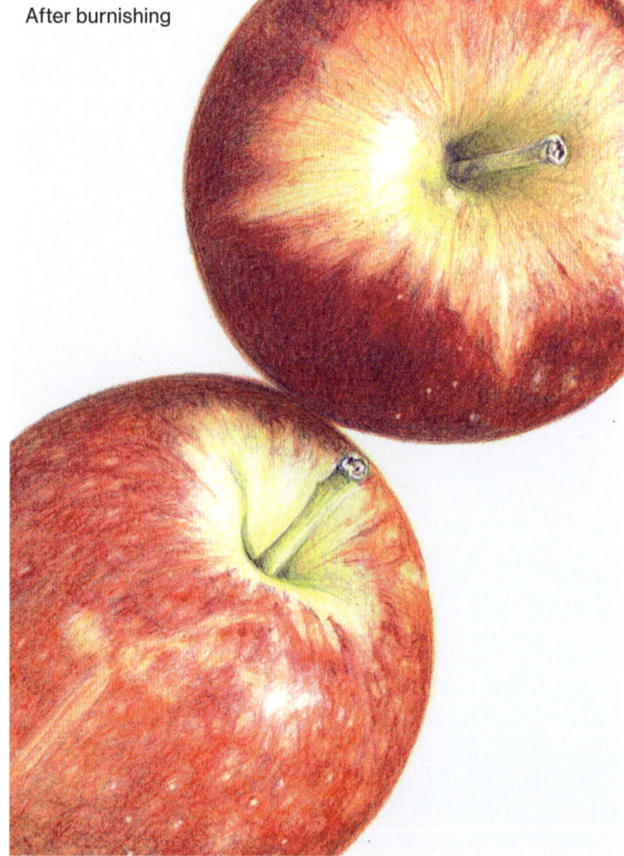

After burnishing

Dry blending

Dry blending refers to blending colored pencils without solvents or liquids but with a tool other than your colored pencils. In addition to the most common tools listed below, you can also experiment with blending powders and colorless pencil blenders.

Household items can be used as blending tools. I often use a piece of tissue to blend, applying varying levels of pressure to get the result I want. Heavy pressure is more effective at blending colors together and gives a very smooth surface finish without damaging the paper. Tools with a smaller surface area, like Q-tips, can be used carefully on a smaller area of detail. Applying a lot of pressure when using cotton swabs risks damaging the paper or the drawing, but used gently on small areas these can be very effective and more precise than using tissue.

Blending stumps and tortillons are inexpensive and commonly used with pastel and graphite. Blending stumps are molded from paper pulp and have two pointed ends. Tortillons are smaller and harder than blending stumps, and are made from a piece of paper rolled into a hollow stick with one pointed end. Stumps are generally used for blending larger areas whereas tortillons are used for small areas of detail.

Brushes can be used for subtle blending. If I'm drawing a light shadow that needs to graduate away from the object and disappear into the paper, I use a brush. I also use a brush if I'm blending two contrasting colors together as the brush encourages the colors to blend initially, then I can go in with a pencil.

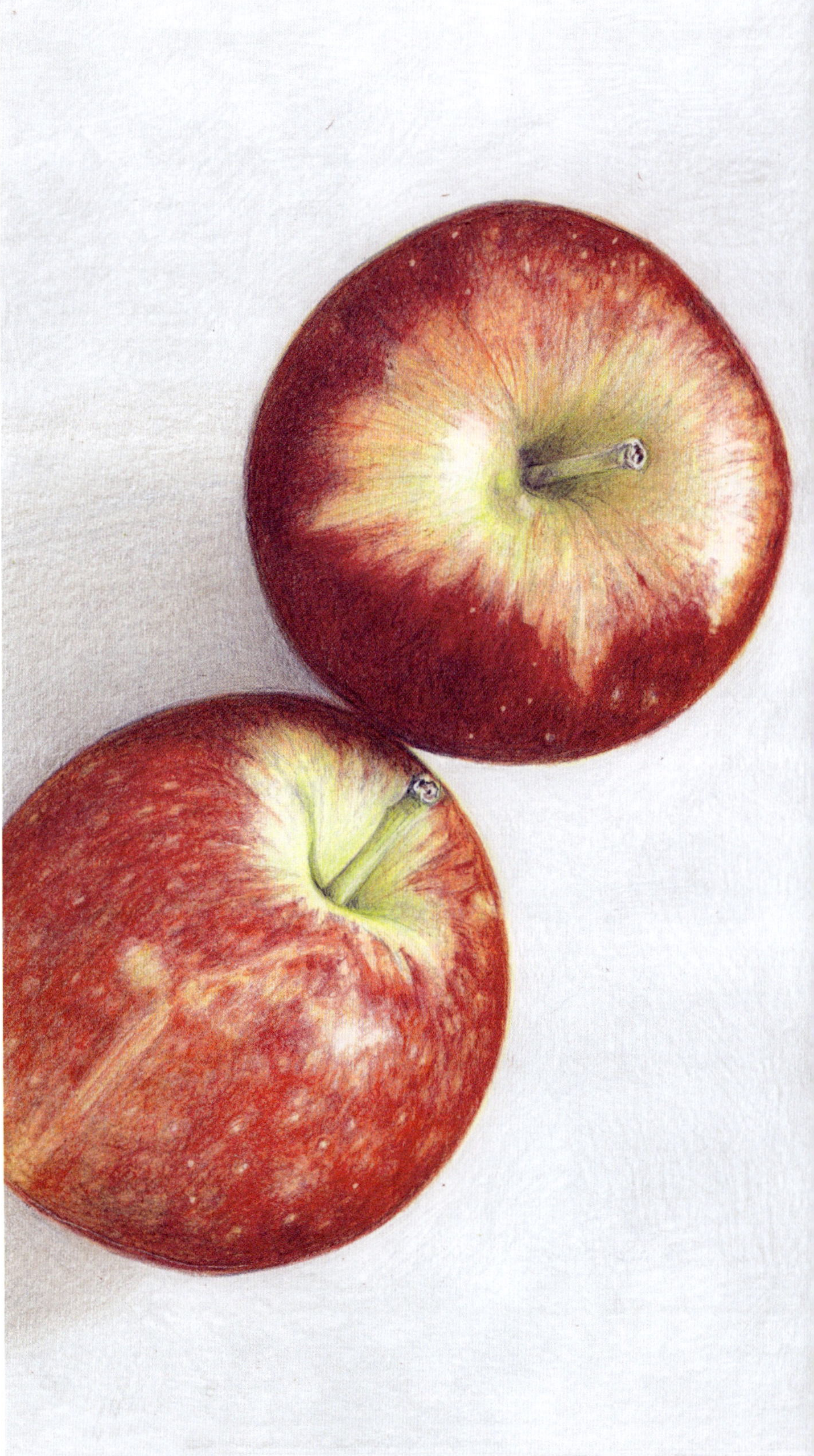

Solvent blending

While I don't use solvents for blending very often, this technique is widely used by many colored pencil artists and is an effective way to achieve great results. Here are the basics so you can experiment with it yourself.

Solvents work by breaking down the wax or oil binders in the pencil, allowing you to move the pigment around like paint. The most commonly used for blending with are rubbing alcohol, odorless mineral spirits, and turpentine.

- Rubbing alcohol is the mildest solvent and works best when there's a lot of color on the paper.

- Odorless mineral spirits will break down the binder more effectively and can be used to create a color wash. If you want to achieve these more painterly results, be sure to use thicker paper.

- Turpentine is the most aggressive of the three and breaks down the wax and oil in the pencil even more effectively than the mineral spirits.

Always test the solvent on a piece of scrap paper first to avoid using something too strong and spoiling your hard work. You can apply solvent with cotton swabs, tortillons, or a small paint brush. If you use a brush, first blot it on some tissue to avoid using too much. I prefer to use a small paint brush and blot often. Work from light to dark so you don't accidentally contaminate a light area of your work with the dark pigment from another area. Let your artwork dry out before you continue to work on it.

Remember: when using solvents, always work in a well-ventilated area.

Colored pencil
blending only

Solvent blending

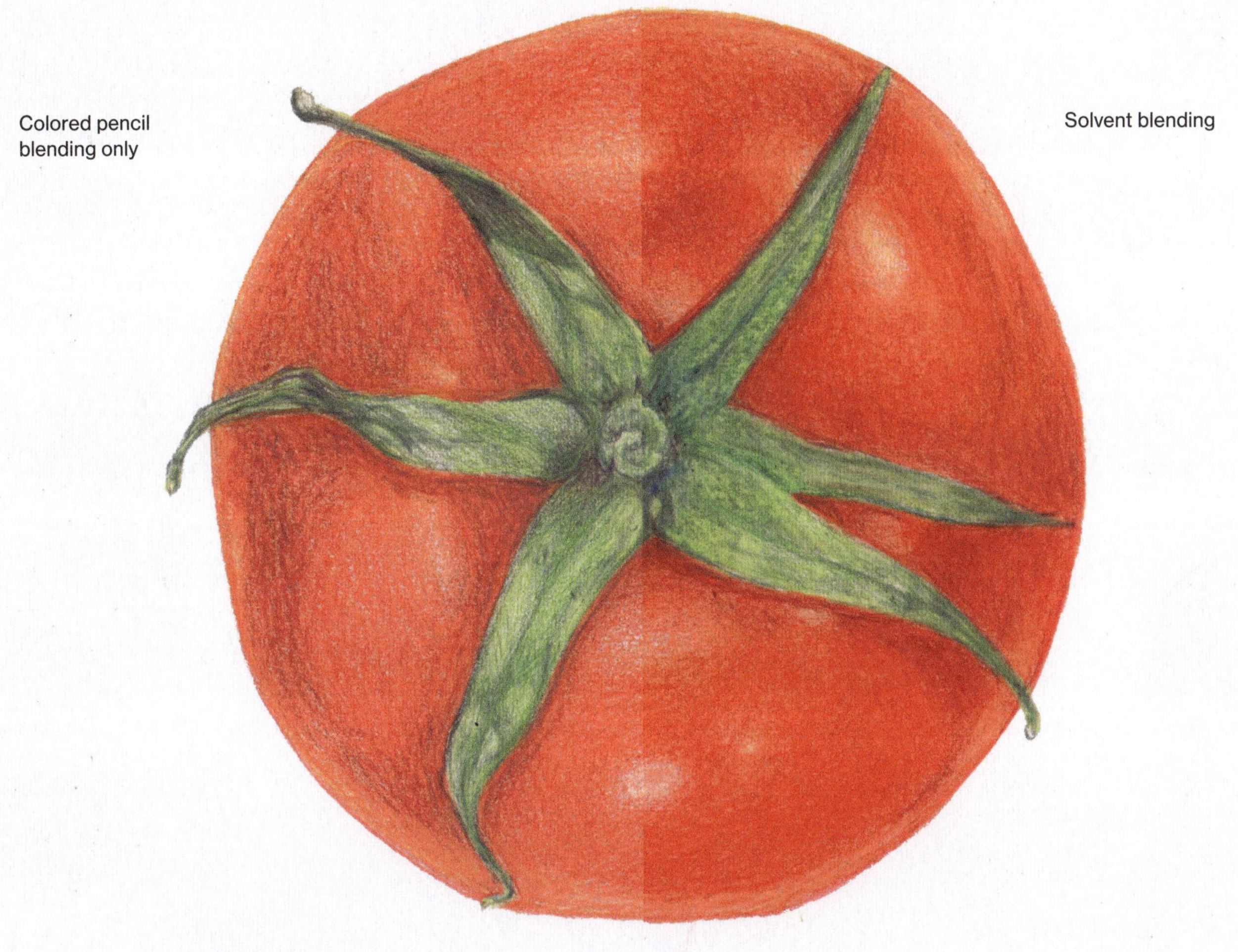

Textures & Surfaces

In order to capture the characteristics of a variety of textures you need to understand how light behaves on their surfaces. Light is absorbed, reflected, and refracted depending on the material or subject you are drawing. It is also important to consider how different materials react to the environment around them.

Fabric

Fabric absorbs light and will have less dramatic contrasting tones than some other materials. Areas where light hits the fabric will always be a lighter shade of the fabric color. Unlike with a hard, shiny surface, you will rarely find any bright white reflective spots on fabric under a light source – the transition from light to dark is smooth and gradual.

You will need to create consistent color gradients across the fabric's surface from the light to the dark areas.

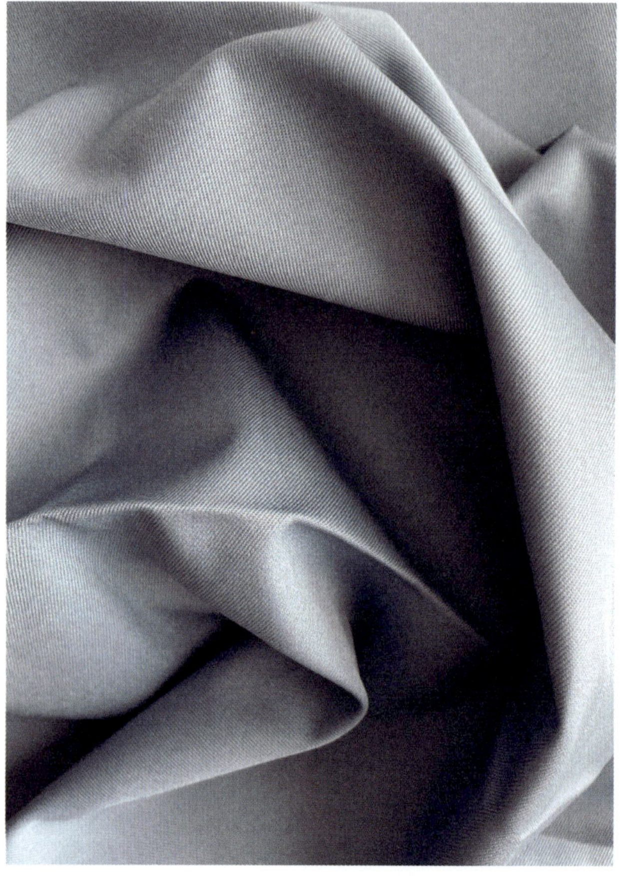

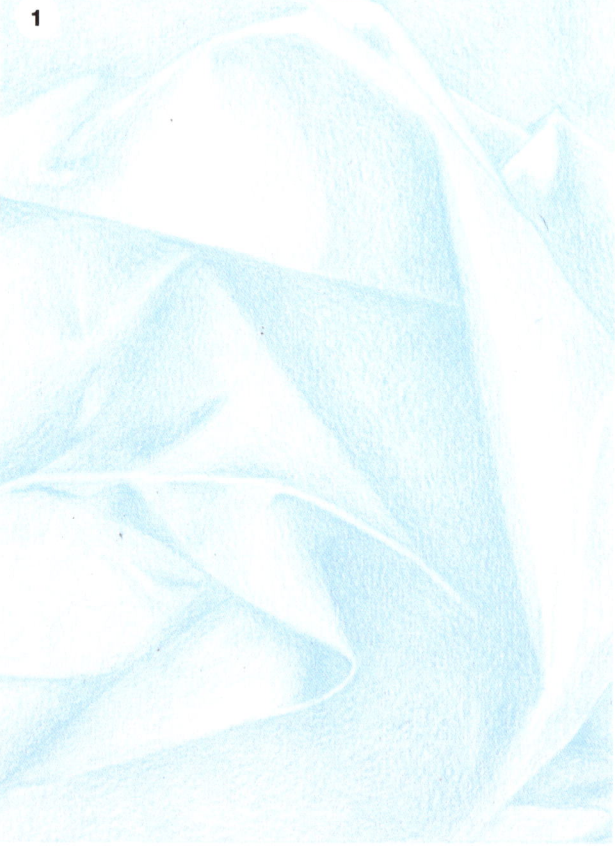

1 Using a single pale color from the palette of your reference image, first draw the guidelines of the fabric and its folds. Lightly apply a layer of the same color, here a light cobalt blue, using more pressure to identify the darker zones.

2 Using a mid-tone, here ultramarine blue, shade over the same dark zones adding another layer of color. Then use mid gray to identify the darkest shadows where the fabric folds. Use consistent circular pencil strokes to blend from the mid blue into the pale blue and from the mid blue into the mid gray.

3 Add more depth to the mid shadows using gray-green, and apply dark gray with light pressure to intensify the darkest zones of the mid shadows. Develop the deepest shadow areas with dark indigo blue and dark gray, carefully blending from these zones to the lighter areas to create a smooth transition from dark to light.

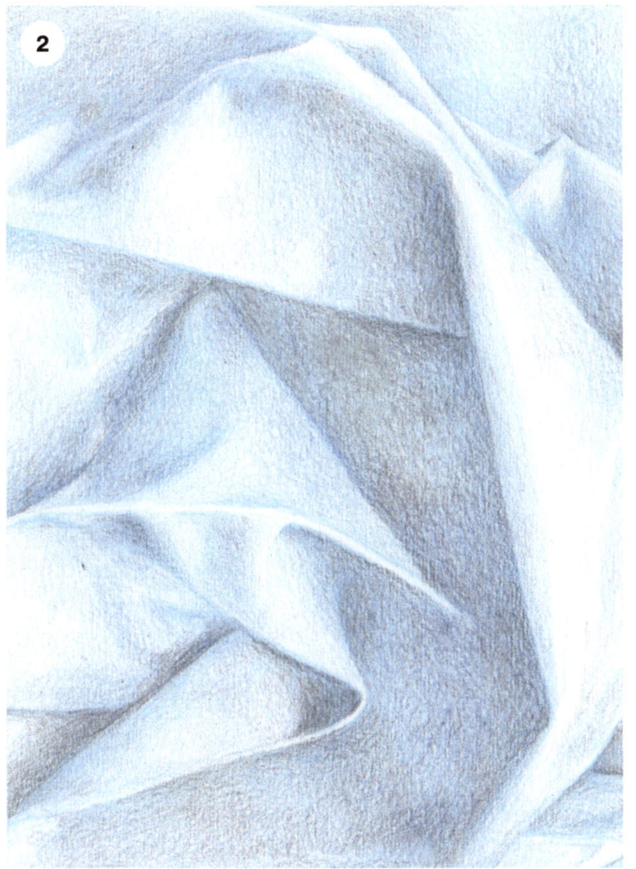

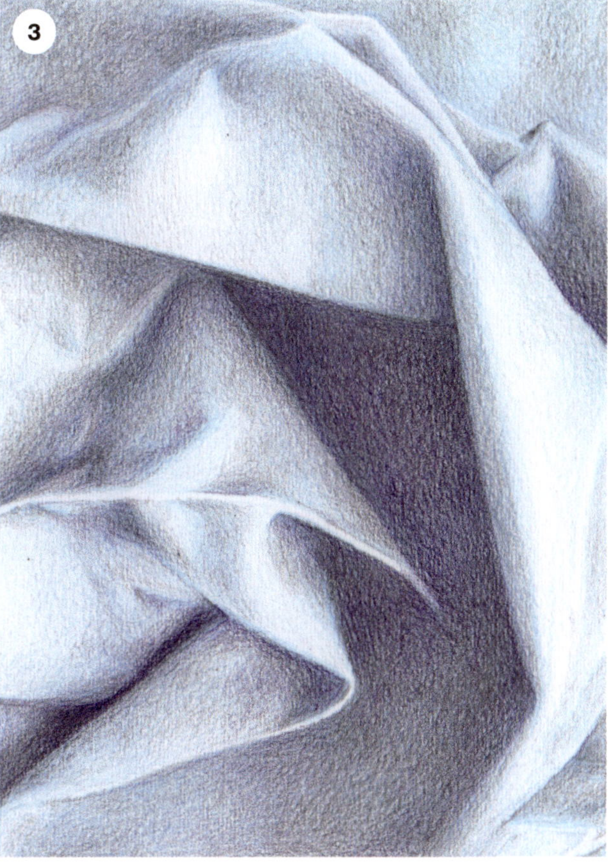

Polished metal

This is highly reflective, and its mirror-like quality will reflect the environment around it so you will need to capture many colors and shapes across its surface. The more complex the shape of the metal object, the more distorted these colors and shapes will be. If the metal has its own color, such as brass or copper, this will bring a yellow or orange hue to the objects reflected on its surface.

1 Set out guidelines using a light color from the palette you wish to use, and select a pale gray to shade in the first light layer for the metal dish. Here, pale orange, yellow, brown, and pink are used to color the candies and their corresponding reflections, applying light pressure. Use dark gray and the very lightest pressure to identify the black licorice.

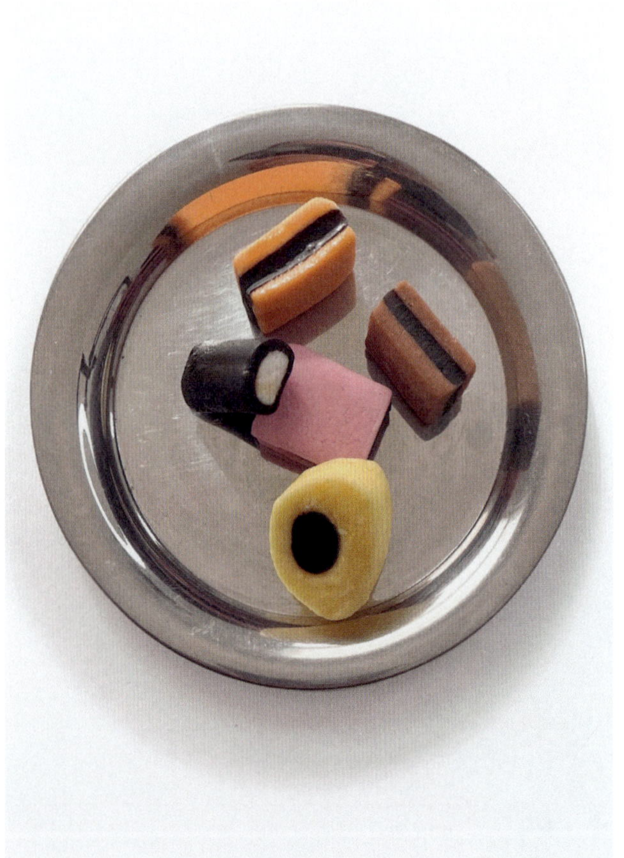

1

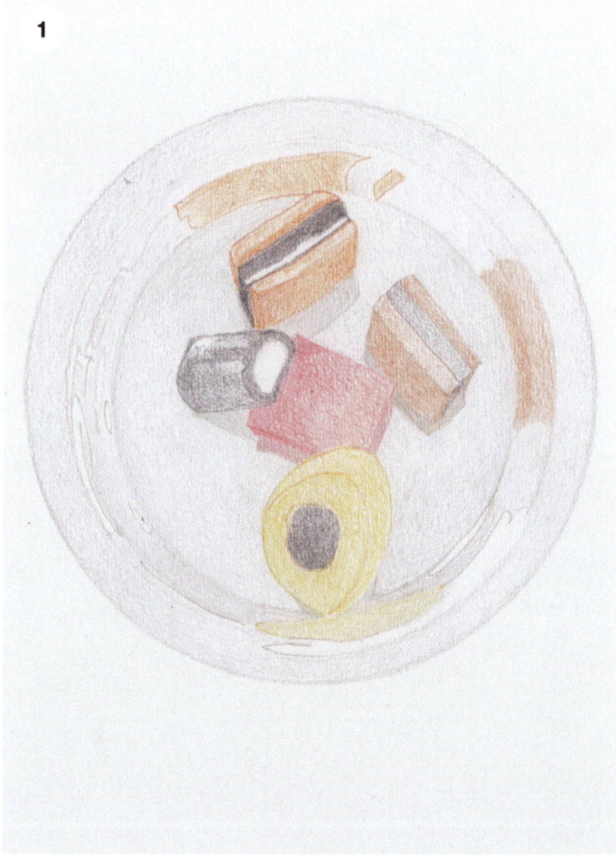

2 Use mid and dark gray to add another layer of color to the metal dish and identify the distorted dark gray reflections around the edge of the dish. Intensify the reflected colored shapes around the edge and blend these into the dark reflections where needed. Add another layer of color to the candies, applying more pressure to darken the surfaces that are in shadow. Use mid gray to identify the reflections in the base of the dish, then shade over this with the corresponding candy color. Add another layer of dark gray with more pressure to the licorice, leaving pale gray or white where there are some lighter reflections.

3 Repeat the previous step applying more pressure, adding more depth of color to all the elements, and give a defined edge to the reflections around the edge of the dish. To give the metal base of the dish a worn appearance, lightly shade in parts with warm gray.

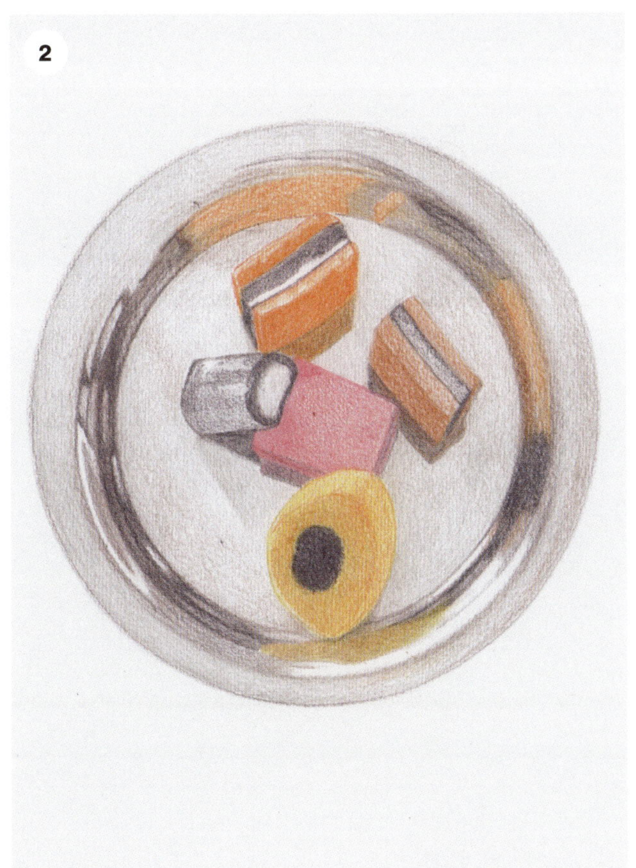

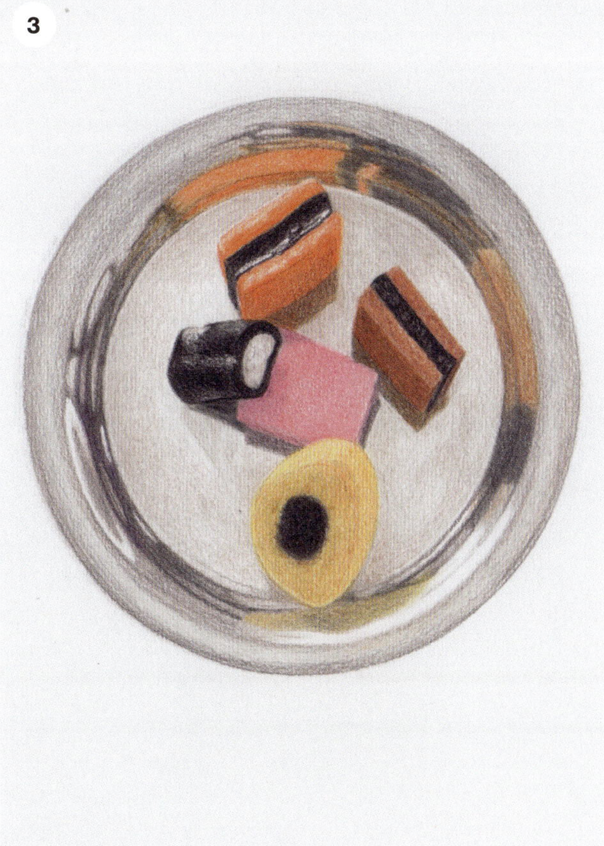

Plastic

Plastic is often hard and shiny and will bounce light off its surface. There will be very distinct white zones of light on the areas of the object closest to the light source, and the drop-off from the palest color of the plastic to the darkest areas will have a consistent and smooth gradient. The areas that are not in direct sunlight or dark shadow will have a flat bold color.

1 Draw the guidelines and lightly add the first layer of color in mid yellow and mid brown. Assess the highlights on the object and make sure that these areas remain completely white – these are the areas closest to the light source. Use light pressure on the areas that catch the light but aren't closest to it. The further away from the light source, the darker the elements will be. Use more pressure on the areas in shadow.

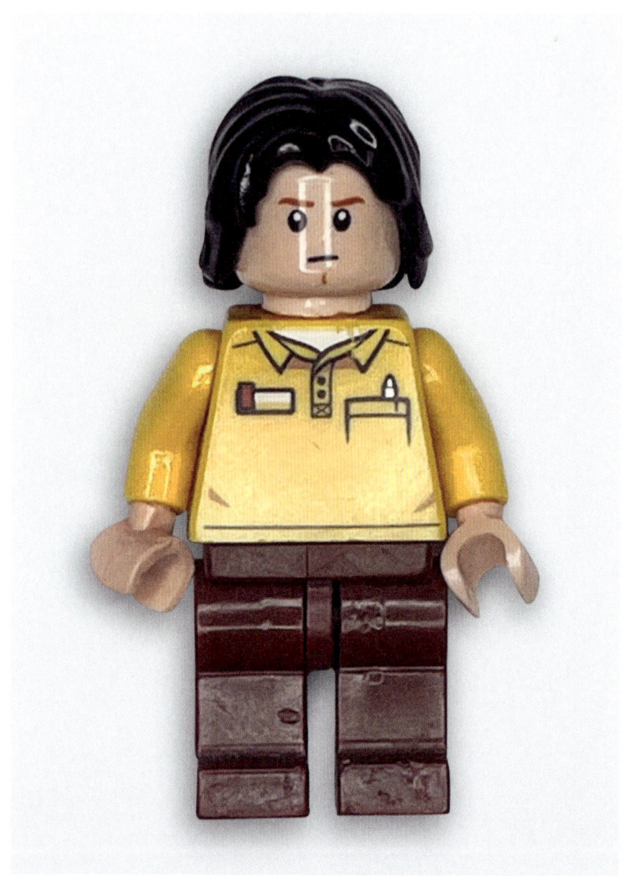

1 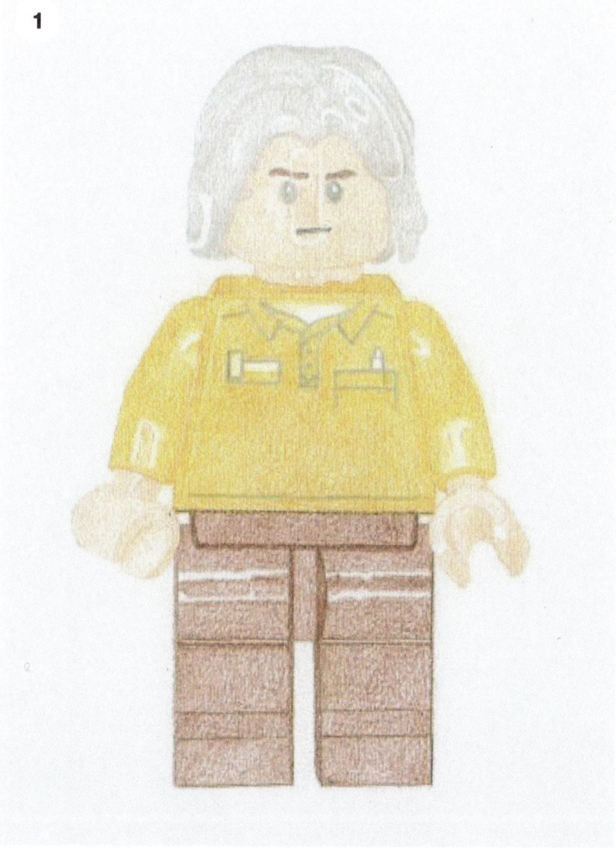

2 Using the same colors, take the whole object a shade darker, carefully working around the highlights and using more pressure to establish the areas in shadow around the neck and on the sleeves and legs. Use black with light pressure to shade in the hair, being careful to avoid the streaks of highlights.

3 Use the mid yellow with more pressure to add another layer of color, and darker ocher for the areas of shadow, blending carefully from the dark to the mid yellow to create a consistent gradient. Use the dark ocher to further define the highlights on the arms and deep brown to add depth to the shadows on the legs. Finally, use black to carefully pressure shade the hair, avoiding the highlights, and to pick out the details on the chest and face. Use an eraser pen to go over highlights if needed to ensure they are crisp.

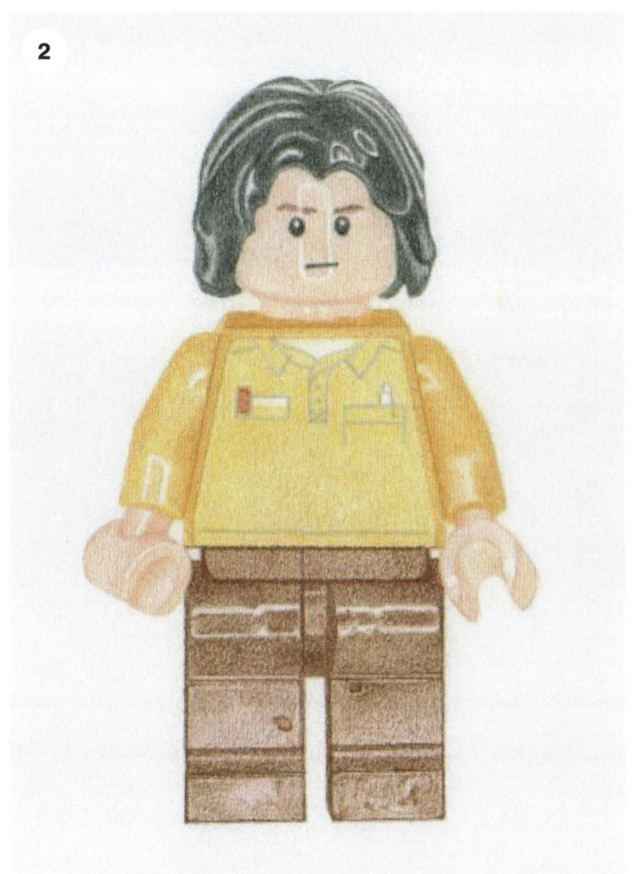

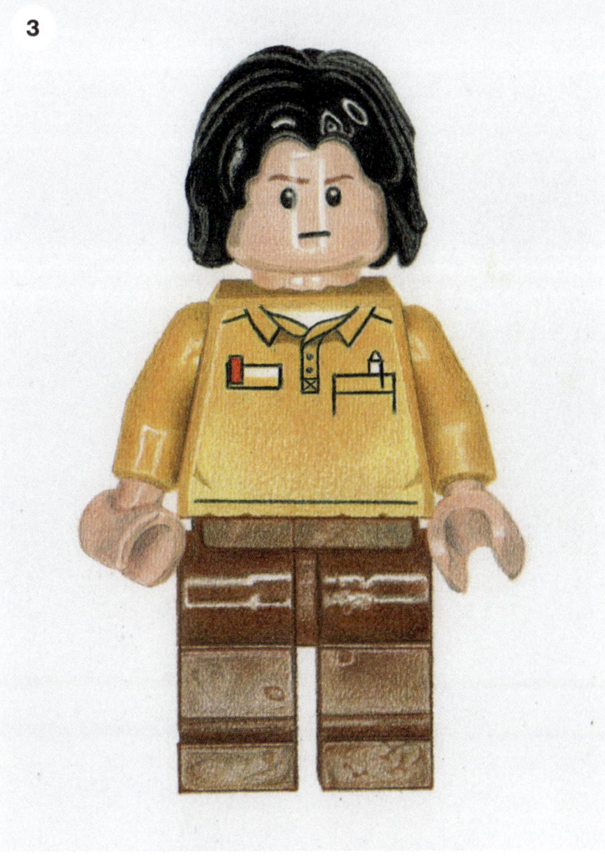

Glass

Glass reflects and refracts the light and distorts objects that are placed inside or behind it. I have found when drawing glass that what you *don't* draw is often more important. Don't be tempted to fill in all the white space, even with the lightest background color.

1 Lightly sketch out the outlines of the glass in pencil, carefully identifying the random shapes at the bottom of the inside of the glass and at its base. Use pale gray to lay down the background color, leaving the areas of white completely alone. Use pale yellow-green with light pressure to partially color the base of the glass: this is the darkest area of the glass, which has green tones in it.

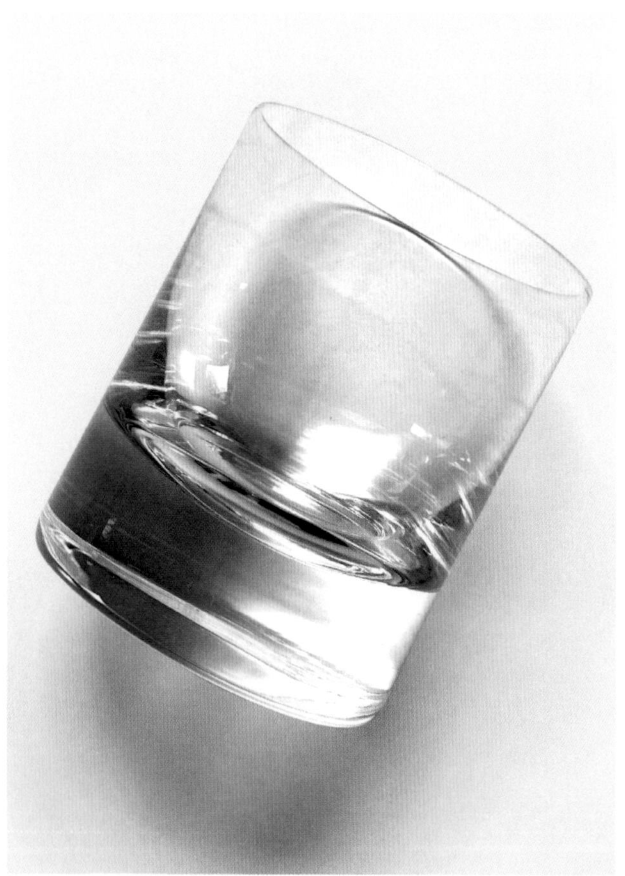

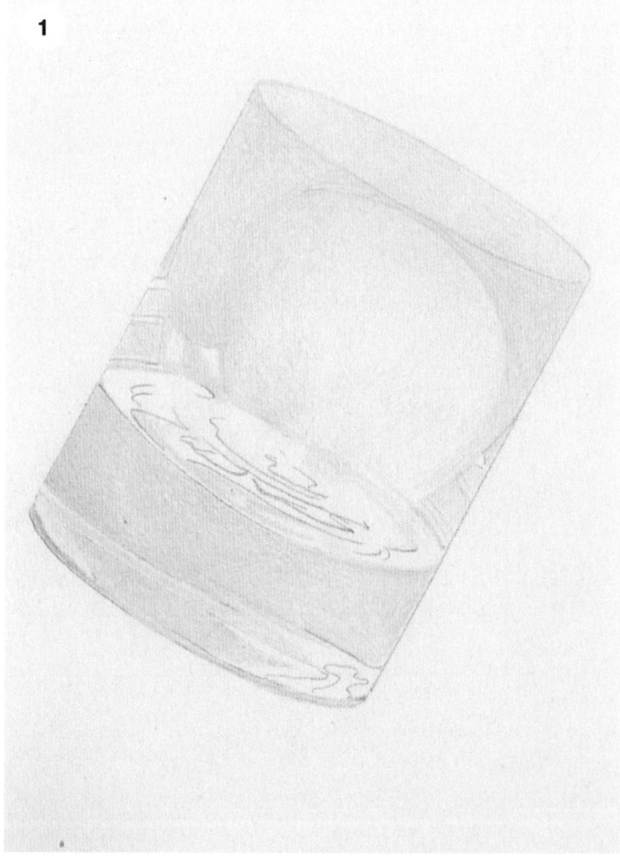

2 Lightly use pale blue and mid blue-green to identify and shade in the shadows and reflections on the glass. Carefully shade in the half moon shadow that the glass creates as it lands on the table, the shapes identified in step one at the bottom of the glass, plus the dark zones on the heavy glass base.

3 Use mid gray to darken all the elements that you shaded in blue-green in the previous step, and add more definition to the random shapes at the bottom of the glass. Take the darker zones on the left of the base of the glass a shade darker, carefully blending out to the lighter areas. Use the same mid gray to create the area of shadow around the bottom edge of the glass. Build up the color gradually using circular strokes, and use less pressure on the light spots.

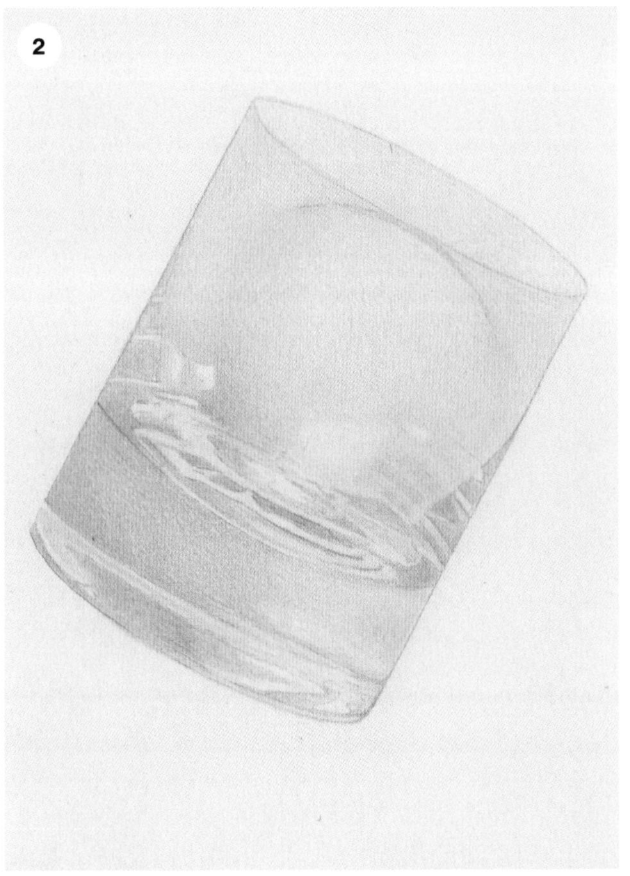

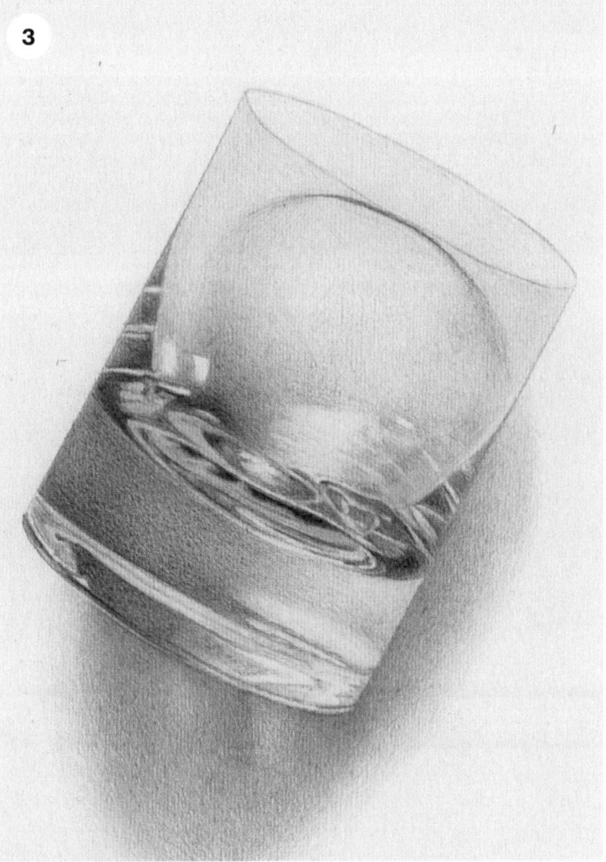

Wood

Wood can absorb or reflect light, depending on how it has been treated; it might be untreated and rough with a matt effect, or polished to a high shine. However, all wood has a grain which produces a textured, patterned surface. The grain is the most important characteristic to capture when you are rendering wood: it immediately indicates that the material in your drawing is wood and not just a brown object.

1 Begin by carefully drawing in the guidelines using a light tone from the palette of your artwork. Focus on setting out as many of the grain lines as possible, and use heavier pressure to identify the darkest and thickest of these. Lightly shade the background color using mid ocher.

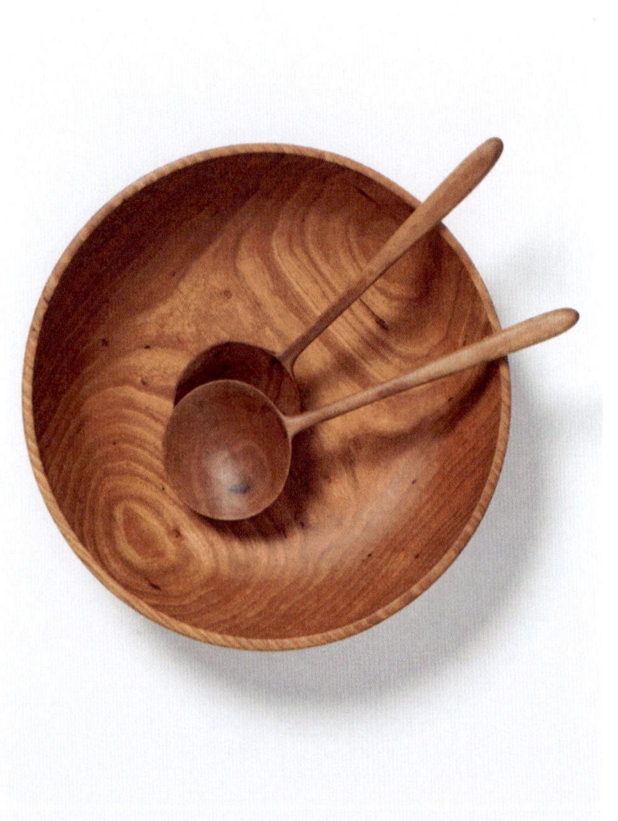

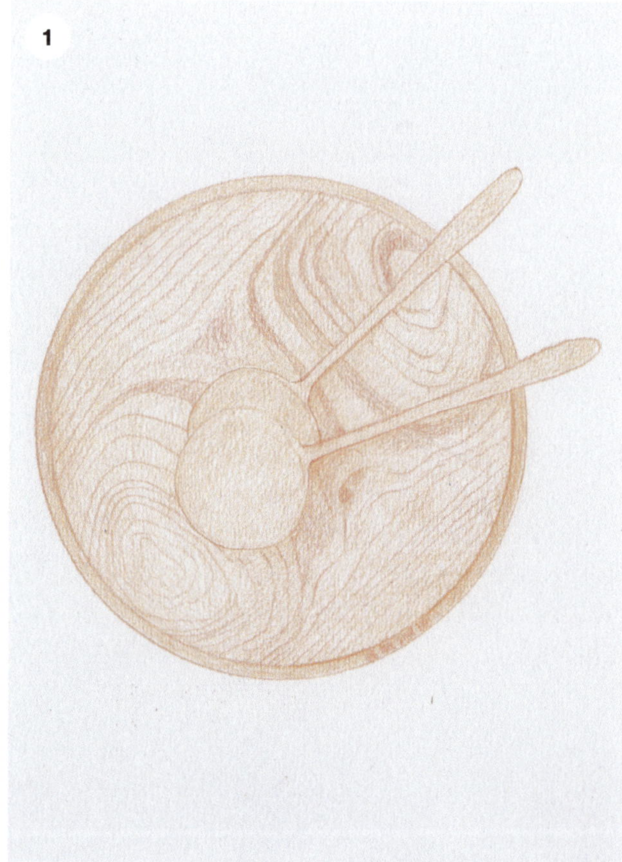

2 Using yellow and dark ocher with medium pressure, add another layer of color to the entire image. Apply the dark ocher with heavy pressure to go over the grain lines, create the thicker grain lines and rings, and identify the dark imperfections in the wood. Use a mid pimento red to add shadows around the spoons and the inside edge of the bowl.

3 Use a mid-toned rusty red-brown with light pressure to add another layer of color to the entire image. Apply more pressure to deepen the shadows around the edge of the bowl and the shadows cast by the spoons. Use the same red-brown along with a chocolate brown to add a darker layer of color to the grain rings, spoon details, and shadows, and chocolate brown to pick out the imperfection spots and flecks in the wood.

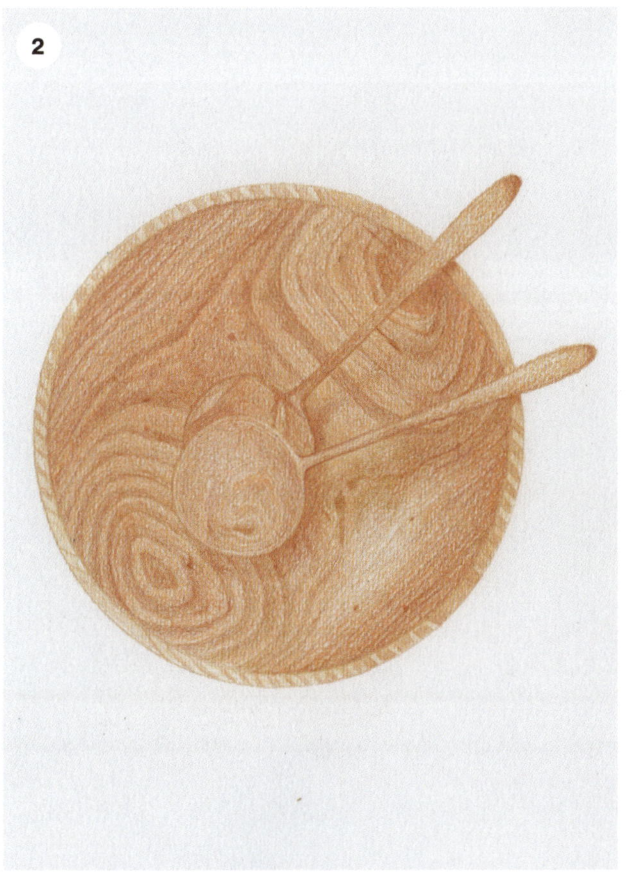

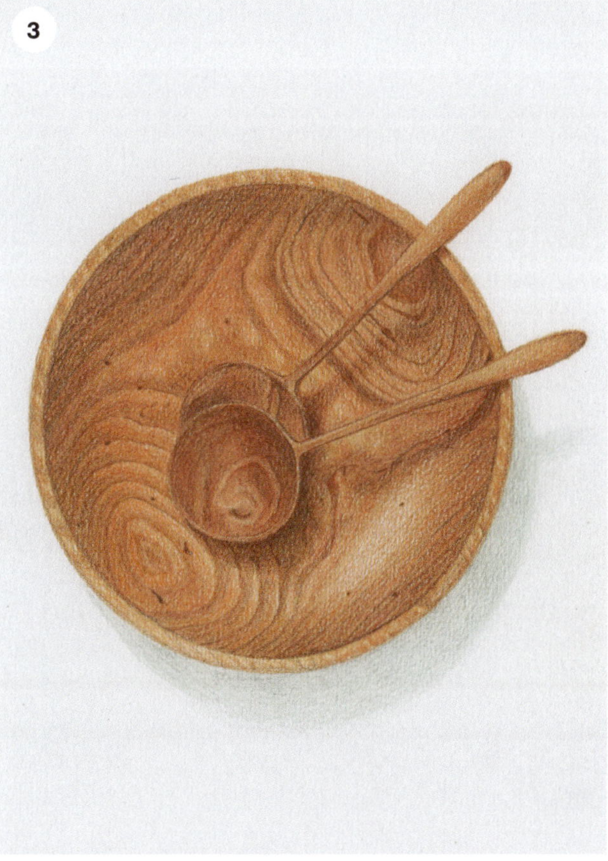

Shadows & Highlights

Shadows and highlights are essential for creating a realistic artwork. Highlights are the areas on the surface of an object that are closest to the light source, and their shape and value – or lightness – will depend on the color, material, and reflectivity of the object. Equally, shadows are not just a spectrum of pale grays to black: the color, shape, and value of a shadow depends on the object.

Identifying

Identify the shadow shape cast by the object at the very beginning of the drawing process. Treat shadows cast on the surface as separate objects that need to be defined early on; shadows on the object, conversely, will be rendered in the later stages.

Carefully build up layers of color to achieve dark shadows, as it is almost impossible to remove dark colors if you have made an error. Begin with the lightest color then layer up until you achieve the desired effect. Shadows can either have a defined hard edge or a soft "drop-off" zone around them, which means that the shadow has a dark area within that gradually becomes lighter toward its edges.

You should also identify the highlights as shapes in the early stages. Just like shadows, the edges of the highlight can be hard or blurry, depending on the reflectivity of the surface and/ or the strength of the light source. If the highlight doesn't have hard edges, simply outline an area that contains the highlight zone. The temperature (whether it is warm or cool) of the highlight will depend on the light source.

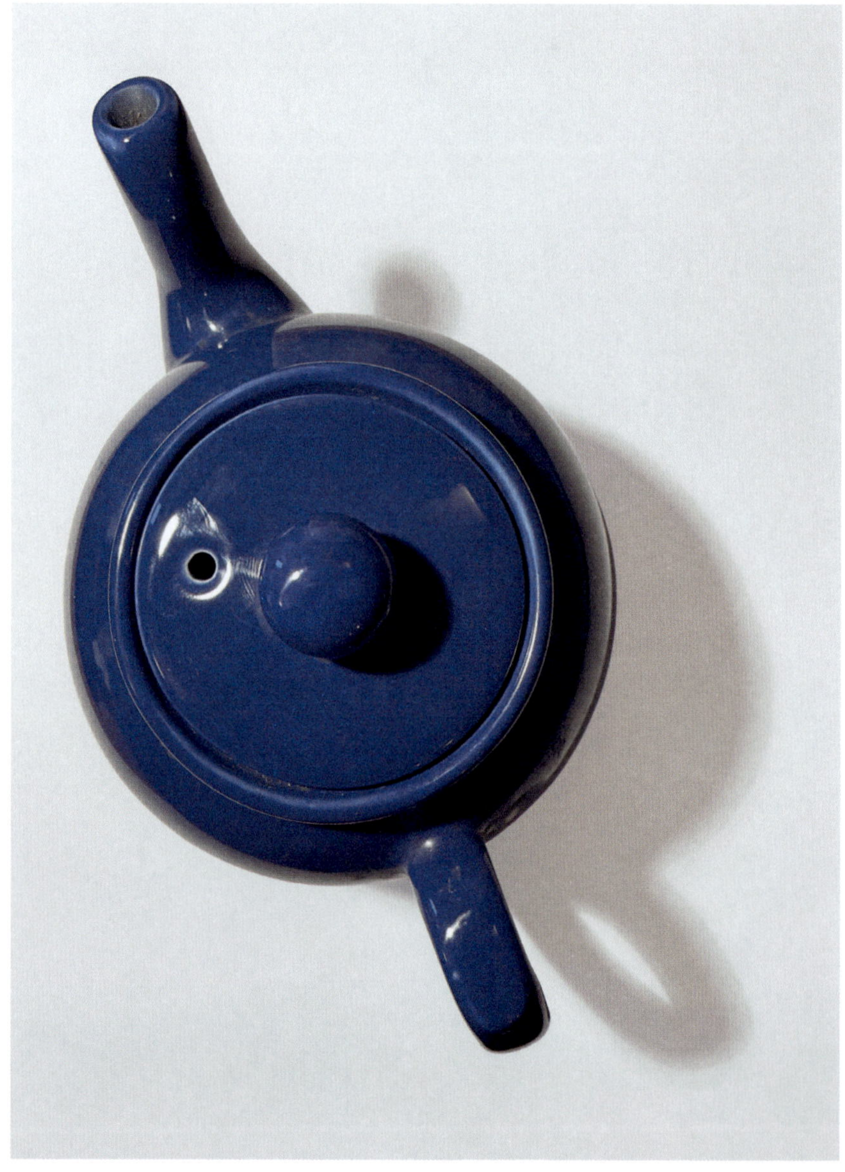

Rendering

1 When drawing the guidelines, outline the shapes of the highlights you've identified. Also identify the shapes of shadows cast on the surface the object is sitting on and outline these too.

2 Lay down the mid blue background color, working around the highlights, and erase any prominent or heavy guidelines where needed. Shade lightly over any highlights that aren't completely white: here there are soft highlights to the left of the spout and around the edge of the teapot body. Use a small eraser pen to make sure that the pure white highlights, such as those on the lid of the teapot, stay white. Use the same background color to identify the darker shadow zones on the object, applying heavier pressure in these areas.

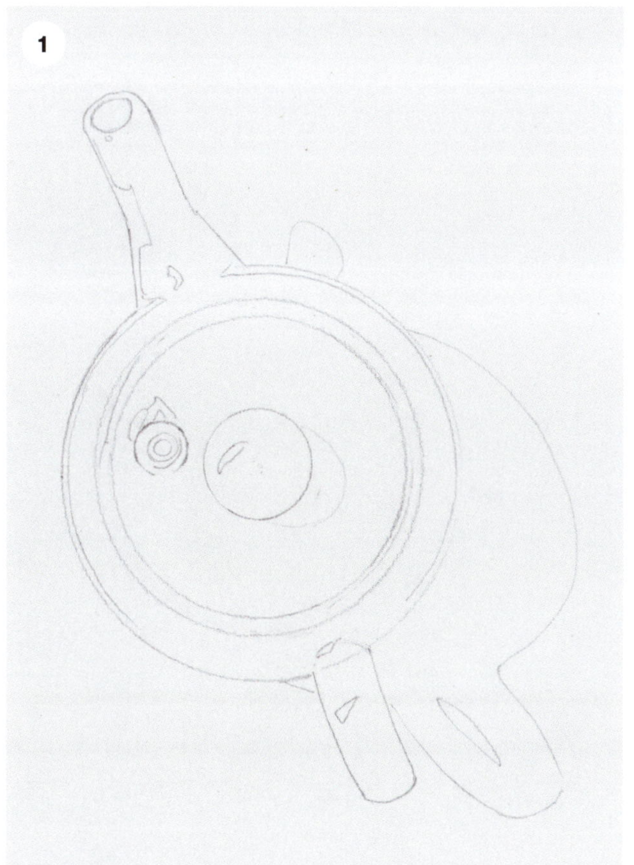

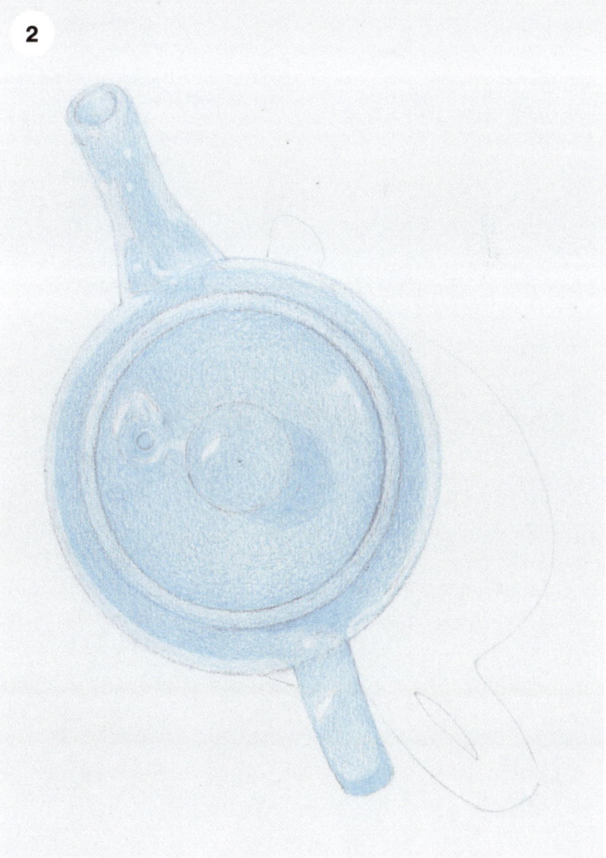

3 Continue to work around the highlights as you layer up more color. Give the highlights a hard edge for more definition, and enhance the shadow zones by continuing to shade these areas using more pressure.

4 Repeat the previous step using darker blue (note that grays and black haven't been used yet). Layer up the color as much as possible to achieve a smooth continuous finish. Now use a very pale gray to color in the shadow cast on the surface.

5 Use mid gray with medium pressure to add more depth to the shadow areas on the object only. Use the same mid gray with light pressure to shade in the shadow cast on the surface, taking it a shade darker. Use circular stokes to ensure the color is even.

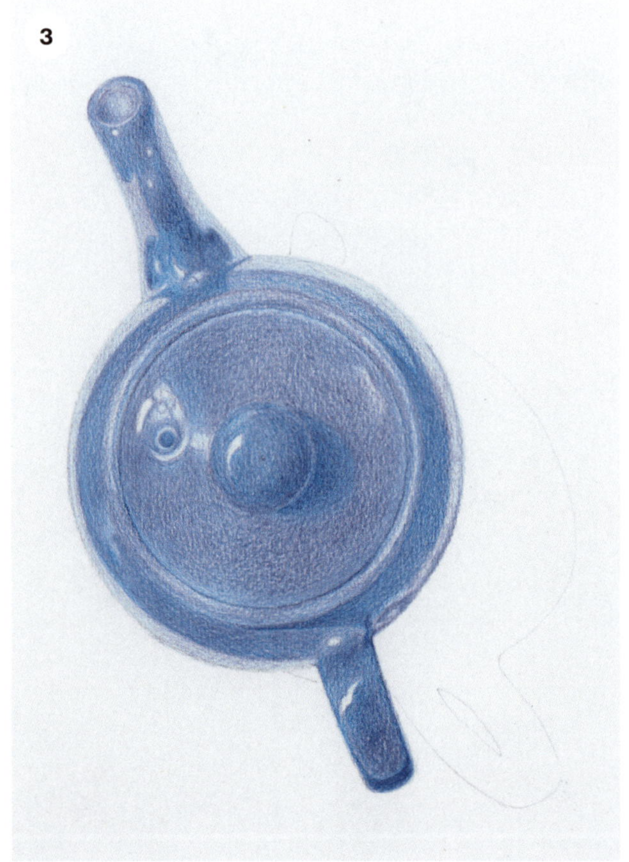

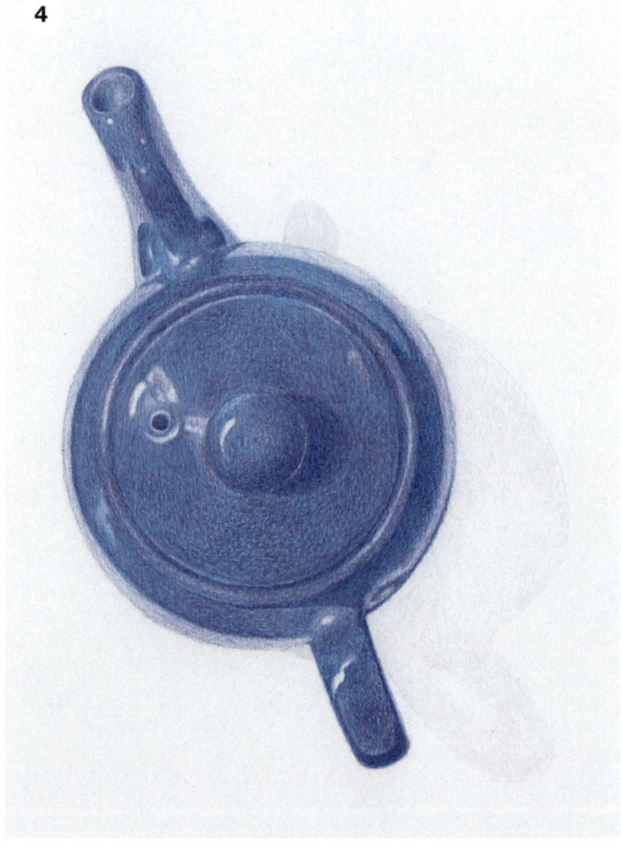

6 With dark gray or black and medium
pressure, take the shadow zones
on the object a final shade darker.
Use your eraser pen to ensure the
brightest highlight spots really stand
out. Use dark gray with medium to
light pressure to take the cast shadow
a shade darker. If there is a drop-off
zone (as here), start the darker zone
just inside the area created in steps
4 & 5 to produce a lighter gradient
of shadow at the edge, using even,
circular strokes for a smooth finish.

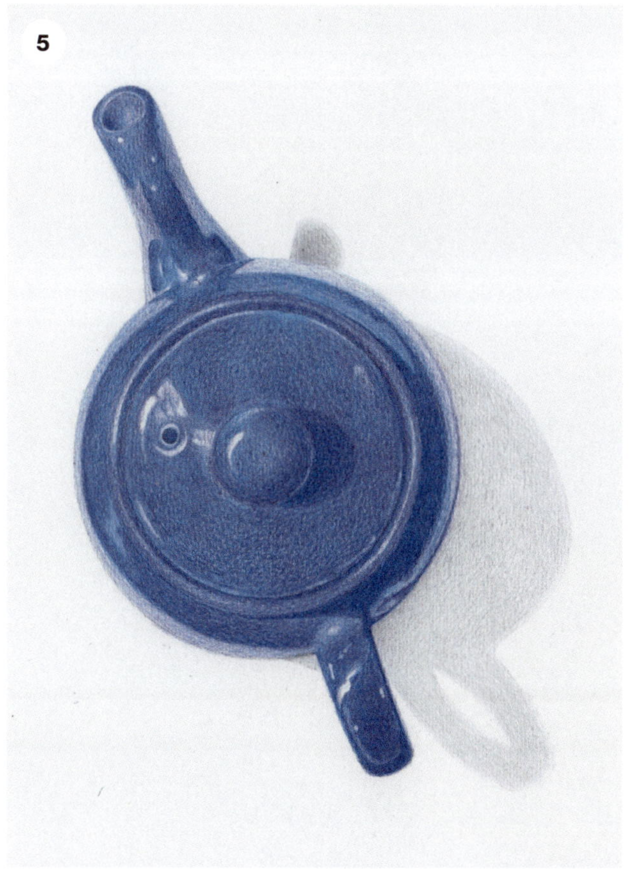

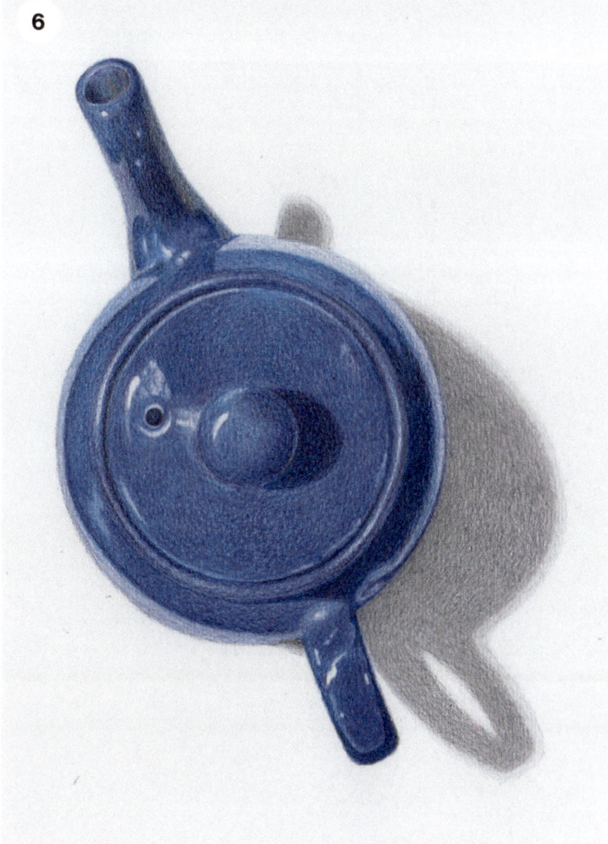

Choosing Colors

The color wheel

Color wheels are a useful tool to help identify colors and understand how they relate to one another. The color wheel can be broken down into primary, secondary, and tertiary colors. It can also be divided into cool and warm colors. Complementary colors are on opposite sides of the color wheel – such as blue and orange, red and green, or purple and yellow – and if you use these color combinations together they appear brighter.

Primary colors: blue, yellow, and red.

Secondary colors: orange, green, and purple. These sit between the primary colors on the wheel, and are created by mixing the primaries either side.

Tertiary colors: yellow-orange, red-orange, red-purple, blue-purple, blue-green, and yellow-green. These are created by mixing primary and secondary colors.

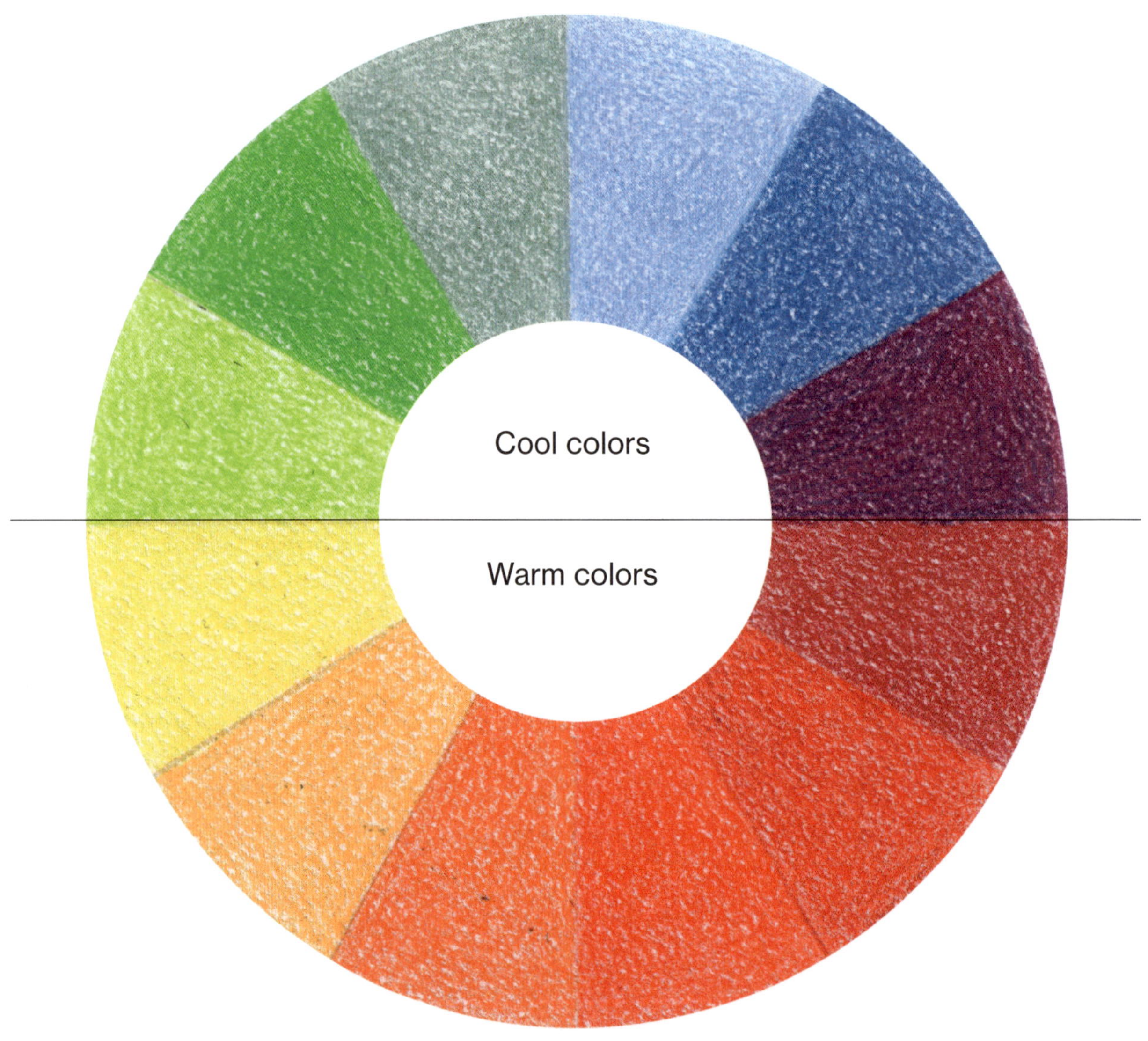

Color, value, & tone

Color is seen when light is reflected off a surface, and it has three main attributes: hue, saturation (or chroma), and value (lightness or darkness).

Hue is simply the pure range of colors and their pigment on the color wheel, such as green, blue, and yellow.

Saturation is a measure of the color's strength – how sharp or dull it appears.

Value is the level of lightness or darkness, determined by the addition of black or white. All colors have a value between black and white.

Tones and tints are variations of hues found on the basic color wheel that are produced when gray or black are added (tones), or when white is added (tints). There is an endless number of these for any hue, but they can be broadly divided into three parts: dark tones, mid-tones, and light tones.

1 Pure red

2 Red tints (mixed with white)

3 Red tones (mixed with gray)

4 Red shades (mixed with black)

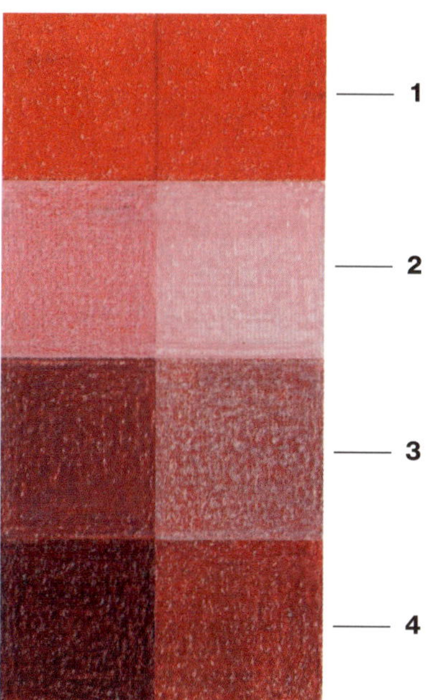

Color charts

All the major colored pencil brands provide a color chart with their ranges, and you can often download these from their websites to help you find the right colors for your artworks. There may be minor differences in the color when you print it out compared to how it looked on your screen. You can also create your own color chart.

Why do you need color charts? They will help you to identify the colors you need and keep track of those you are using for a particular artwork. I would recommend creating your own as you build up your pencil collection. Different brands will produce the same color in name, but often an indigo produced by Derwent Lightfast, for example, may slightly differ from an indigo produced by Caran d'Ache. The added benefit of producing your own color chart is that you can show swatches of the same color with light, medium, and heavy pressure.

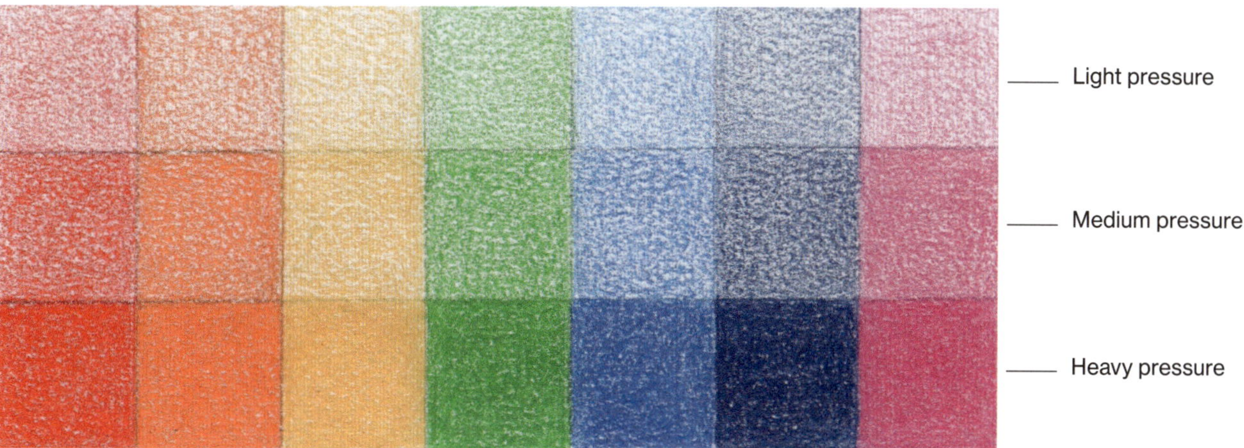

Identifying color & tone

There are different ways to identify colors and tones in a physical image (whether a photograph or a still life set-up) and in a digital image on a backlit screen. If your image is digital and you have access to Photoshop or a similar photo-editing program, you can use the Color Picker tool.

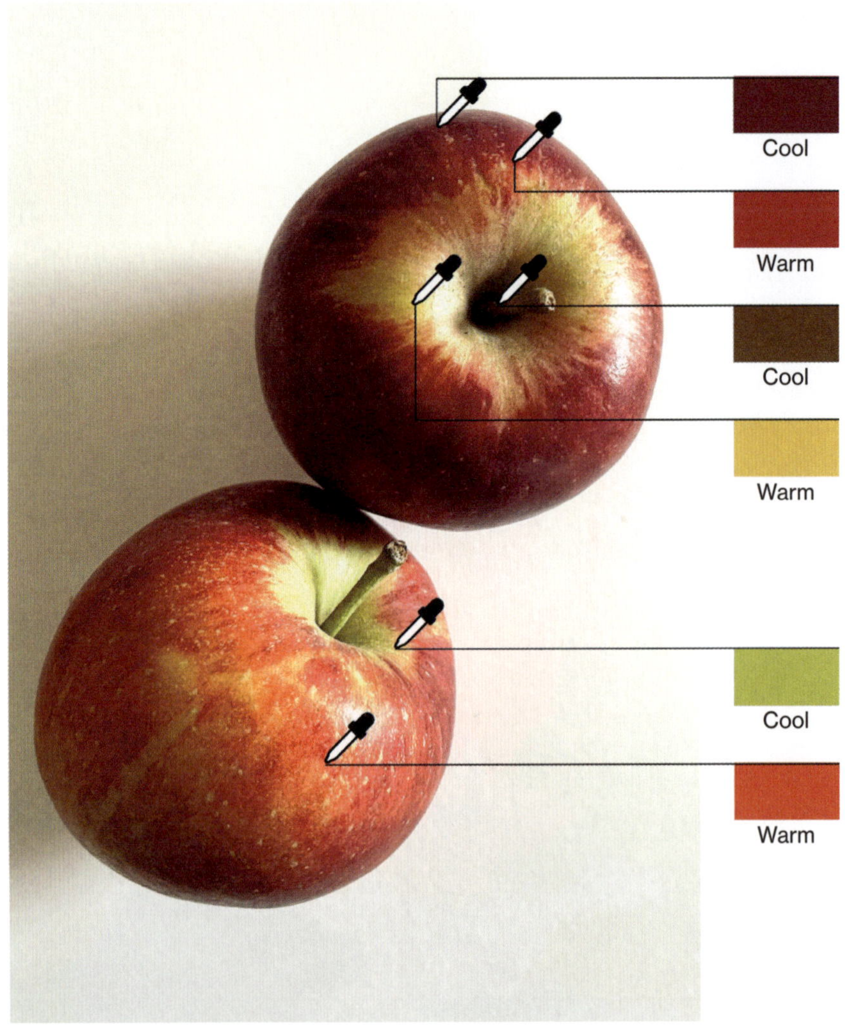

Using the Color Picker in Photoshop

The Color Picker can be used in the same way to identify both color and tone in your image. To identify tones you will need to turn your color image into a grayscale image. Using the Color Picker is simple, but it is not as precise as it looks – there is an element of trial and error, especially when there are many different shades of colors across the surface of an object, as in the example shown here.

Choose the areas of color you wish to identify and then use the picker to sample the colors in those areas, saving each swatch. The same method applies to the tones. This will produce a palette of colors and tones that you can use to match with the colored pencils in your collection and as a guide for the areas of shadow and light.

If you prefer to work from a physical image or you don't have access to these types of programs, there are other analog methods you can use, shown opposite.

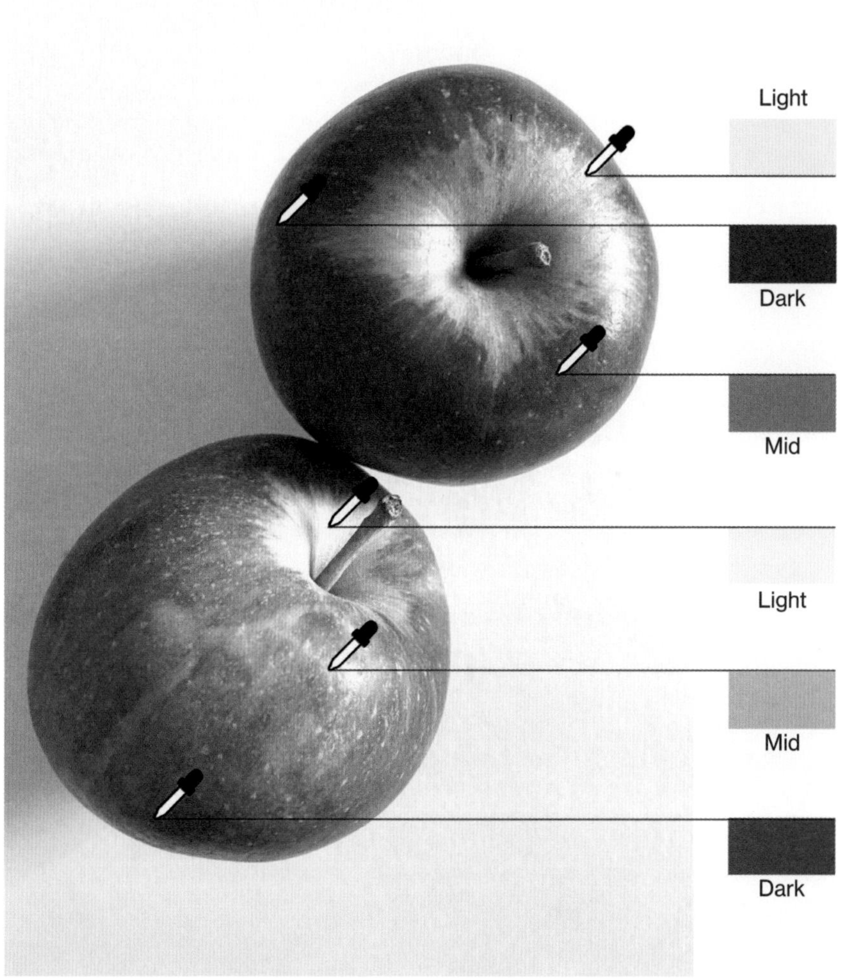

Grayscale & value finders

These are simple tools that allow artists to identify the value of blacks, whites, and colors. There are many versions available, and the one I use is a simple card gadget by the Color Wheel Company which can be bought inexpensively from art shops or online.

Value finders, like this one, isolate an area of an image, which helps to focus on the color more easily. The value scale will then help determine whether the tone is light, mid, or dark.

Place the value finder over the area of the image you are working from and move it left or right until you find the value closest to the color you are identifying. I find it helps to squint as it allows you to focus on the light or dark. If you are working with a color image you won't find an exact match: this tool is intended to help find the closest in lightness or darkness to your color.

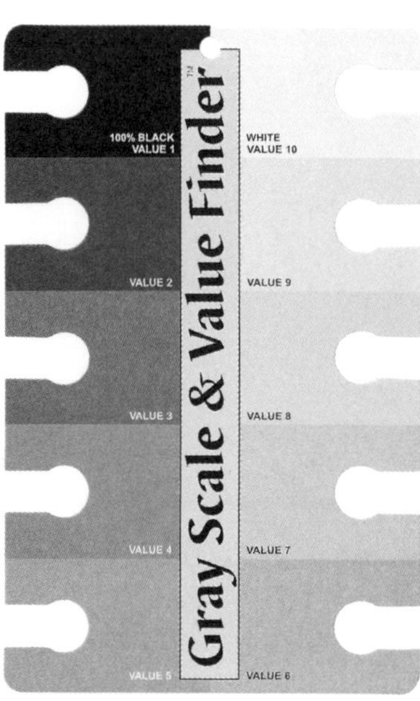

Projects

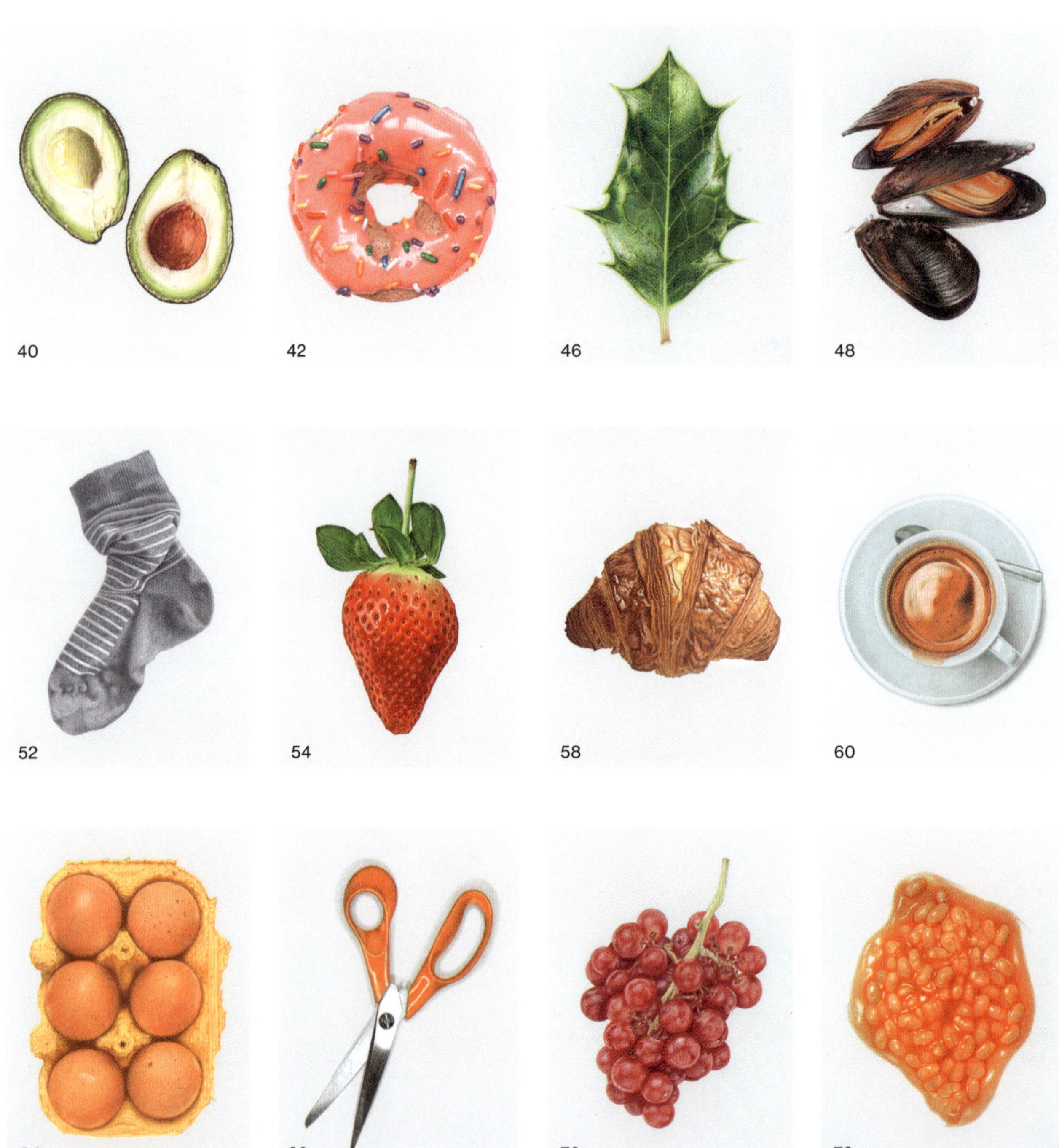

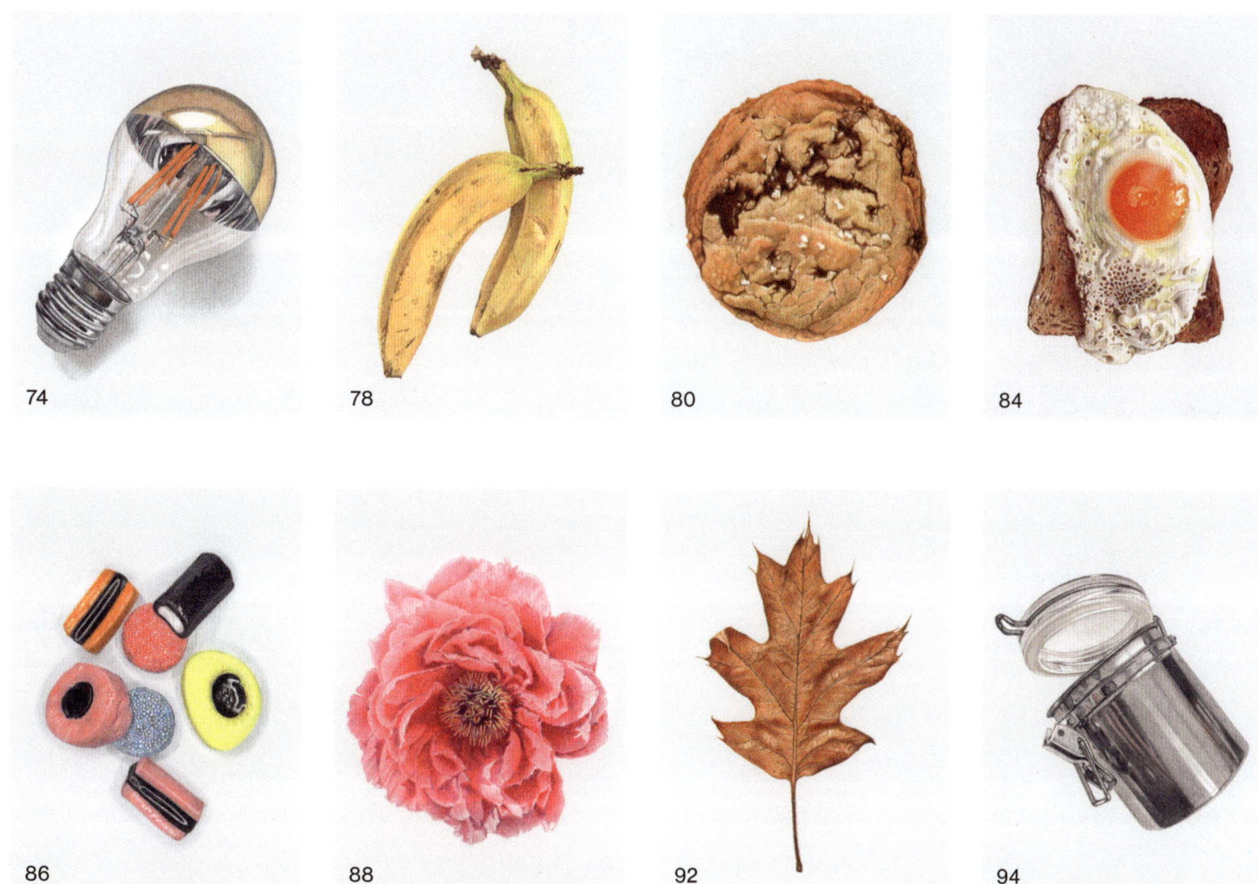

74
78
80
84
86
88
92
94

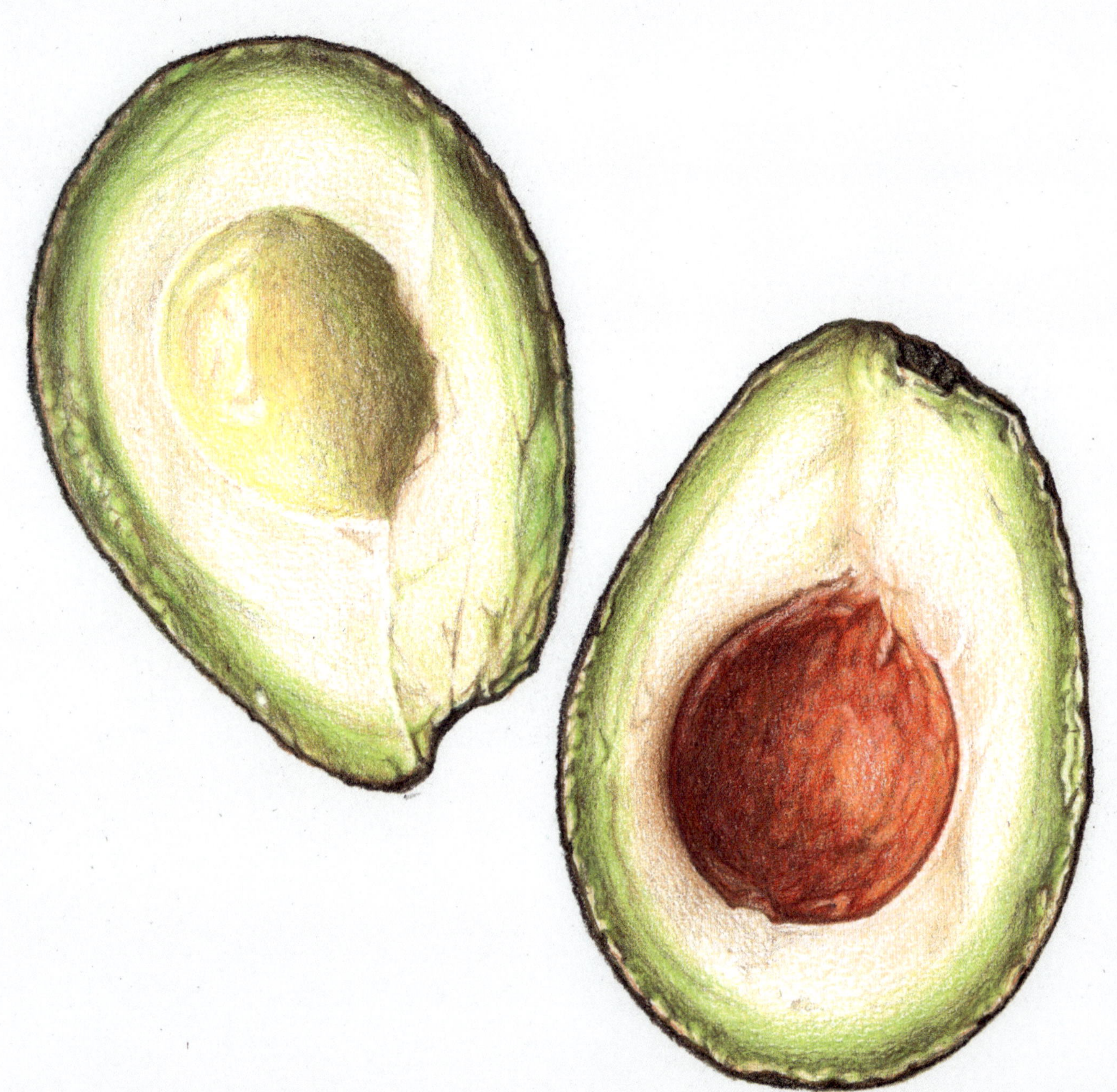

Avocado

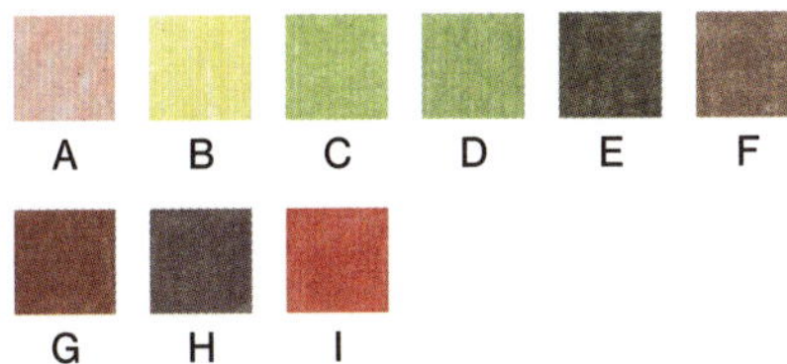

A B C D E F

G H I

1 Use a light tone (A) for the linework.

2 Lay down the base for the flesh and stone with light pink (A) and brown (F).

3 Use dark sage (E) to define the outlines, emphasizing bumps along the skin. Add zesty yellow (B) around the edge of the flesh and in the empty stone cavity. Use pale olive green (C) to shade around the inner edge and add shadow to the cavity. Pressure shade the stone in brown (F) and lightly shade dents in the flesh.

4 Use mid green (D) on top of the pale green and create a gradient toward the inner edge. Lightly emphasize lines and divots on the flesh with dark sage (E), and add another layer of shadow to the cavity.

5 Add a zesty yellow (B) layer to the cavity, leaving the highlights alone. Use the sage to add more shadow, starting with light shading in the middle and applying more pressure toward the edge.

6 Add a layer of terracotta (G) to the stone, working around the highlights. Use brown (F) to deepen the area in shade and to lightly draw the lattice-like pattern over the surface of the stone, and pimento red (I) to pick out the pattern. Finally, further define the skin around the edge in black-brown (H).

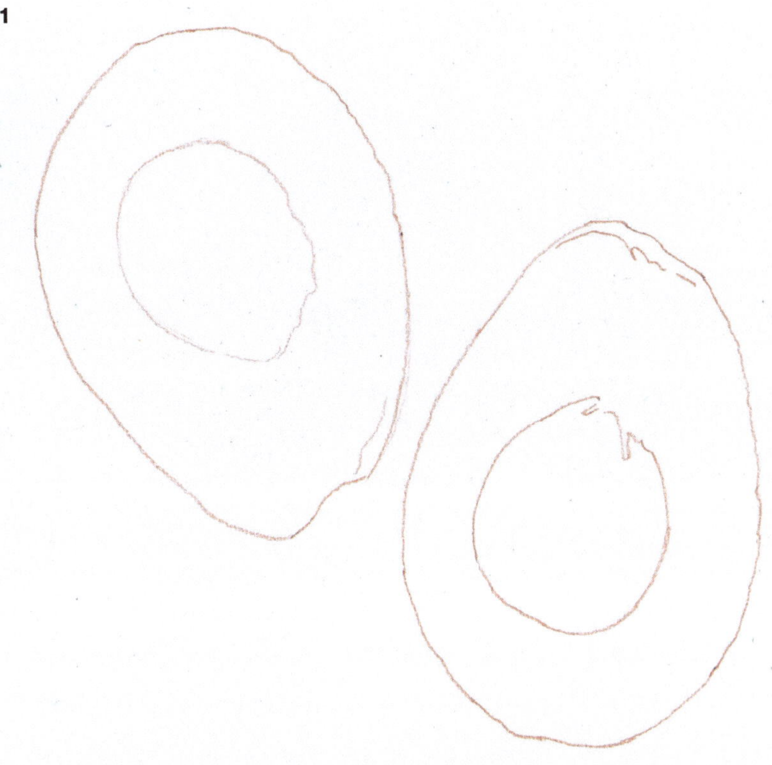

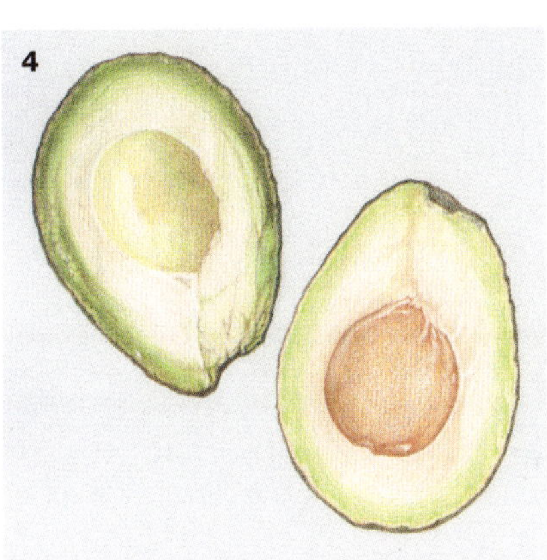

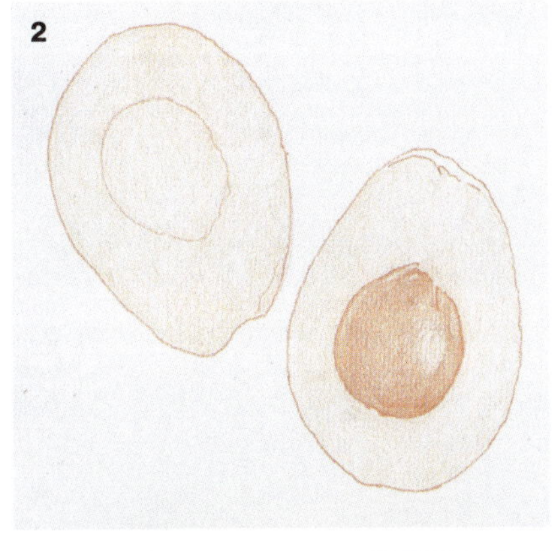

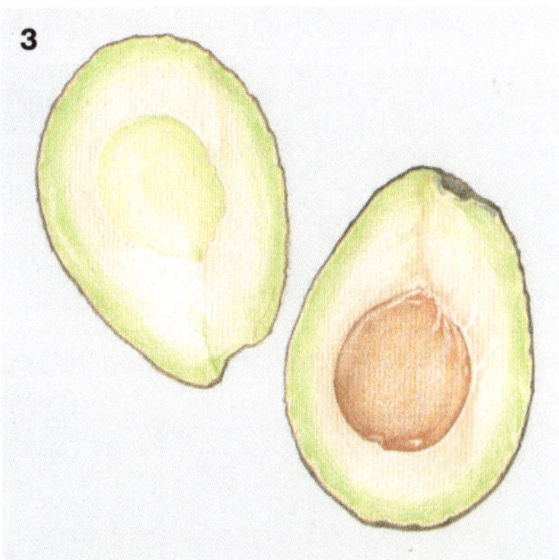

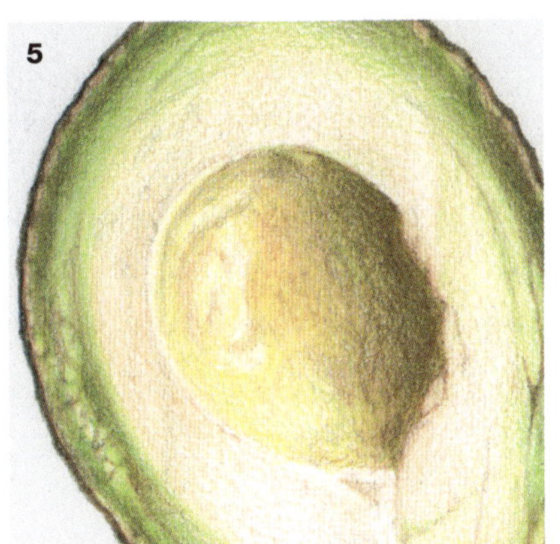

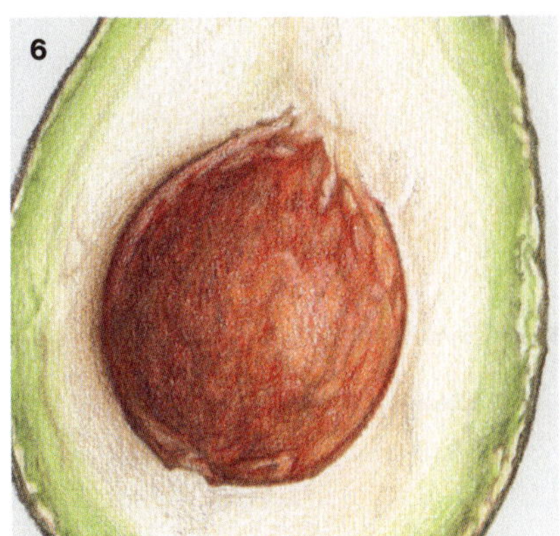

Glazed donut

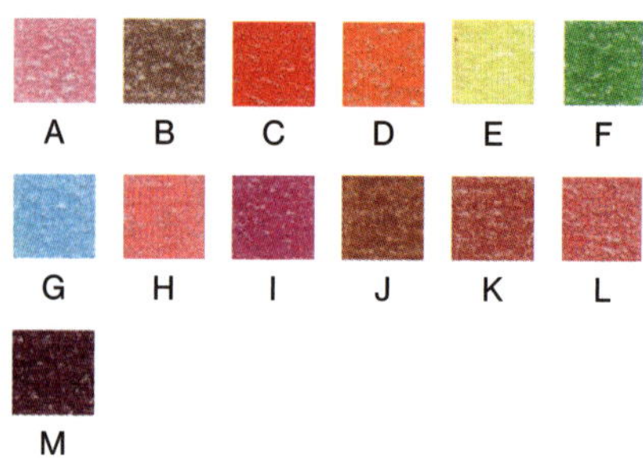

A B C D E F

G H I J K L

M

1 Choose a pink tone, here it's mid pink (A), for the linework, making sure you clearly outline all the individual sprinkles on top of the icing as well as highlight areas.

2 Use the mid pink with light pressure to shade in the base color of the icing, being careful to avoid the outlined sprinkles and any highlights that you've identified.

3 Select a pale brown (B) and, using light pressure, shade in the sponge area of the donut where it's not covered by icing.

4 Color the sprinkles using bright red (C), orange (D), yellow (E), green (F), blue (G), bright pink (H), and purple (I), leaving highlights on each where they occur.

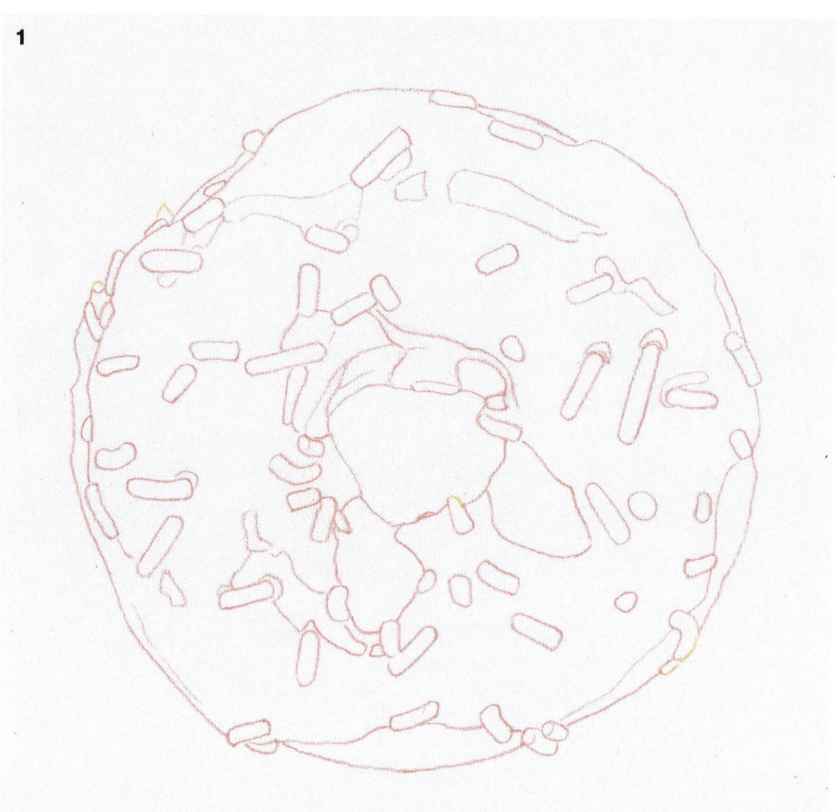

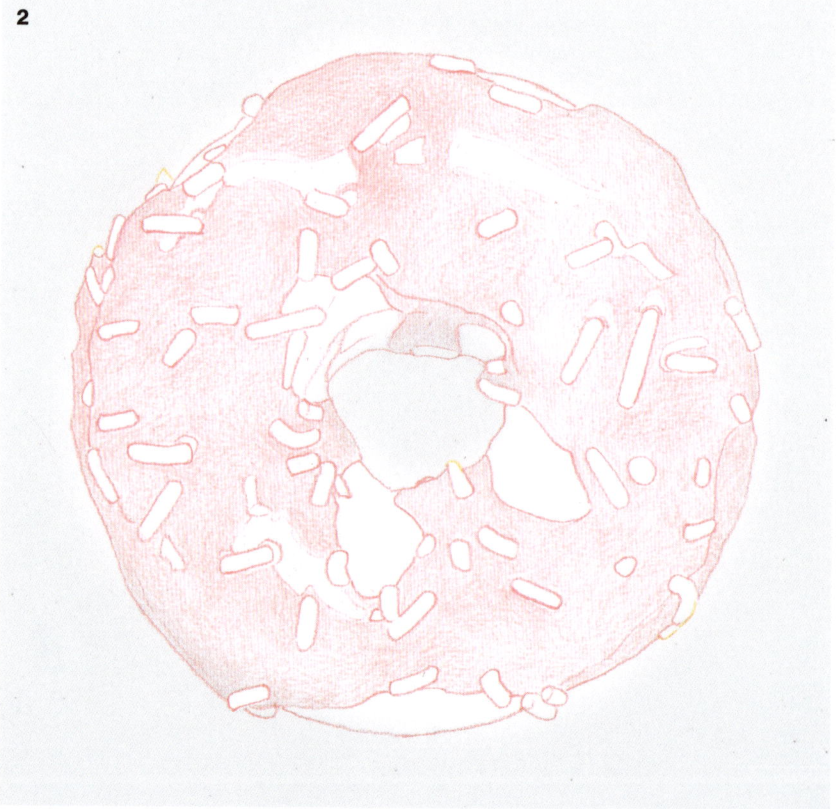

3

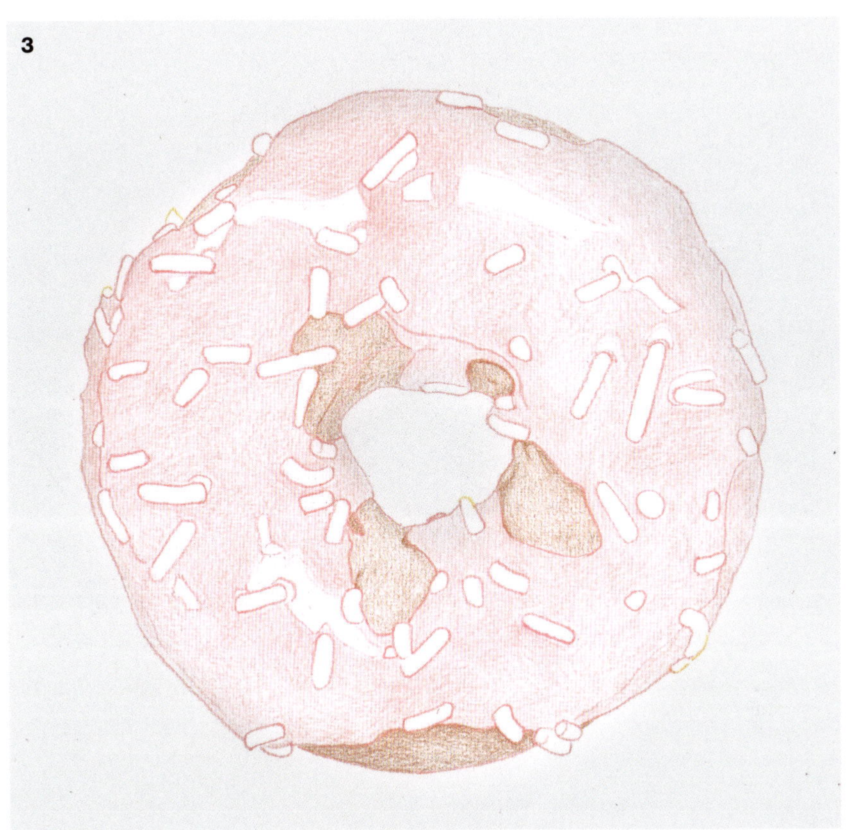

4

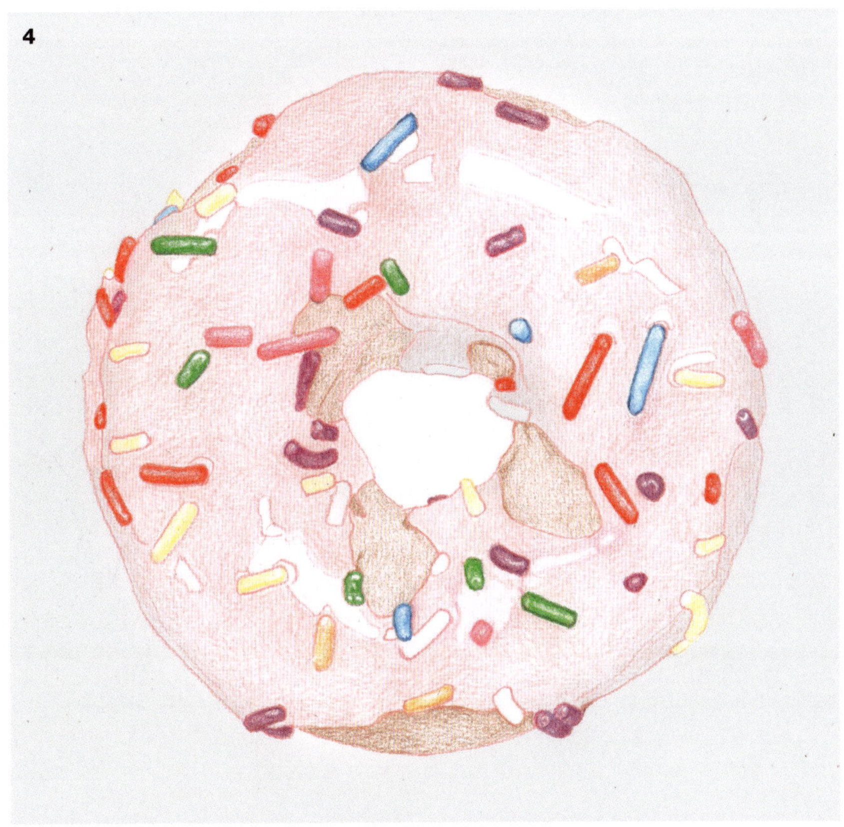

5 Use bright pink (H) with medium pressure to take the icing a shade darker, applying extra pressure to darken the areas immediately around the edges of each sprinkle and the edges of the icing drips. Further define the highlights to make them stand out.

6 With mid brown (J) and rusty red-brown (K), add texture, dark pockets, and shadows to the sponge, applying more pressure where the sponge and the icing meet.

7 Take the icing a further shade deeper using dark pink (L), again using more pressure around the sprinkle edges and icing drips. Define the highlight edges. Use bright red (C) with medium pressure to add extra depth to the shadows on the icing, focusing on the center of the donut and around the bottom edge.

8 Using the sprinkle colors from step 4, applying heavy pressure, add another layer of color to the sprinkles, avoiding the highlights. Use extra pressure around the edges of each sprinkle where it is embedded in the icing.

9 Use blackberry (M) with light to medium pressure to add depth to all the shadows. Carefully blend the darker color into the icing shadow areas, focusing on the icing folds around the center of the donut.

10 Finally, give extra definition around the edges of the sprinkles and icing drips, and use your eraser pen to clean up the highlights if needed.

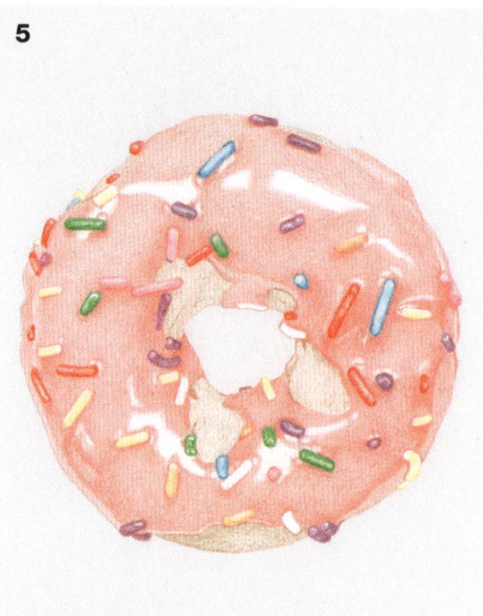

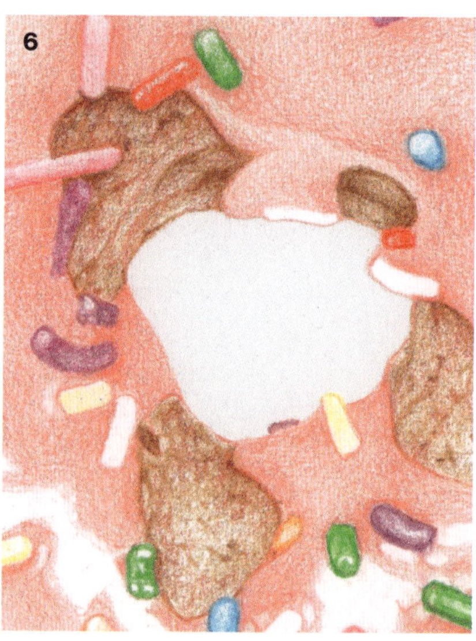

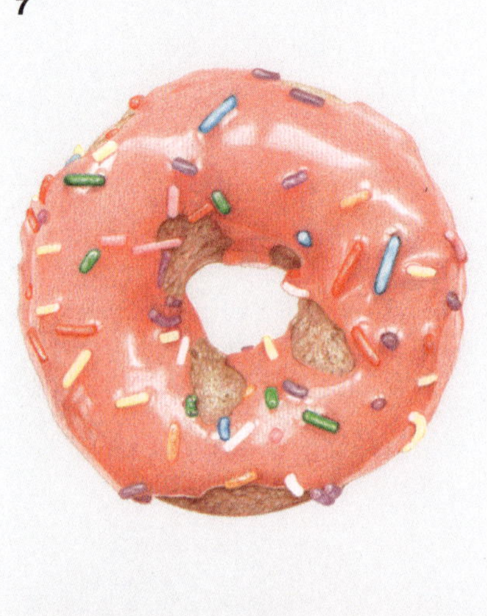

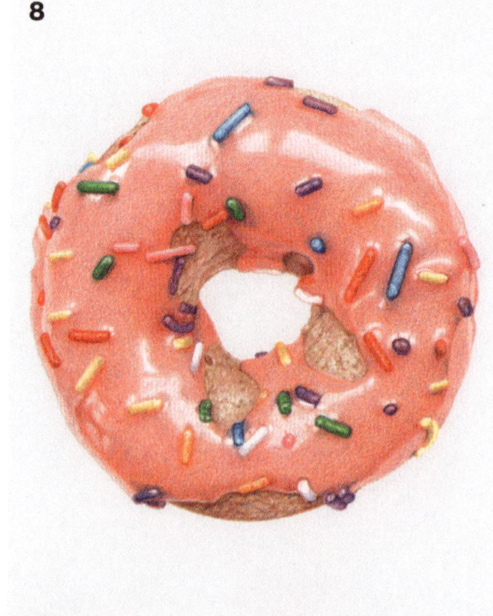

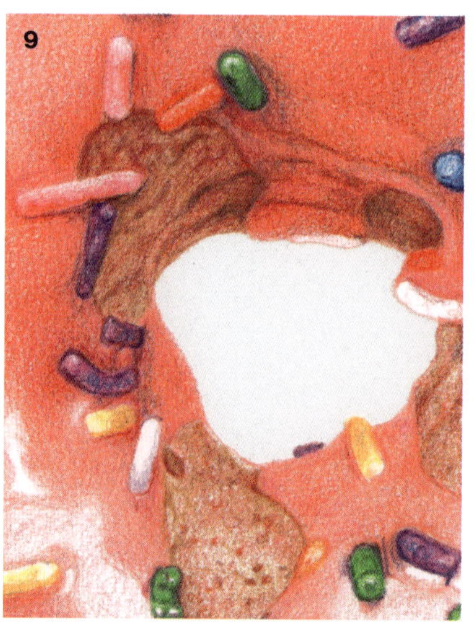

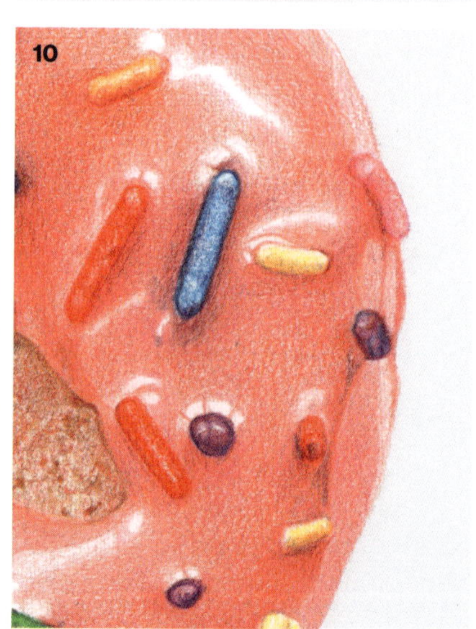

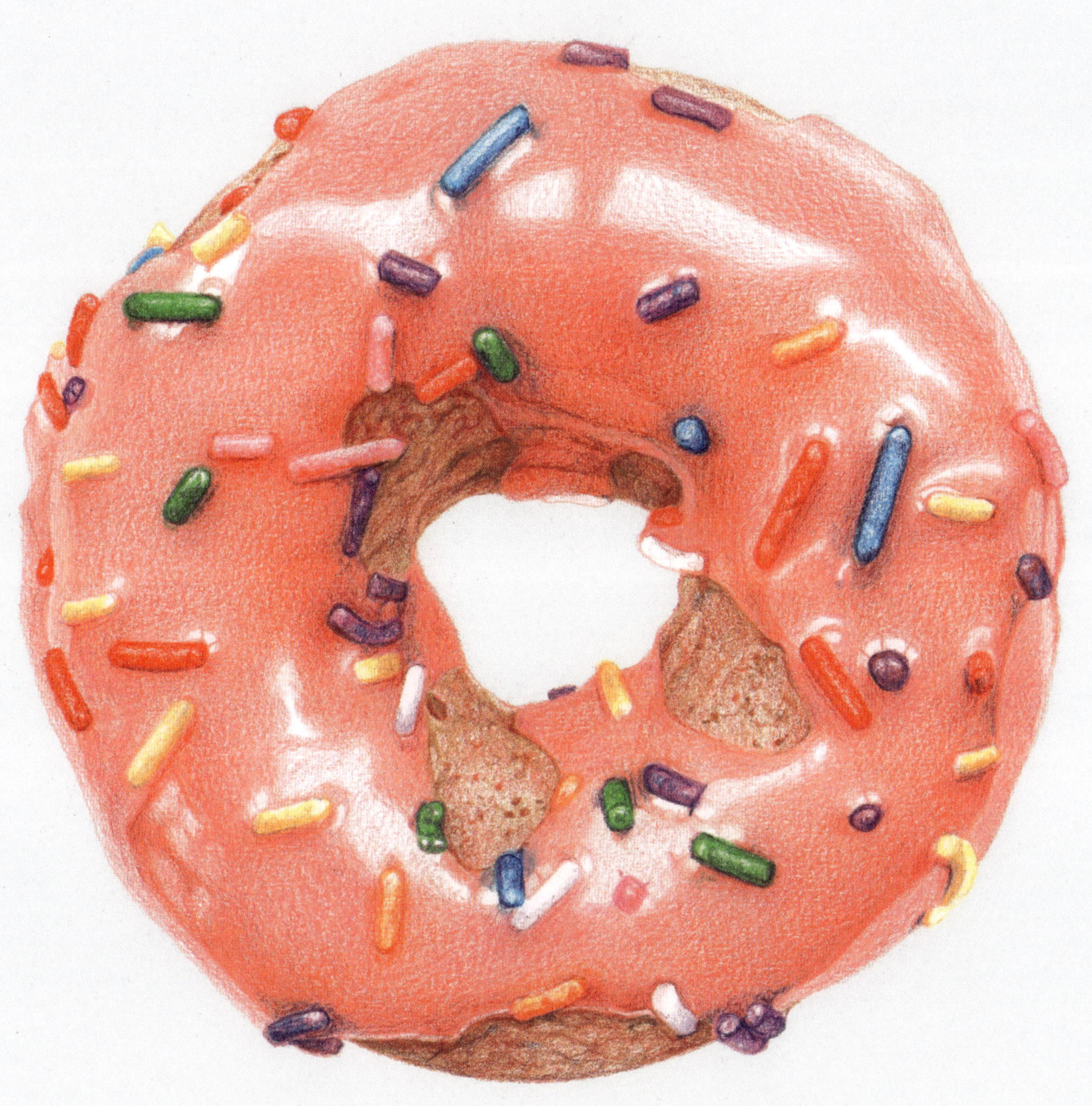

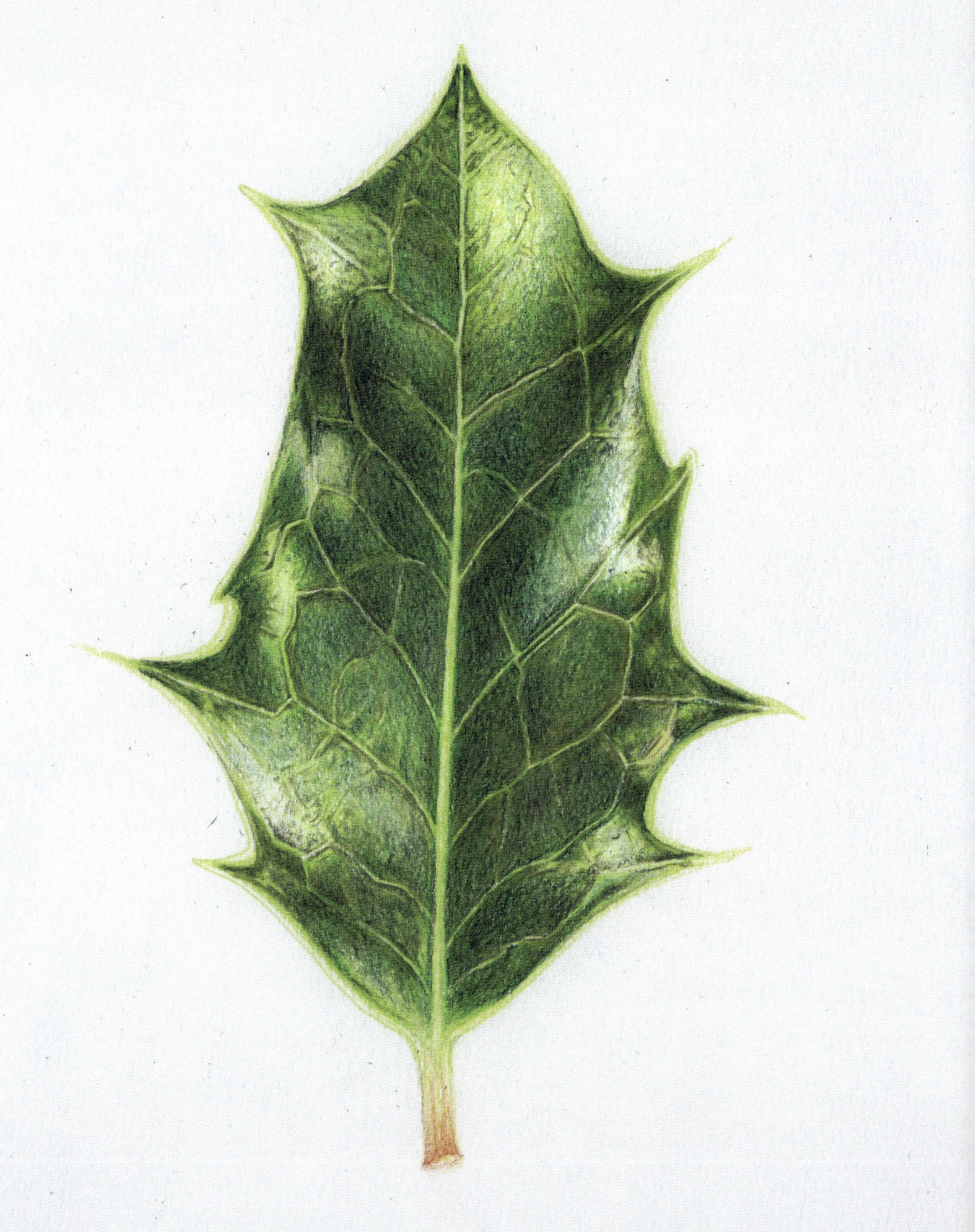

Holly leaf

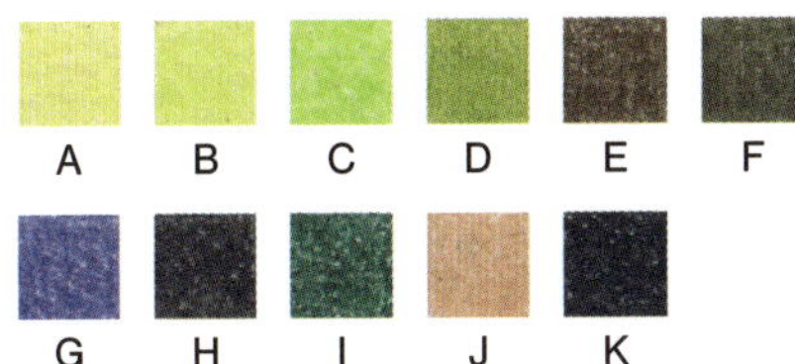

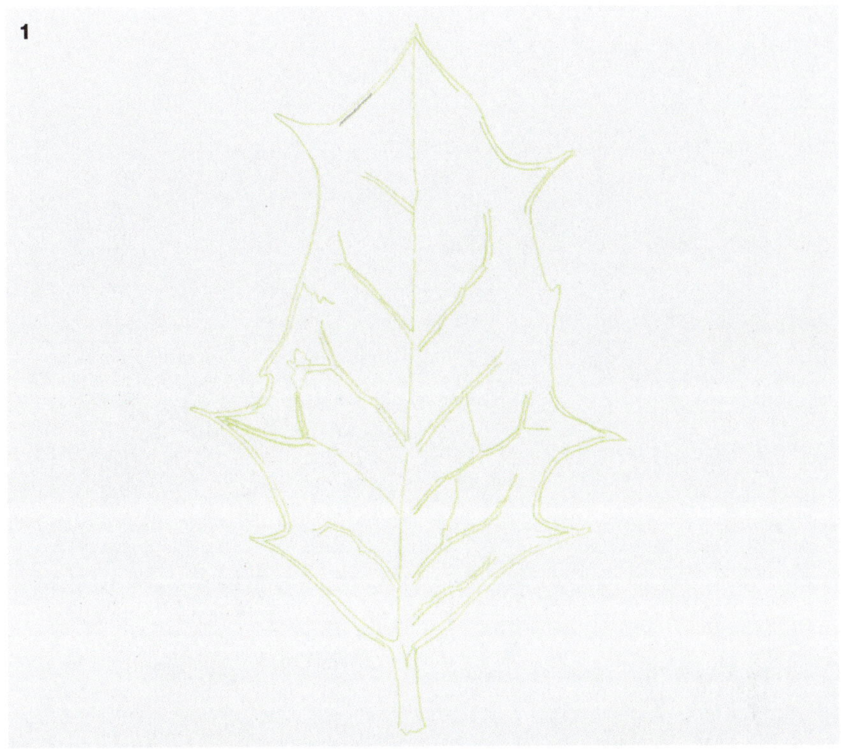

1. Use a light yellow-green (B) for the linework, adding as much of the vein detail as you can, as this makes shading easier later.

2. Shade the leaf in the same light yellow-green, leaving the central stalk white. Leave a slim white strip along one side of the smaller veins so that you don't lose them. Use zesty green (C) to add another layer of color, leaving the same white areas. Leave a thin line of light yellow-green all the way around the leaf edge, and shade around the highlights. Use pale yellow (A) to shade the stalk and veins.

3. Add a layer of pale olive green (D) with medium pressure, avoiding highlights, veins, and stalk. Use mid olive green (E) with medium pressure to create darker shadow areas, and focus extra pressure around the leaf edge. Shade the bottom of the stalk in light ocher (J).

4. Add depth to the shadow zones using sage green (F), applying pressure to define the edge of the leaf and veins. Use mid blue (G) with light pressure in the highlight zones; when the light catches these areas the blue tones in the leaf become visible. Use sage green again to give a speckled texture to these highlights.

5. Add a layer of darker sage green (H), allowing some of the lighter sage green to show through. Use bottle green (I) with medium pressure to enhance the blue tones in the leaf, using circular strokes to blend the colors together. With a very dark bottle green (K), add depth to the darkest zones and definition to the edges of the veins and stalk.

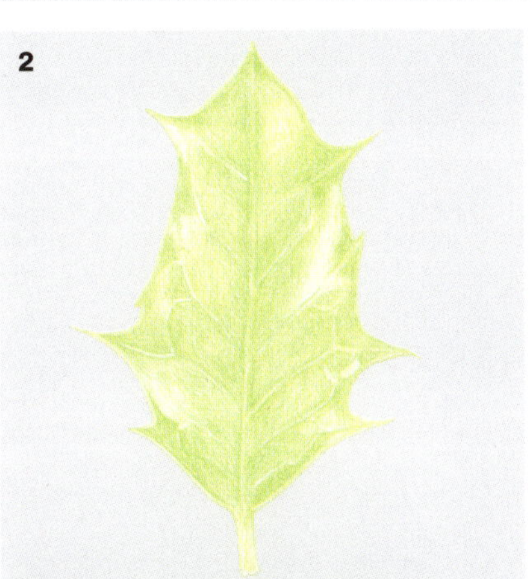

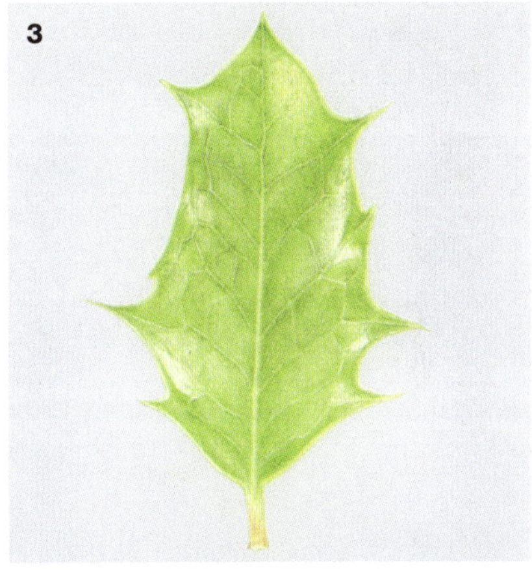

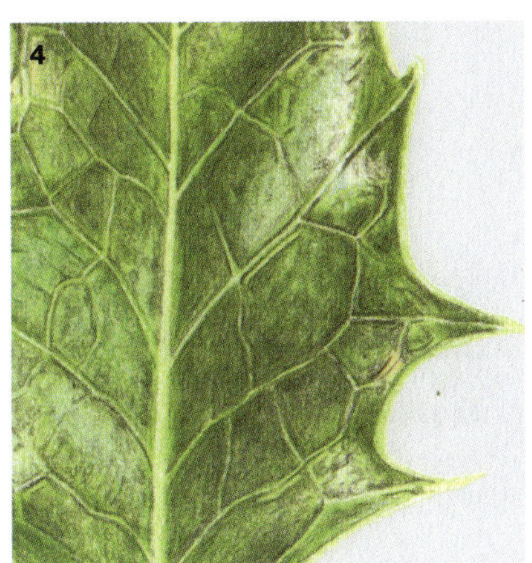

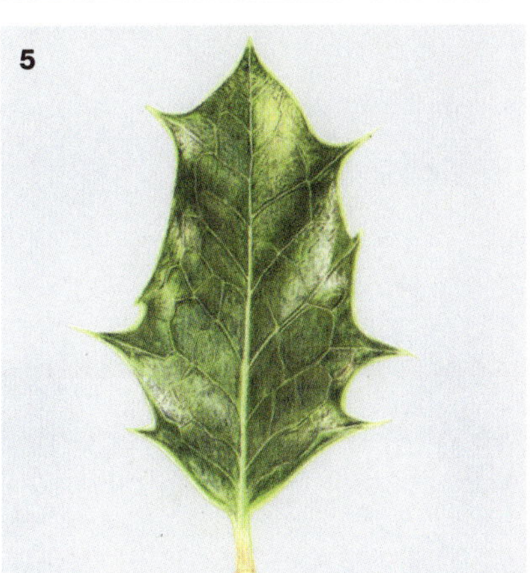

Mussels

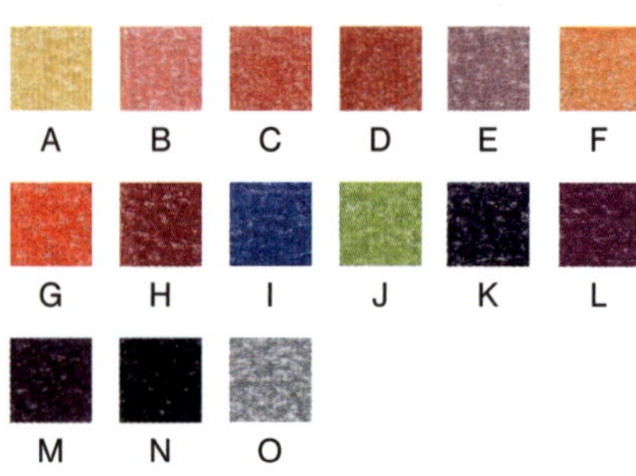

1 With pale gray (O) or a graphite pencil draw the guidelines for the shells, using mid orange (F) to create guidelines for the flesh.

2 Use flesh pink (B) and mid orange to shade in the outer shell, leaving the highlights white. Identify the darker areas of the shell with the mid orange. Use warm mid yellow (A) to shade in the flesh. With pale gray and light pressure, shade the inside of the shell and the highlights on the middle outer shell.

3 Shade in the outer shells with light pimento red-brown (D). Outline the small barnacle areas on the middle and lower shells and leave them in the light flesh pink background color. Use pressure to create the ripples, lines, and darker shadow zones on the shells.

4 Use lavender gray (E) to add another layer of color to the shells. Don't completely cover the red-brown you laid down in the previous step. Use pressure to define the shadow zones and add darker shadows and tonal variation to the internal surface of the shells. Remember to work around the highlights.

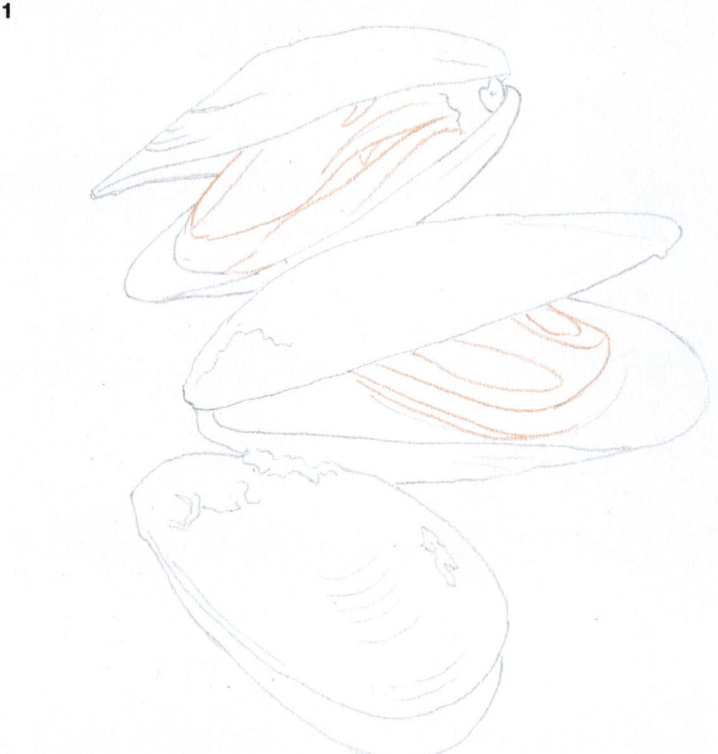

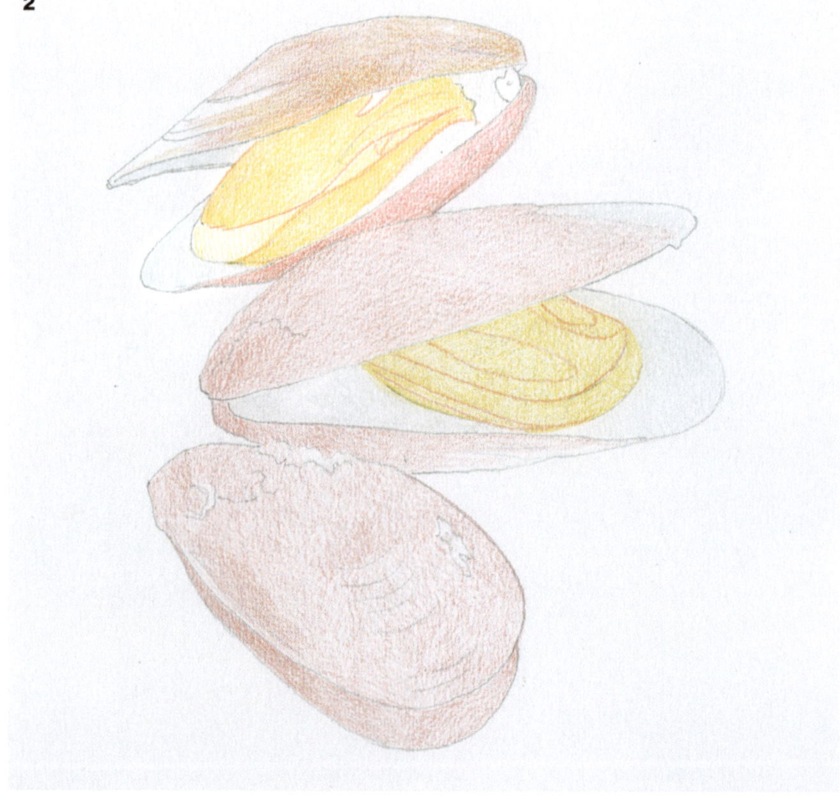

3

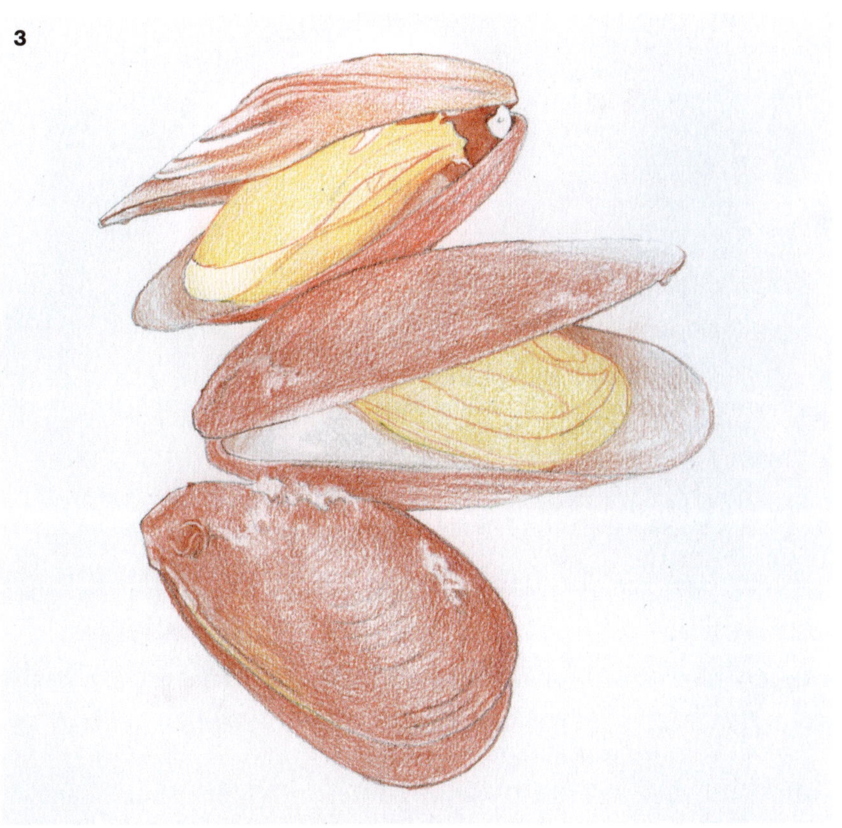

4

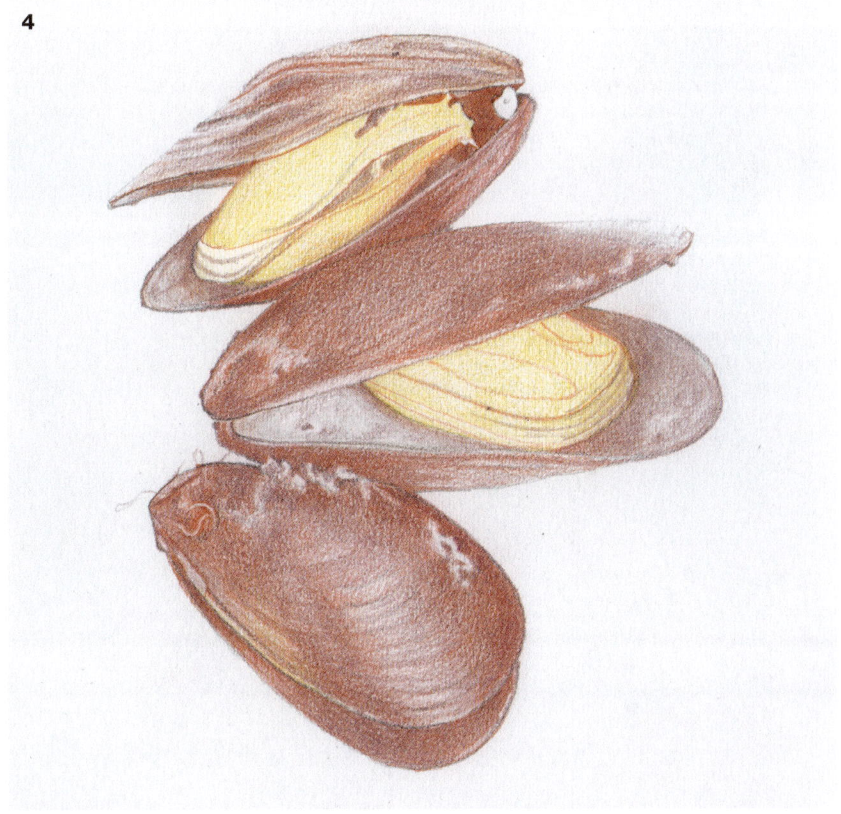

5 Shade in the flesh using mid orange (F) and deep orange (G). Use mid orange first to take the mussels a shade darker, then deep orange for the darkest areas. Blend carefully, producing a smooth gradient between the two. Use deep cranberry red (H) to color the dark details on the flesh and shade around the edges where it meets the shell. Use the same color with light pressure to give depth to the shadows and add warm reddish hues to the rest of the outer shells.

6 Lightly use royal blue (I) to add blue tones to the shells' surfaces, both internal and external. Don't entirely shade over the layers of pink and reddish brown: allow these colors to bleed through around the highlights. Focus pressure on the shadows and accentuate lines and ripples on the external surfaces. Use light olive green (J) to pick out the green detail along the edges of the middle shell.

7 With the same royal blue, add darker shadows to the internal surface of the shells. Focus more pressure around the edges of the flesh where it sits in the shell. Apply pressure to define the sharp edges of the shells.

8 Use dark purple (K) and mid purple (L) to add another layer of color to the shells. Again, don't completely shade over the layers of color beneath. Apply pressure to create darker shadows: use the dark purple on the inner shells and the mid purple predominantly on the external surfaces. Add color to the barnacles with flesh pink (B).

9 Use blackberry (M) to further darken the shadows inside the shells. Build up the color on the outer shells slowly, focusing pressure on the darker areas and allowing previous layers to show through. Work around the barnacles, adding definition and detail this time. Shade over the blackberry using black (N). Finally, use a small eraser pen to make the highlights stand out.

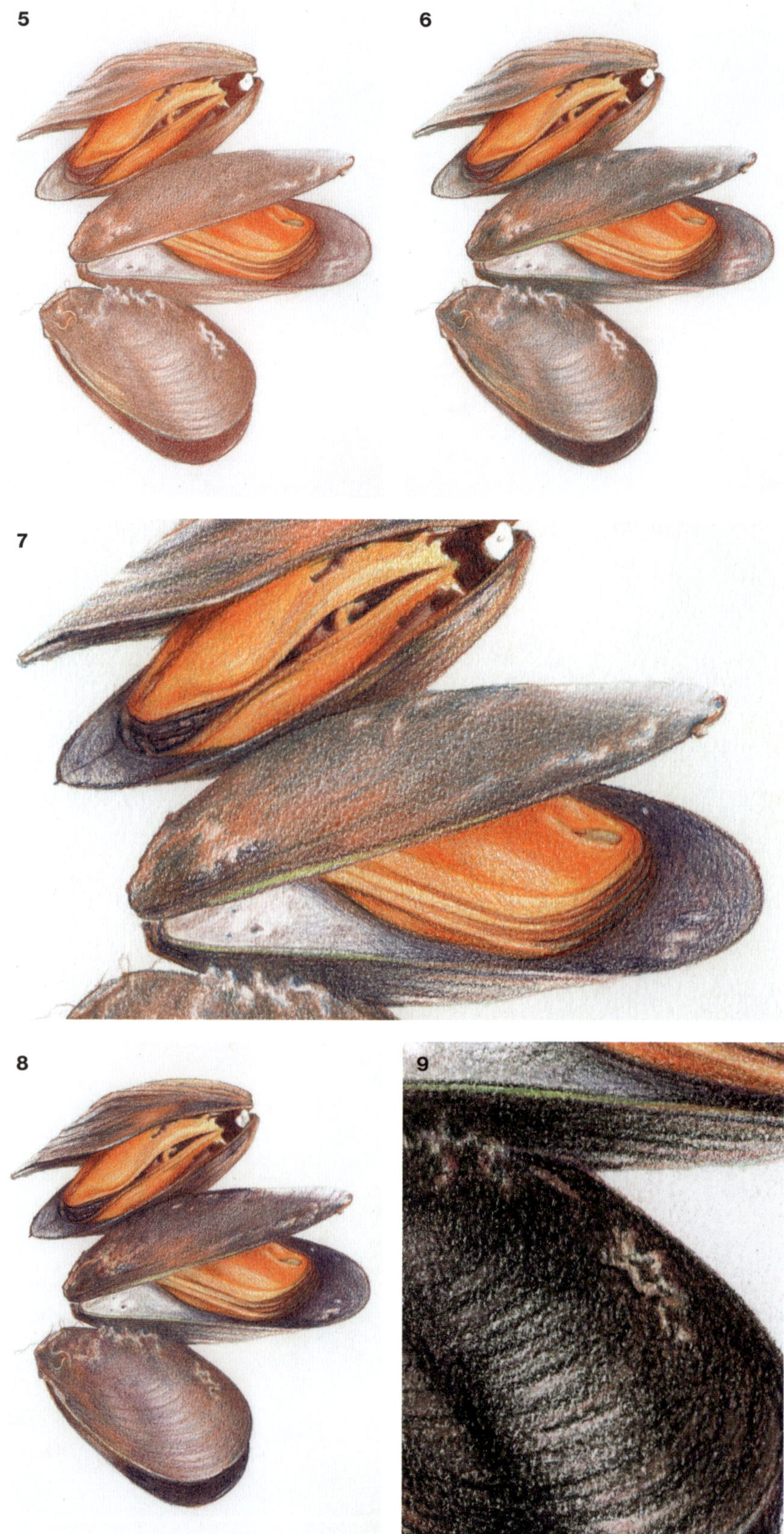

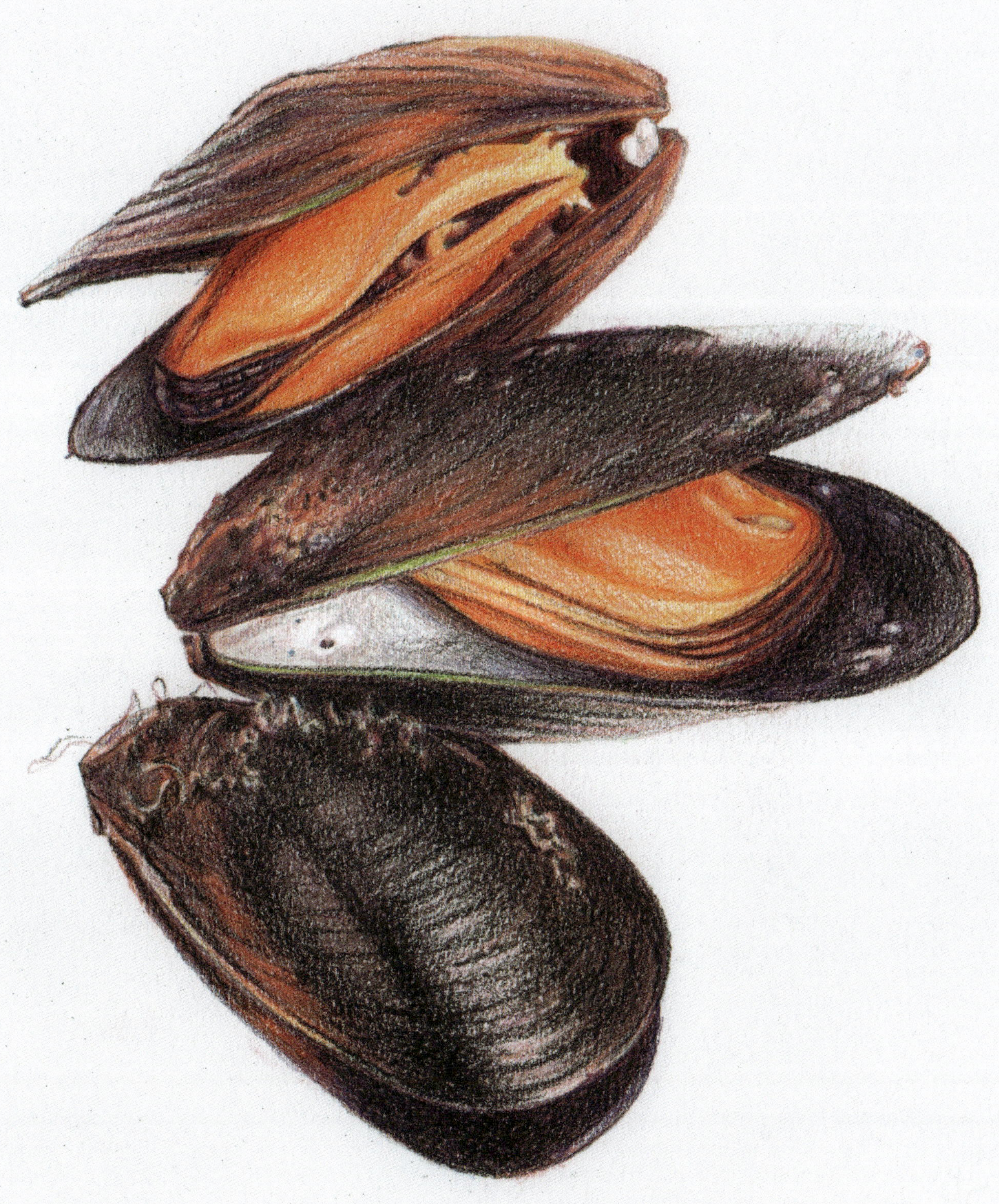

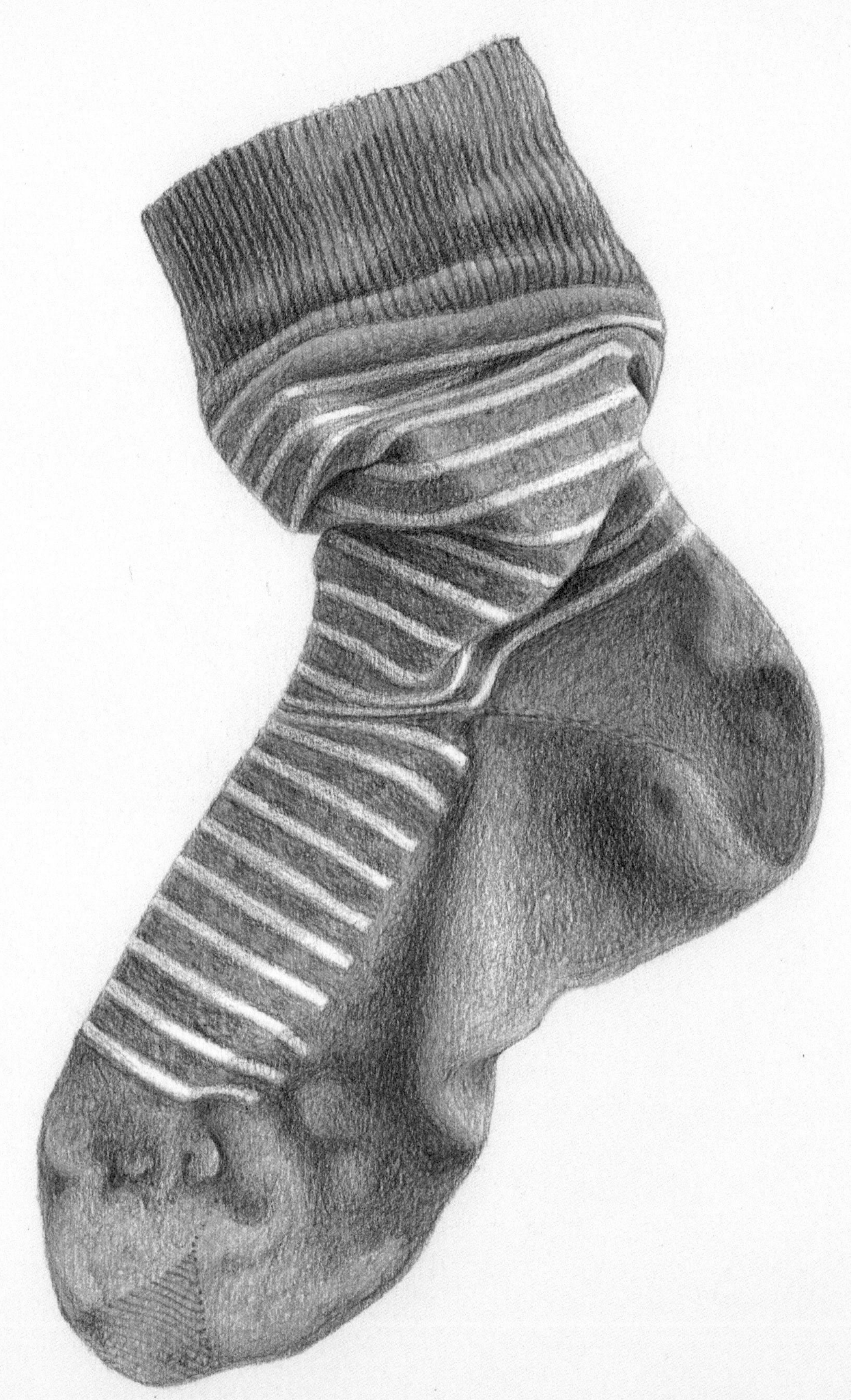

Sock

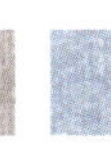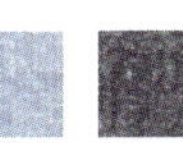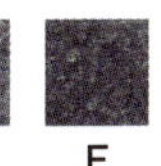

A   B   C   D   E   F

1 Lay down linework using mid gray (B).

2 Shade the background of the whole sock in light silver-gray (A), avoiding the stripes. Apply greater pressure to identify the shadows and folds on the sock.

3 Use the mid gray (B) with medium pressure to add another layer of color. Work carefully around the stripes, using your eraser pen to remove any heavy guidelines as you go, and apply heavier pressure to darken the shadows and folds.

4 Add a sepia tone using pale brown-gray (C), which will make the sock look nicely worn. Use light pressure over the whole sock and heavier pressure in the darker gray areas. Use mid gray (B) with heavy pressure to make the ribbed cuff a shade darker, and dark gray (E) to accentuate the ribs and the shadows created by the folds in the cuff.

5 Use the dark gray to take the shadows created by the creases on the rest of the sock a shade darker, blending into the lighter areas with circular pencil strokes. Give depth to the shadows using light blue-gray (D) with medium pressure over the whole sock, avoiding the stripes. Use dark gray with heavy pressure to take all the shadows a shade darker, and gray-black (F) to add a final layer of shadow to the darkest creases and folds.

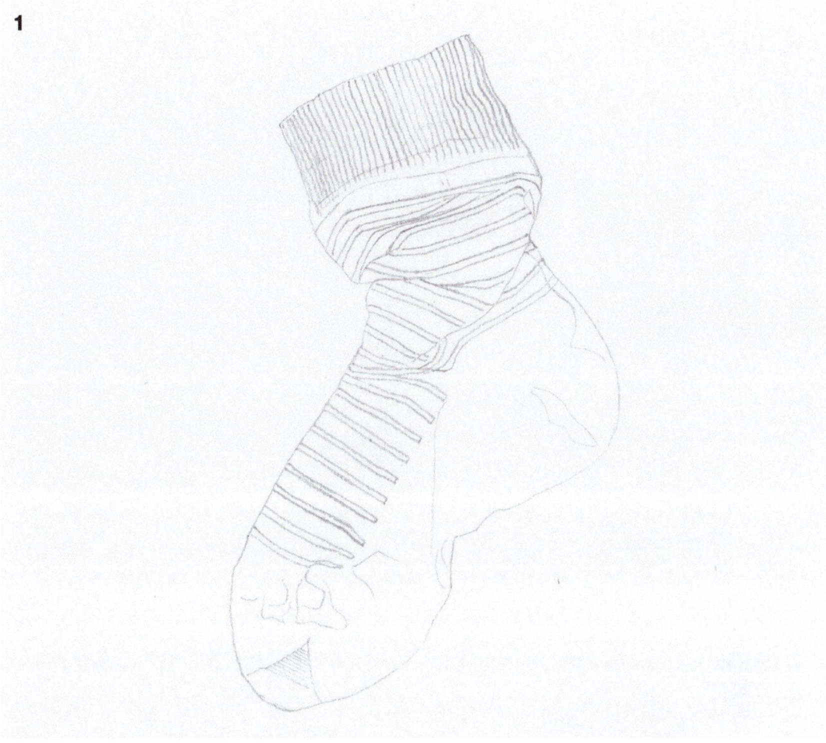

1

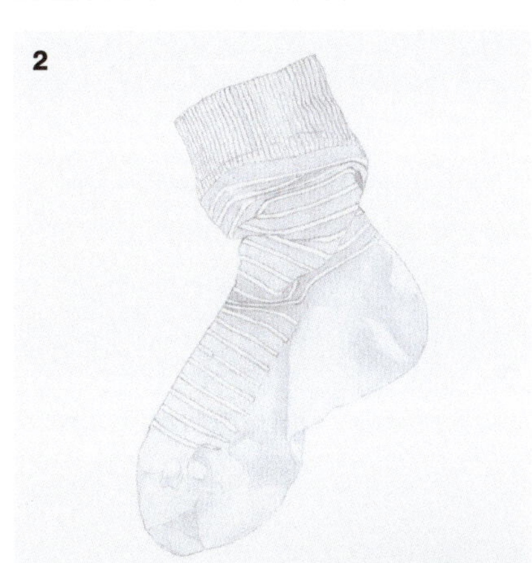

2

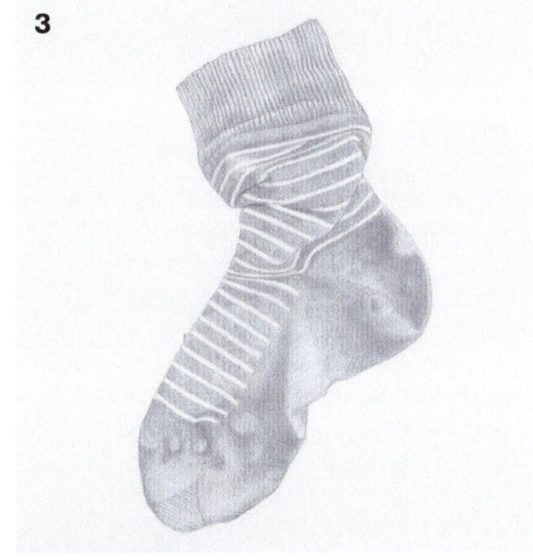

3

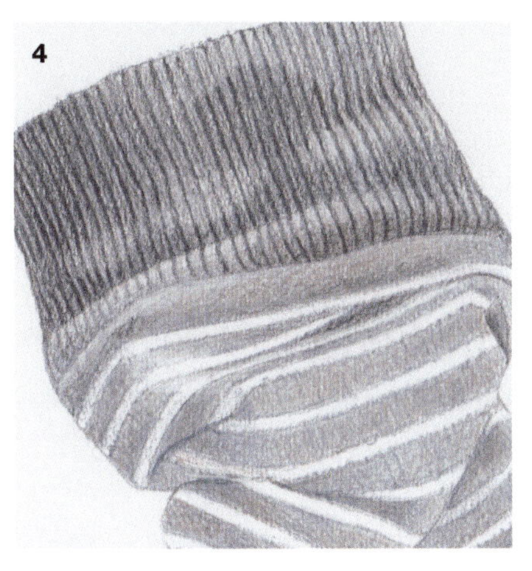

4

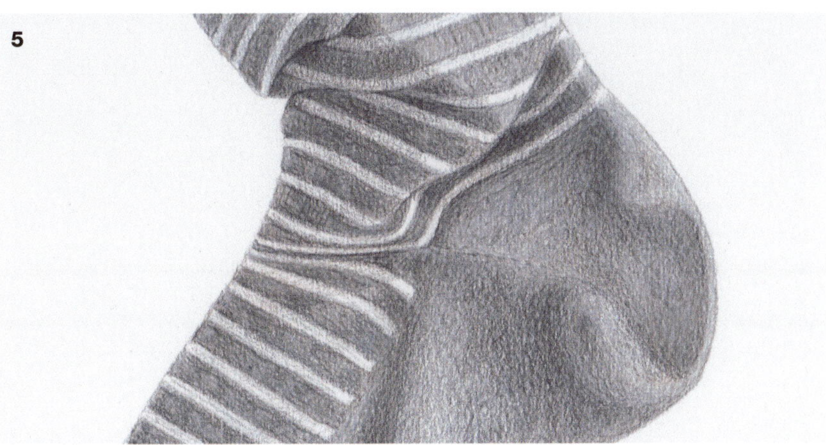

5

Strawberry

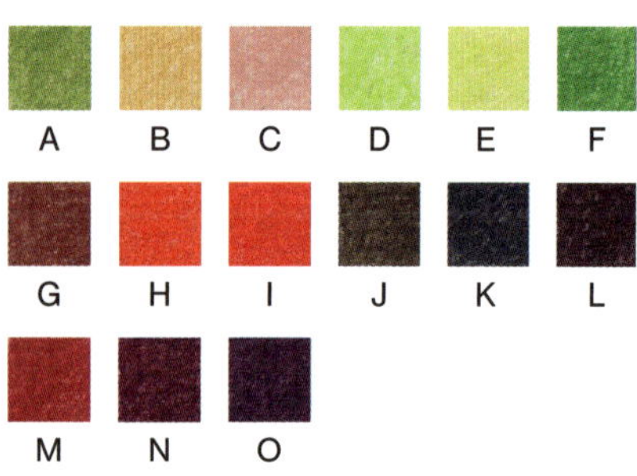

1 For your linework, select light tones from the color palette for each of the different elements of the strawberry. Use mid green (A) for the leaves and stalk, mid yellow (B) to outline the seeds, and light flesh pink (C) for the strawberry outline and to define the highlights.

2 Color in the seeds with mid yellow, and use light green (D) with light pressure to shade in the leaves and stalk. Use the light flesh pink to lay down the background color of the strawberry, avoiding the seeds and the flesh at the top just below the leaves: lightly shade this area with yellow-green (E) and shade the right-hand half of the strawberry on top of the flesh pink background.

3 With bright green (F), identify areas of shadow on the leaves and stalk, applying a little pressure to indicate the more prominent leaf veins. Use mid brown (G) with light pressure to add color to the tips of the leaves and stalk. Draw over the seed outlines with orange-red (H) and use this color to lightly shade over the right-hand side of the strawberry.

4 Use the orange-red with medium pressure to shade in the red flesh. Define the highlights, drawing their shapes first then coloring around them. The light source is to the left of the strawberry, so use lighter pressure down the left side, shading around the seeds to achieve a paler zone. Use medium pressure to add shadow around the edges of each seed "pocket." Blend carefully into the pale green zone at the top of the strawberry.

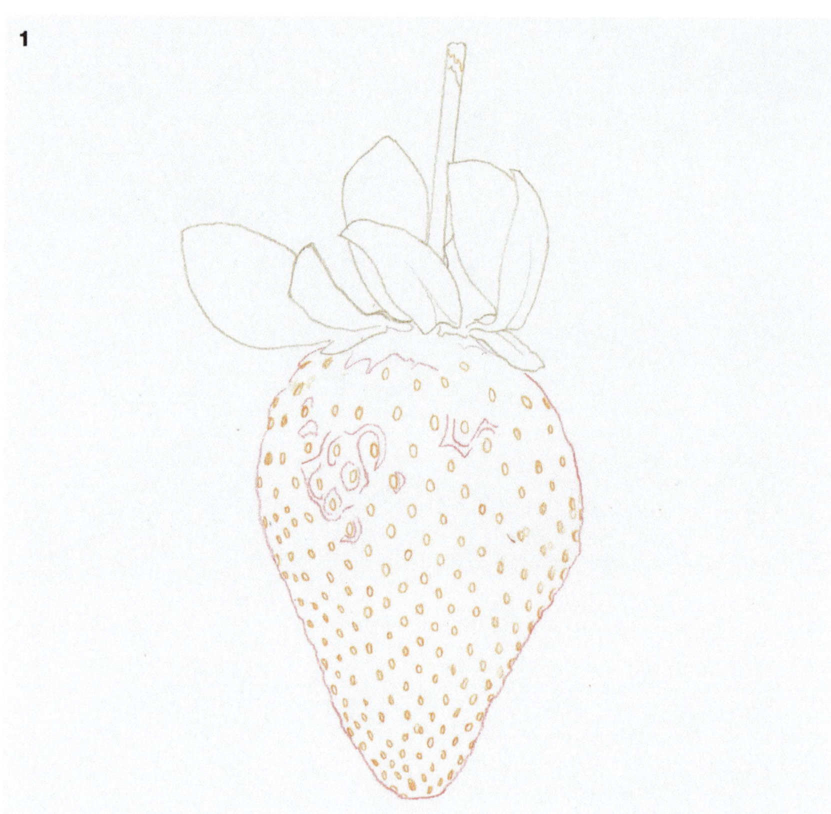

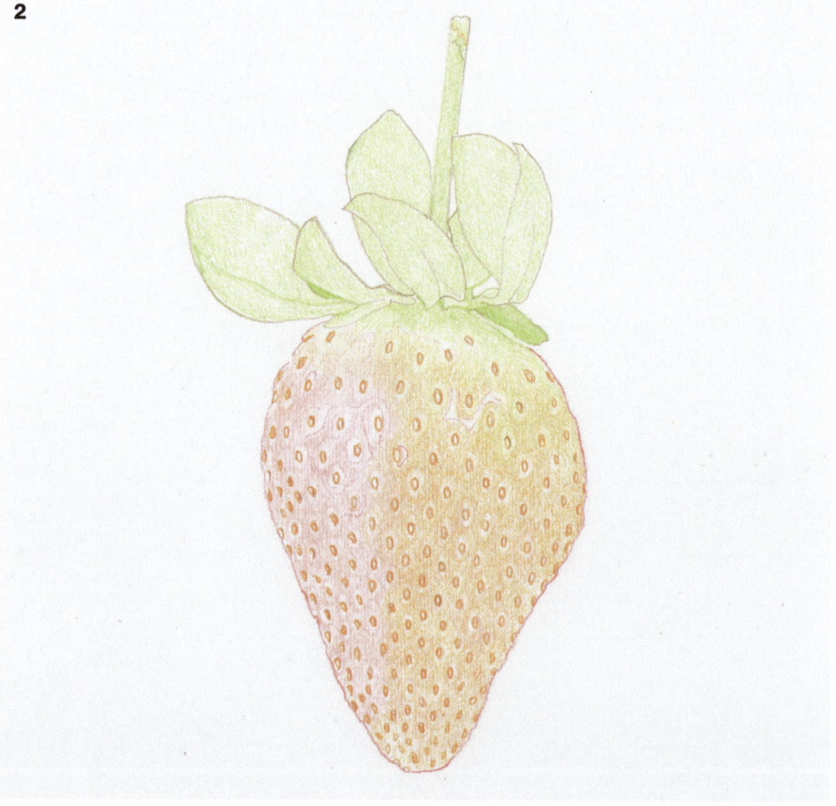

"

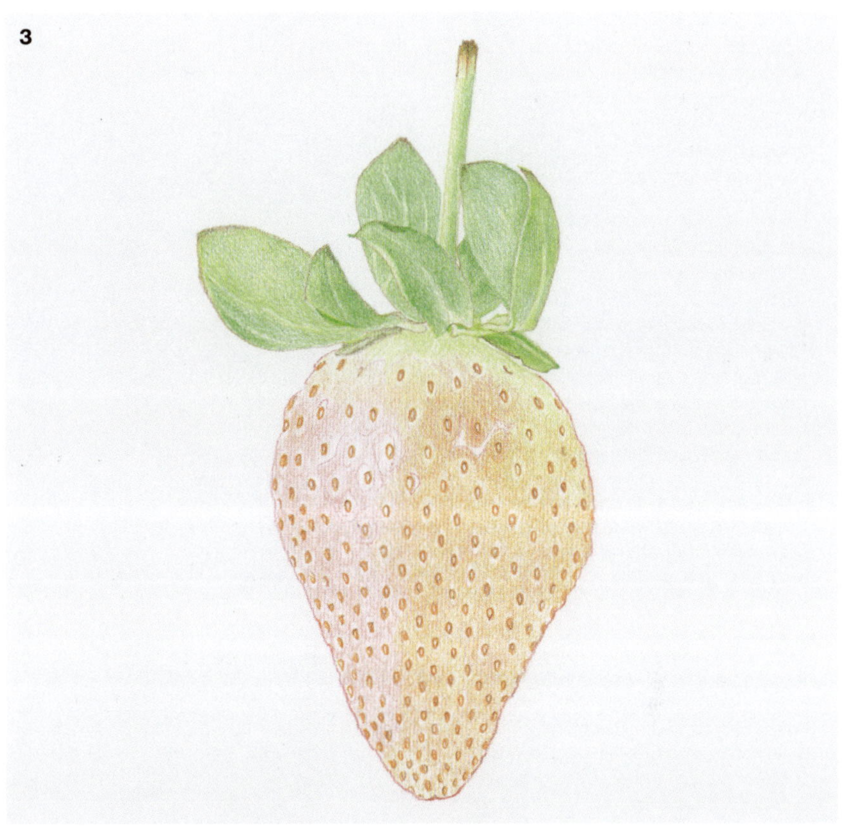

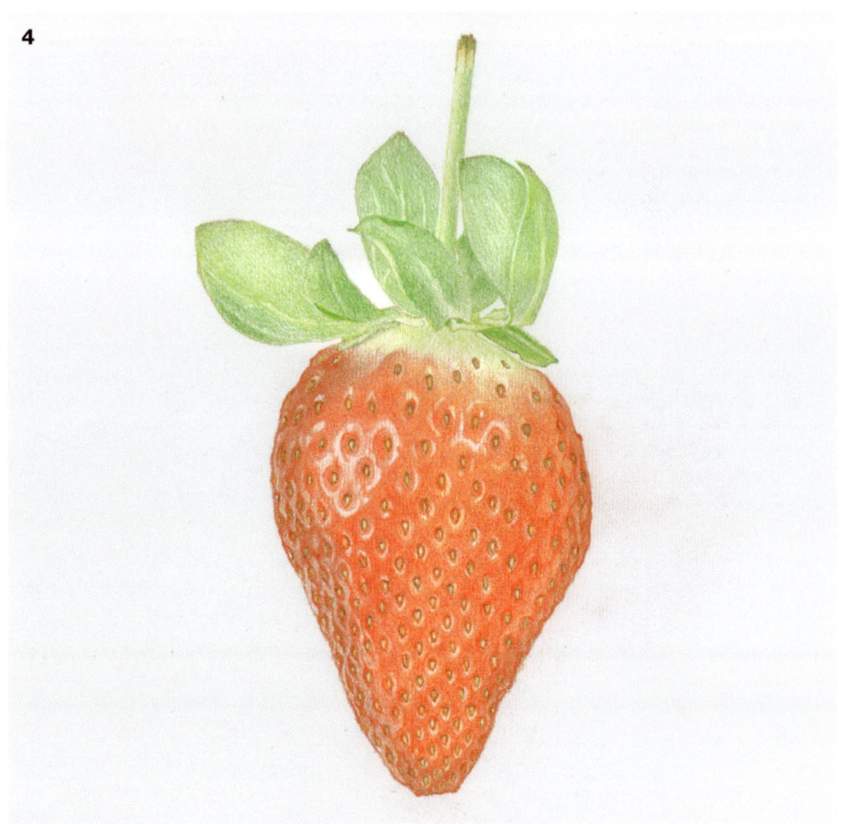

5 Apply bold red (I) to take the whole strawberry a shade darker, avoiding the highlights that you have carefully created. Use yellow-green (E) to add another layer of color to the leaves, using pressure to emphasize the darker zones.

6 Use dark olive green (J) with light to medium pressure to add another layer of color to the leaves. Add definition to the veins on the leaves and further darken the tips where the leaves are browning. Use this color to add more shadow to the right side of the stalk. On the flesh, use the bold red heavily to build up more color and create a smooth and consistent red finish.

7 With deep blue-green (K), define the edges and shadows of the leaves. Identify darker patches on the leaves and add more shadow to the stalk. Use dark brown (L) for the tip of the stalk and the browning edges of leaves. Use dark red (M) with pressure to shade in darker zones on the right side of the strawberry.

8 Add more depth and shadow to the strawberry using dark purple-red (N) with medium pressure. Use consistent circular blending strokes to layer on the color in the darkest areas and blend into the lighter green zone at the top of the strawberry. Carefully work around the seeds and highlights and use pressure to define the thin shadow pocket line around each seed.

9 Using the dark olive green (J) with medium pressure, take all the leaves a shade darker. Apply heavier pressure to add more depth to the shadows on the stem and leaves.

10 Use blackberry (O) to intensify the shadow zones on the strawberry, focusing on the right side where the shadows are darkest. Use the blackberry to darken the lines around the seeds in this area particularly.

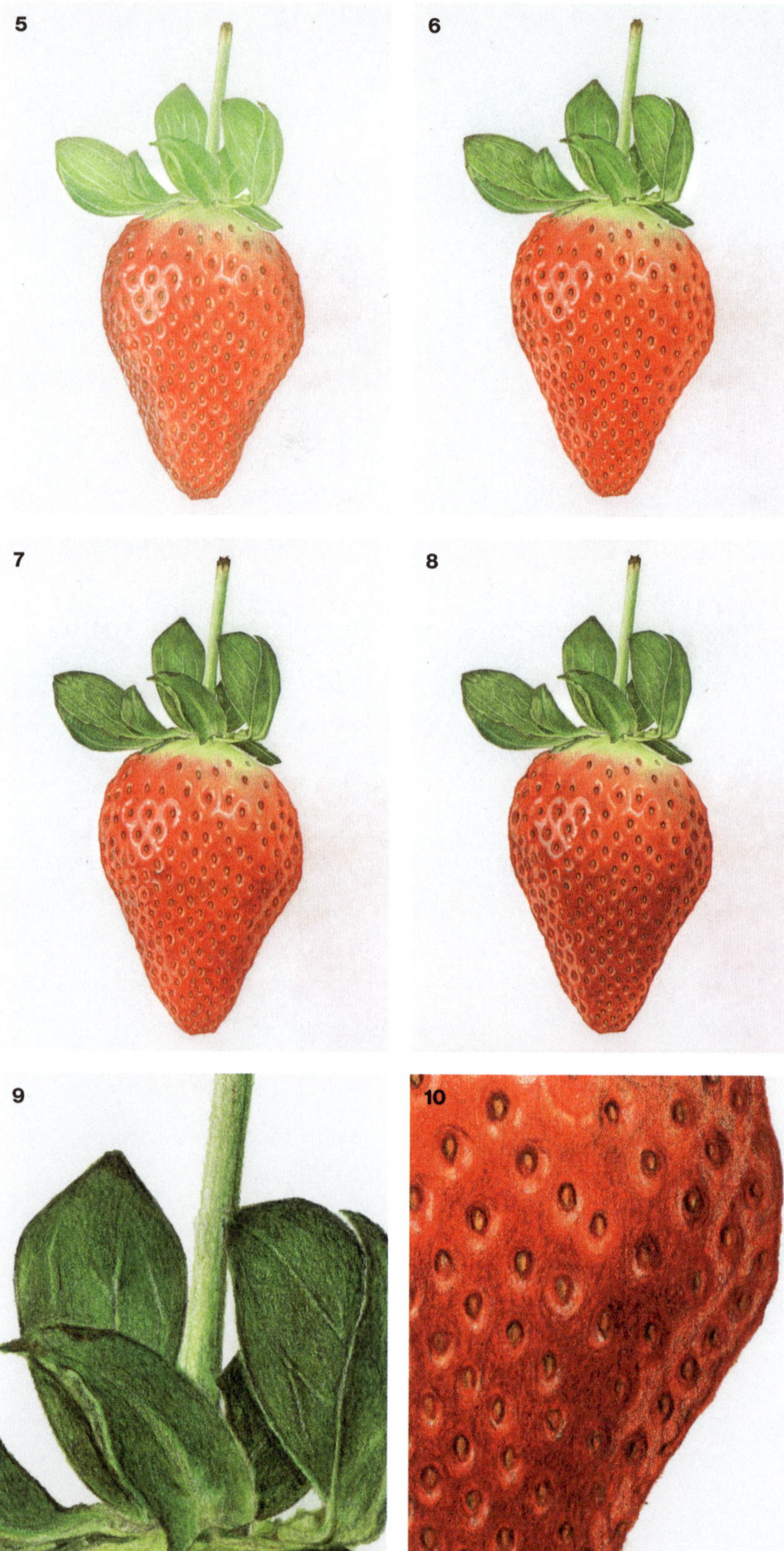

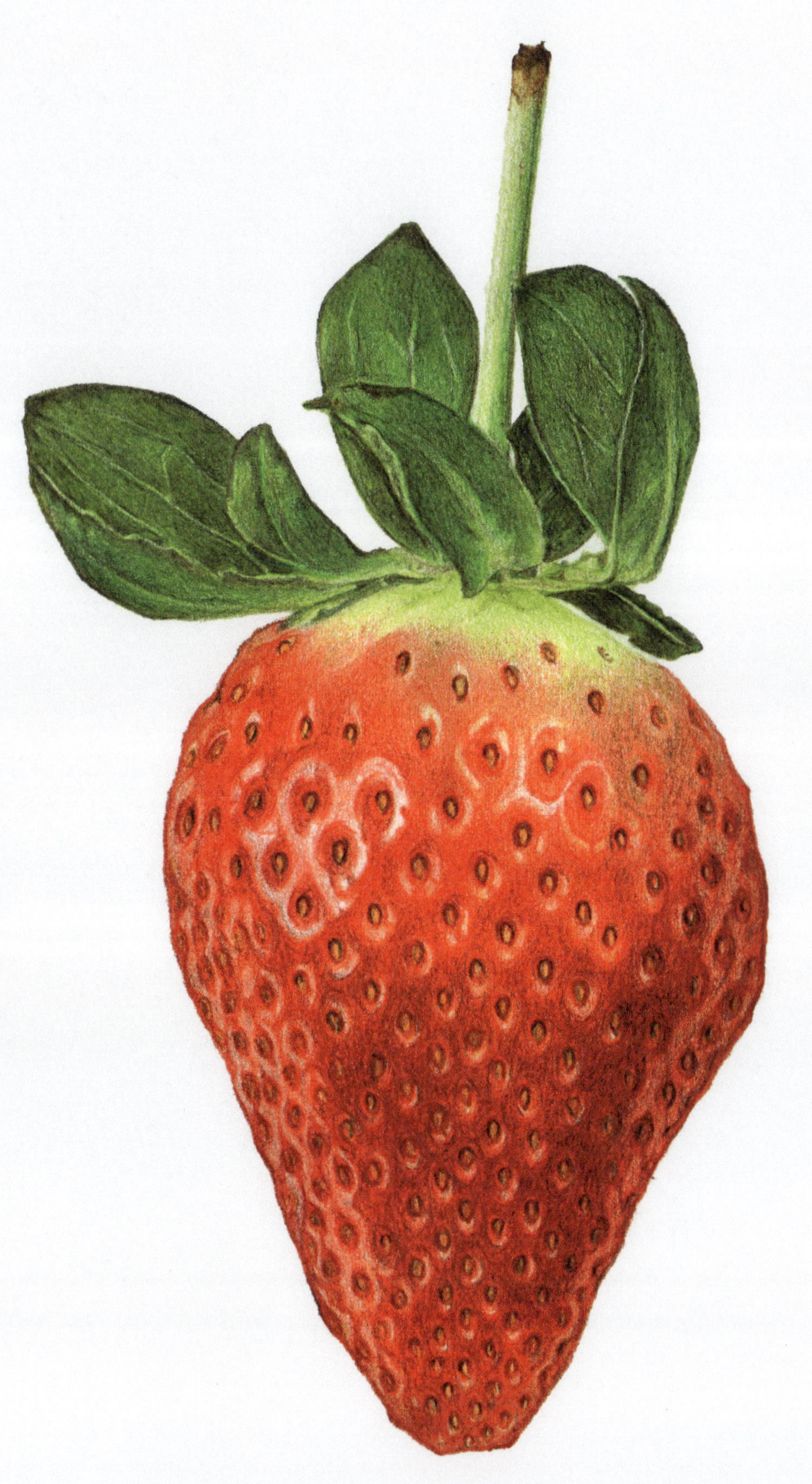

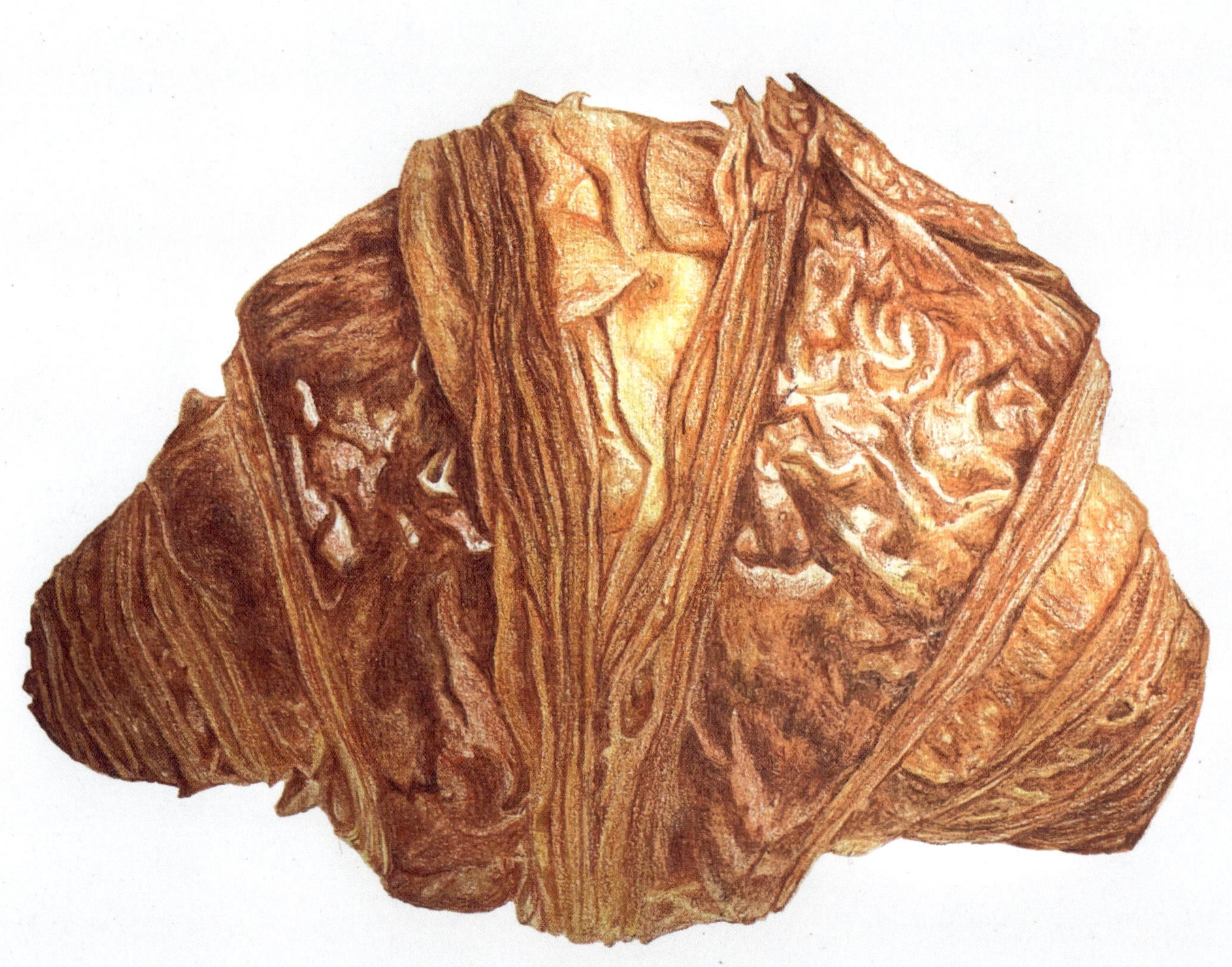

Croissant

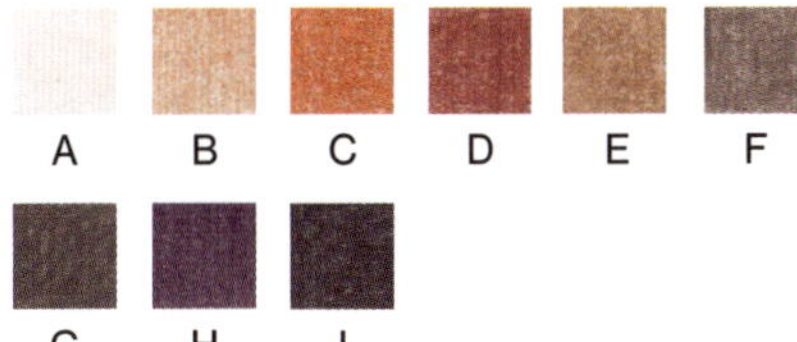

1 Use a light tone (B) for the linework.

2 Add a pale peach base across the whole of the croissant (A), and use light brown (E) to pick out the flaky folds and ridges.

3 Use terracotta (C) to add depth and definition to the same edges, flakes, and folds. Pick out the lowlights and darker spots with a bit more pressure.

4 Leaving the central area of flaky pastry alone, use the terracotta to take the two sides a shade darker, applying more pressure over the darker areas to ensure detail isn't lost.

5 Work into the shaded areas across the whole croissant with brown (F) and pimento red (D). Pick out flaky edges and shaded areas with dark brown (G). Don't completely cover the previous brown and red, just accent these with the dark brown. Finally, use blackberry (H) and black-brown (I) to add a final layer of dark shadow, making the left side of the croissant a shade darker.

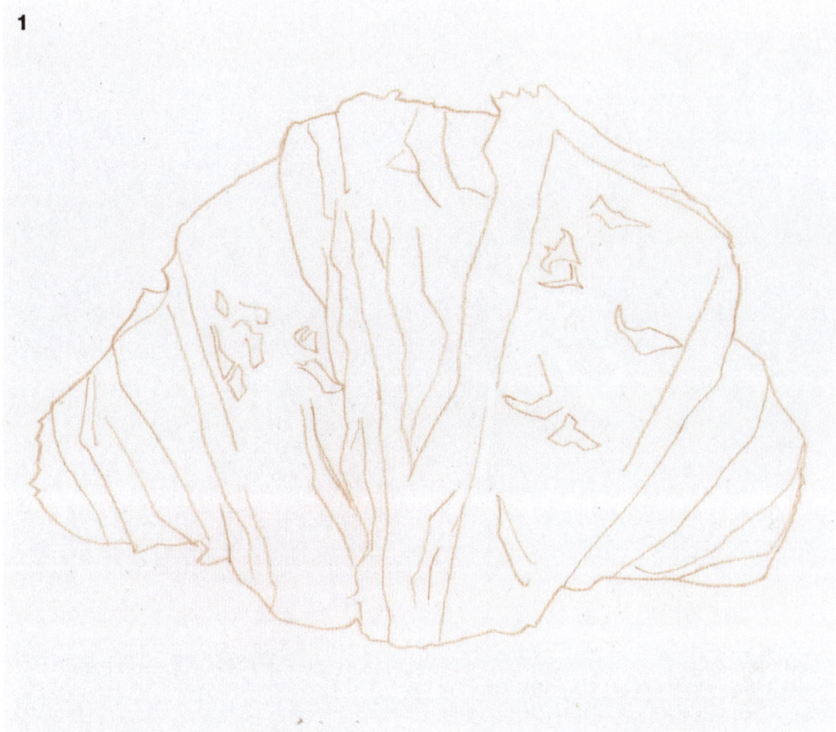

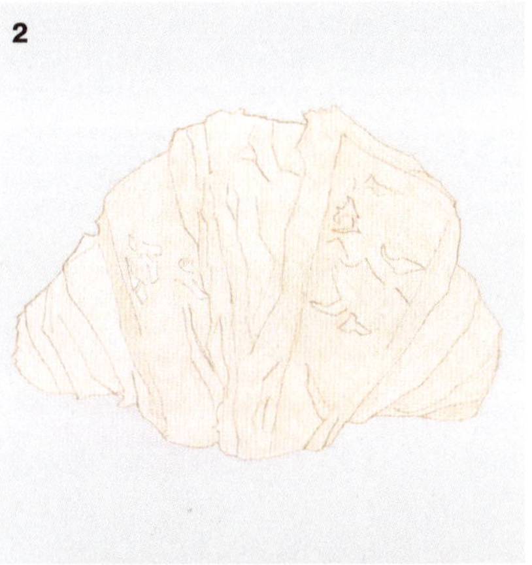

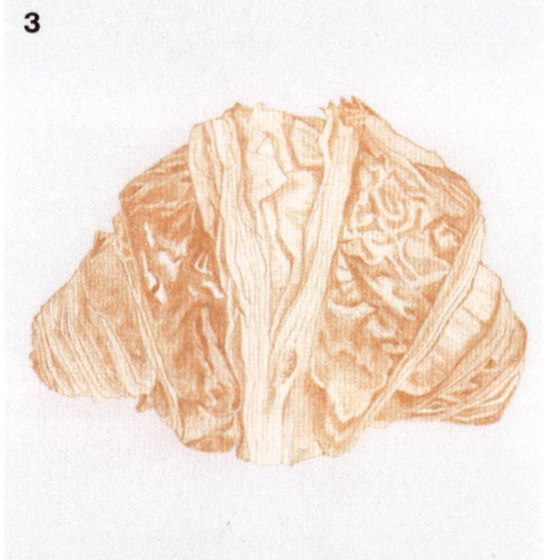

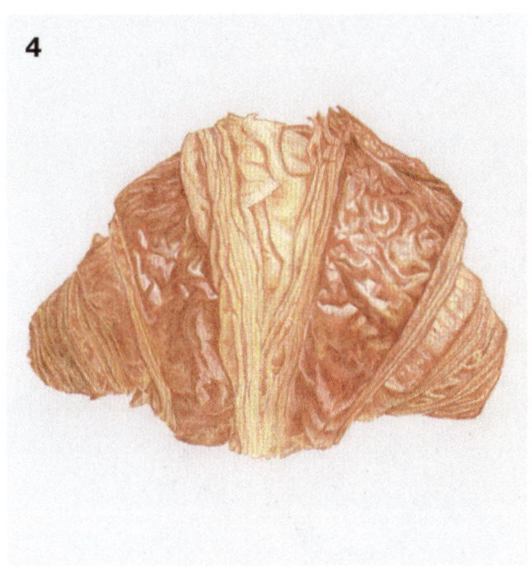

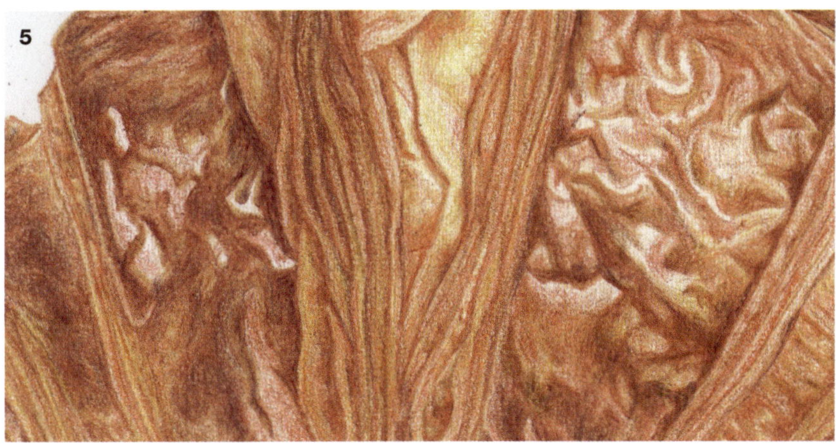

Espresso

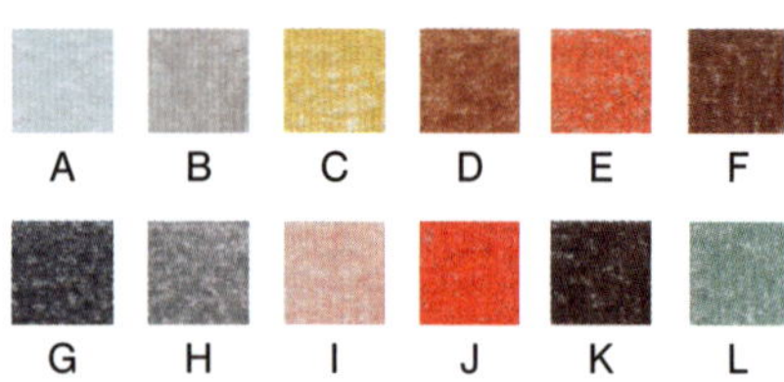

A	B	C	D	E	F

G	H	I	J	K	L

1 For the linework, use pale blue-gray (A) to draw the cup and saucer, and dark orange (E) for the coffee. Outline the different color zones on the surface of the coffee.

2 Using the pale blue-gray, shade in the background of the cup and saucer, leaving the highlights white. Color the spoon in pale silver-gray (B). Use mid yellow (C) with light pressure to shade in the coffee, and pale peach (I) to add a layer of color to the coffee foam areas.

3 Apply the pale blue-gray (A) with more pressure to take the cup and saucer a shade darker. Add the shadow zone to the inside of the coffee cup in the same color using medium pressure. Use a light warm brown (D) to shade in the coffee, working around the foam.

4 Shade in the dark zones on the spoon with dark gray (G), applying medium pressure. Lightly use mid gray (H) to identify the shadow zones on the saucer and cup. Use dark orange (E) to give another layer of color to the coffee, lightly blending smaller shadow areas into the foam as necessary. Use mid brown (F) to shade around the edge of the coffee and the top edge of the coffee ring.

1

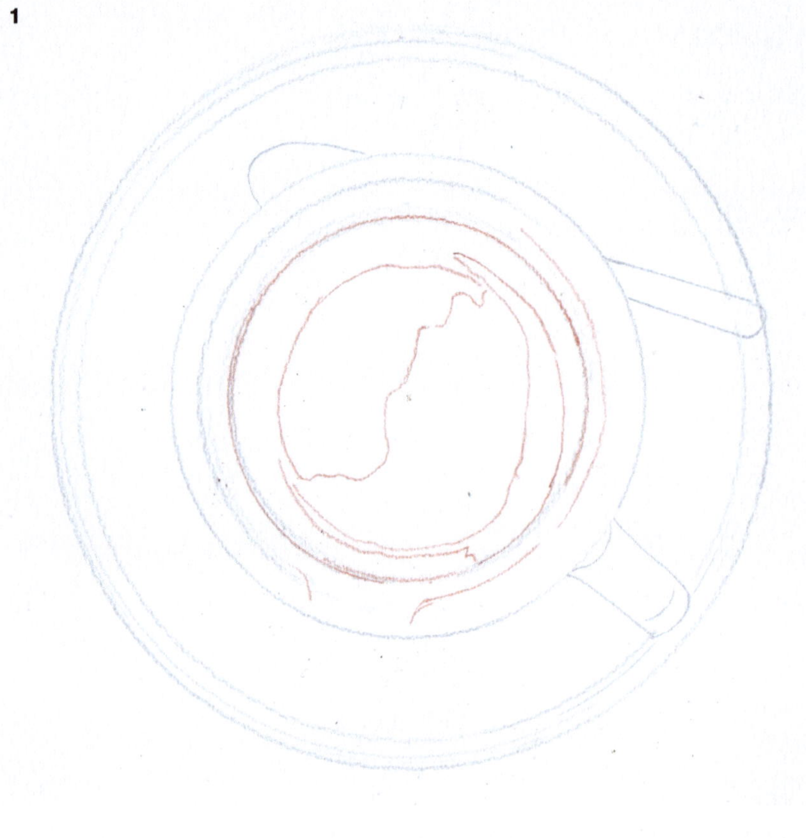

2

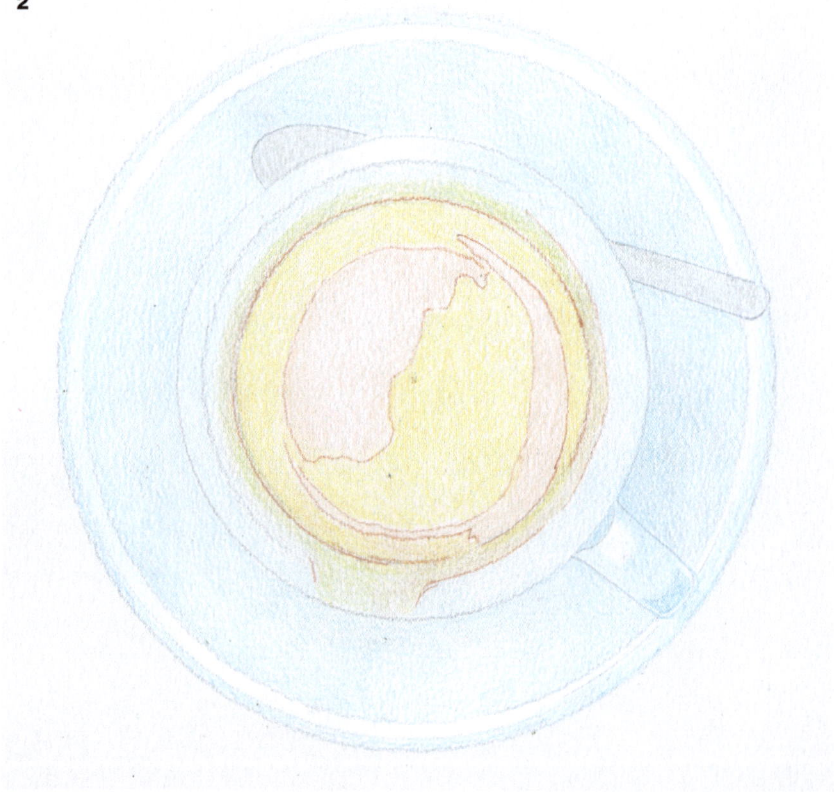

3

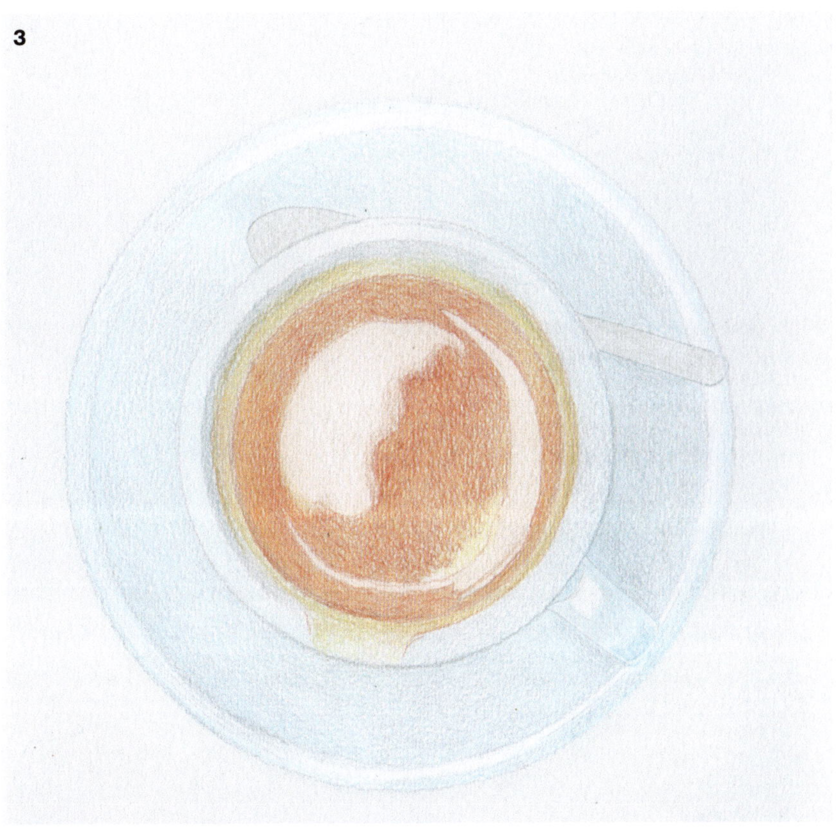

4

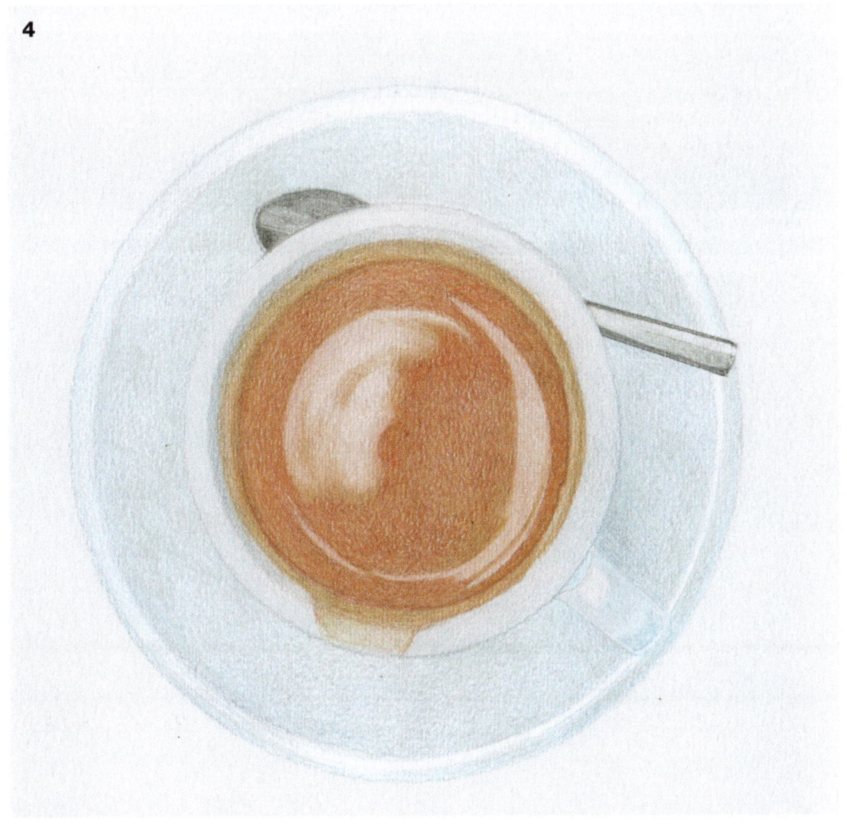

5 Use mid gray (H) with medium pressure to add another layer of shadow to the cup and saucer, focusing on the area around the cup handle and the inner edge of the saucer where the shadows are darkest. With mid brown (F), take the coffee ring around the edge of the coffee a shade darker. Lightly apply dark orange (E) to take the coffee a shade darker, blending into the foam as you did in step 4.

6 With dark terracotta (J) use medium pressure to add more depth to the coffee, blending around the edges to create a richer orange-brown tone. Use dark brown-black (K) to shade in the areas where the black coffee shows through the foam in the center and around the edge. Blend carefully into the terracotta orange, creating a smooth gradient.

7 Use mid blue-green (L) to shade in the pale gray zones on the head of the spoon and to shade around the edge of the dark gray areas on the spoon handle. Darken all the shadows on the cup and saucer using the mid gray (H) with heavy pressure.

8 Use dark brown-black (K) with heavy pressure to add the small bubbles in the coffee, and the same color with heavy pressure to darken the black coffee. Blend some of the brown-black into the foam shadow areas. Use the dark orange (E) to add flecks of dried foam around the inside of the cup. Use dark gray (G) with medium pressure to add a final layer of shadow on the saucer around the handle, and mid gray (H) to add a narrow cast shadow just beyond the saucer. The shadow should follow the line of the saucer, producing a thin crescent shape that tapers off at either end.

5

6

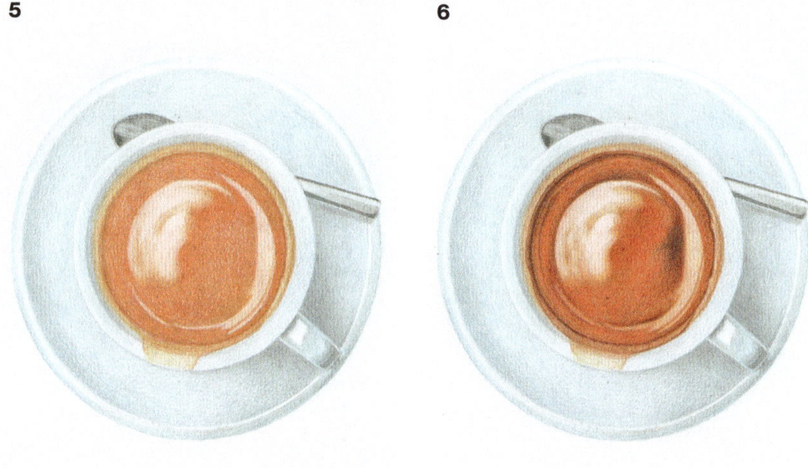

7

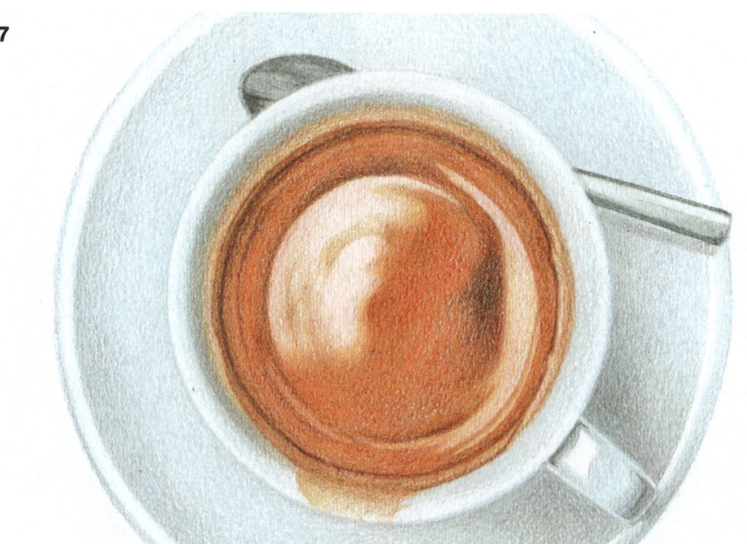

8

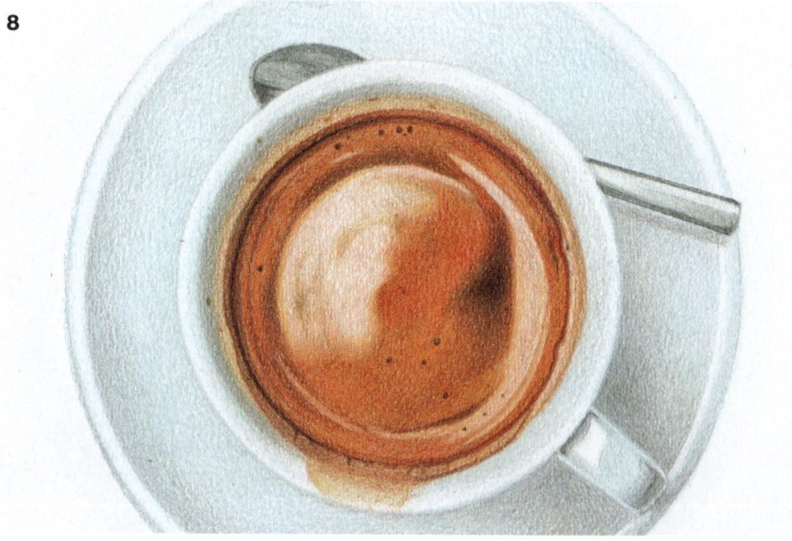

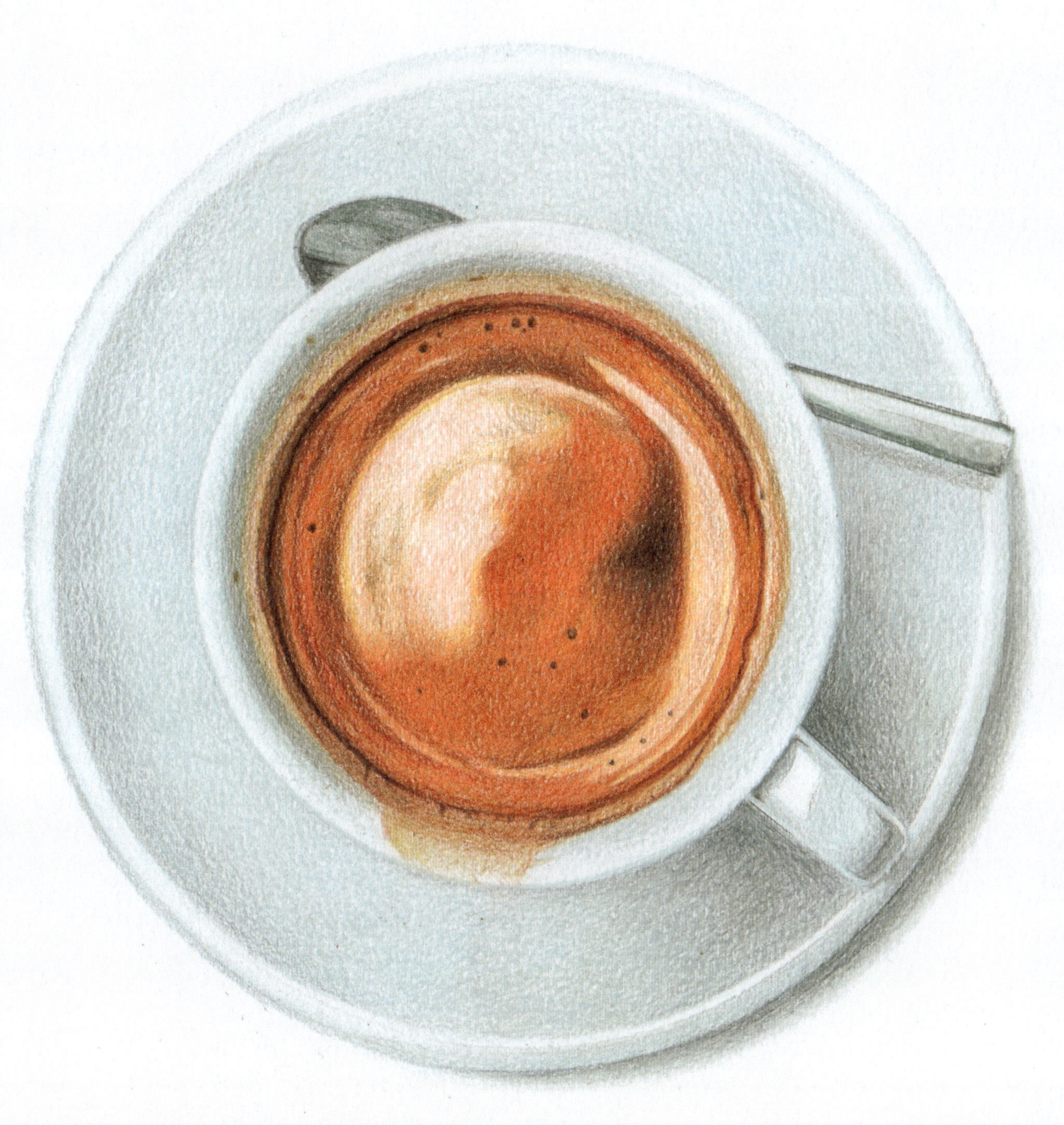

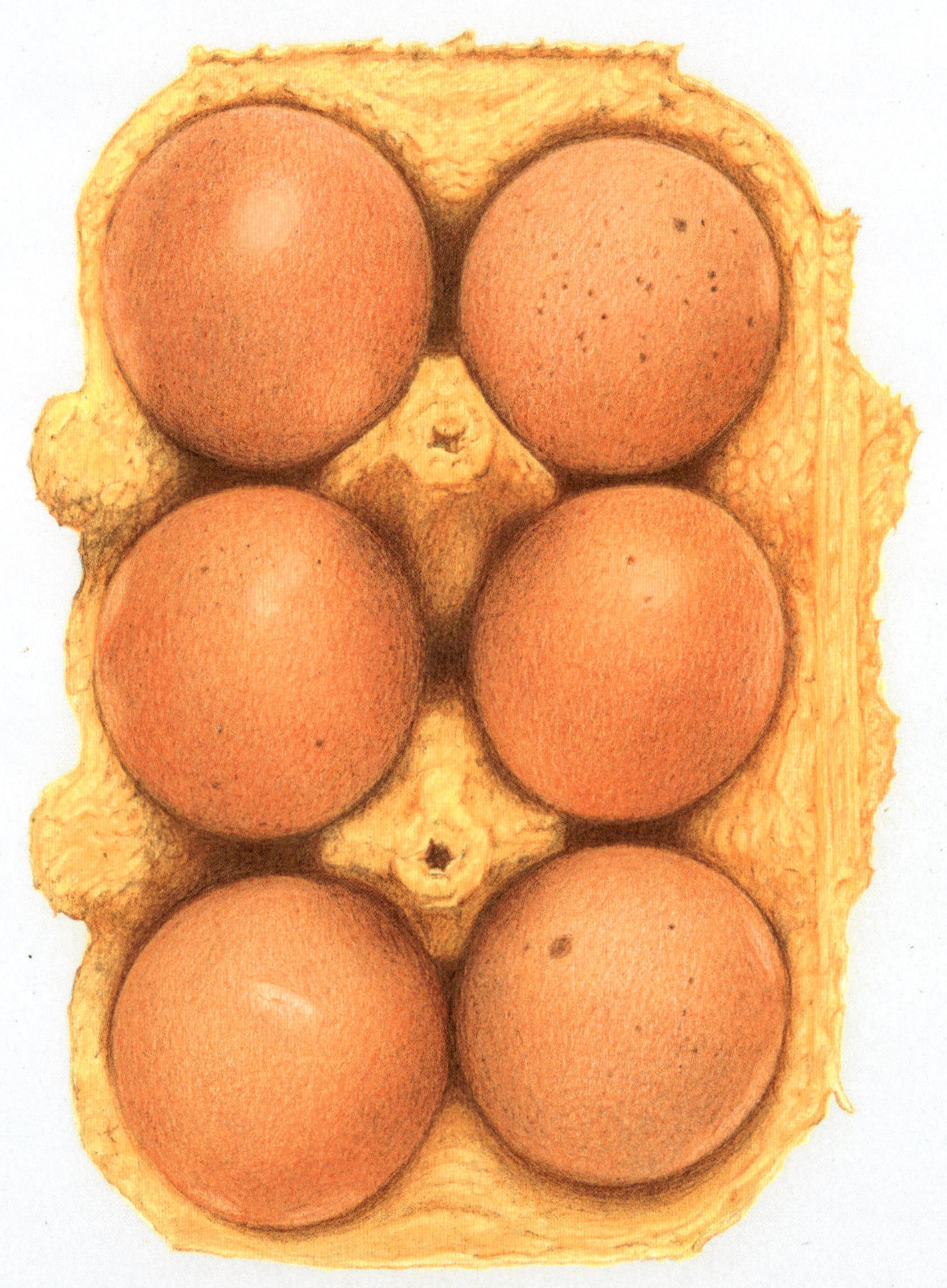

Egg box

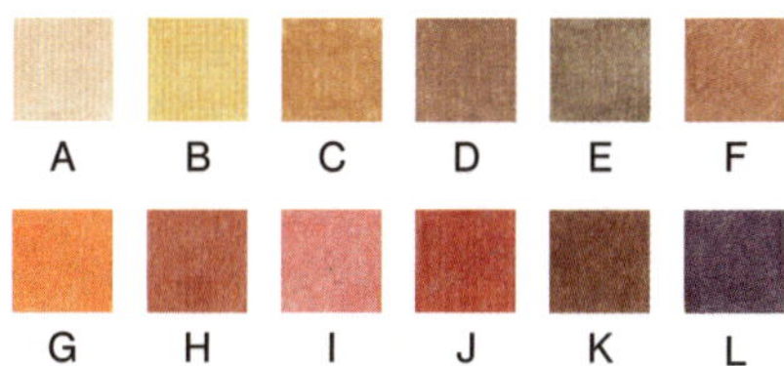

1 Select a light tone from the color palette for your linework (C is used here).

2 Lightly shade in the eggs with a flesh color (A), and use pale yellow (B) to shade the egg box, applying more pressure to identify shadows.

3 Add a light layer of shadow to the eggs in yellow ocher (C). Work around the edges and leave the highlights in the flesh color.

4 Use mid terracotta (H) to add another layer of shadow to the eggs, and dark terracotta (J) and pale brown (D) with light pressure to develop the color.

5 Use burnt ocher (F) to add shadow to the egg box, focusing on the edges and between the eggs. Add more shadow and pick out the details on the egg box in pale brown (D) and orange (G).

6 With mid brown (E), add a darker layer of shadow and define the divots in the box. Use dark flesh pink (I) to bring depth to the darker tones on the eggs, and dark brown (K) to add the speckles on the shells. Use the same dark brown and blackberry (L) to build shadow in the darkest areas of the egg box.

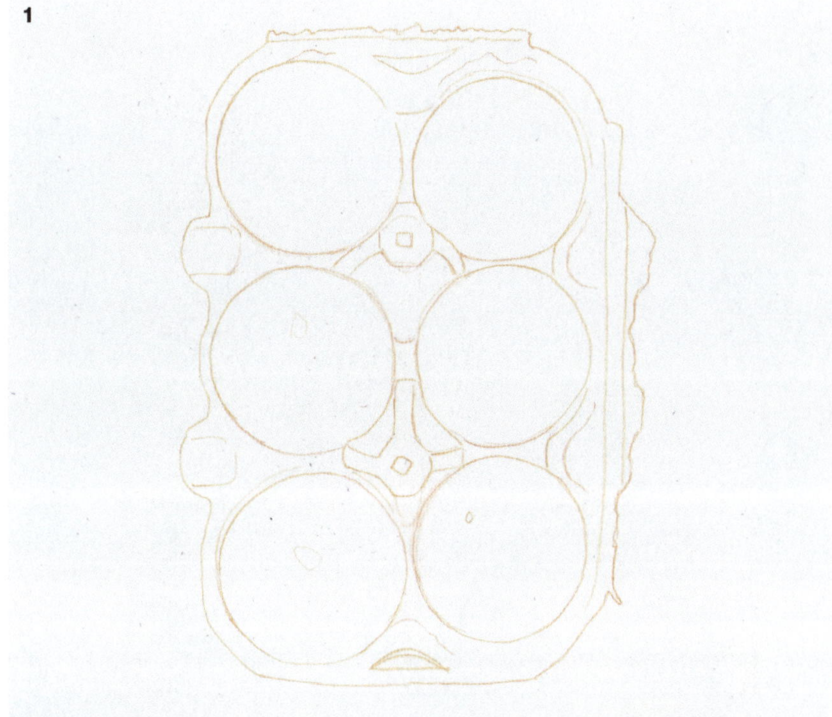

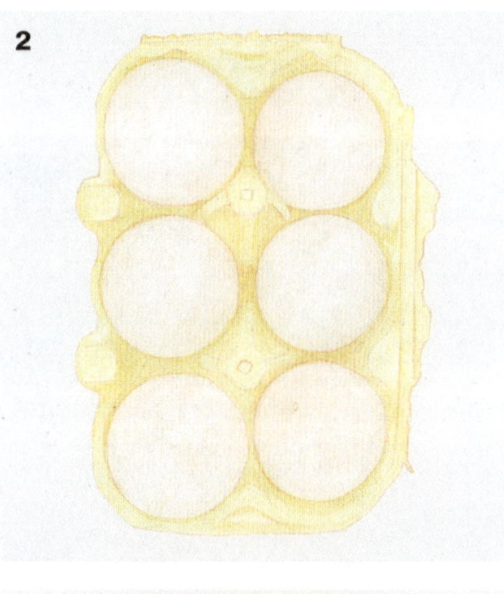

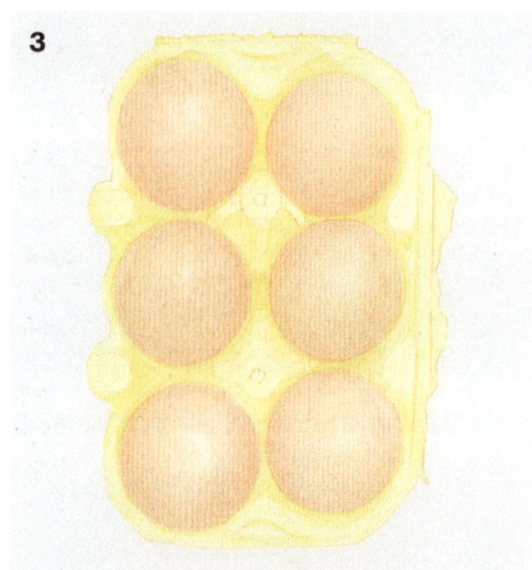

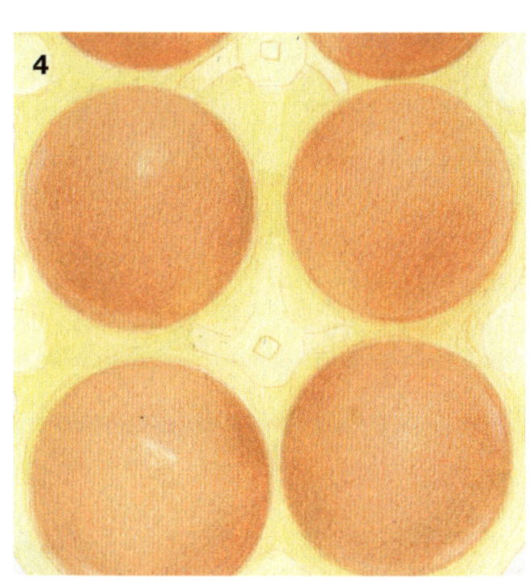

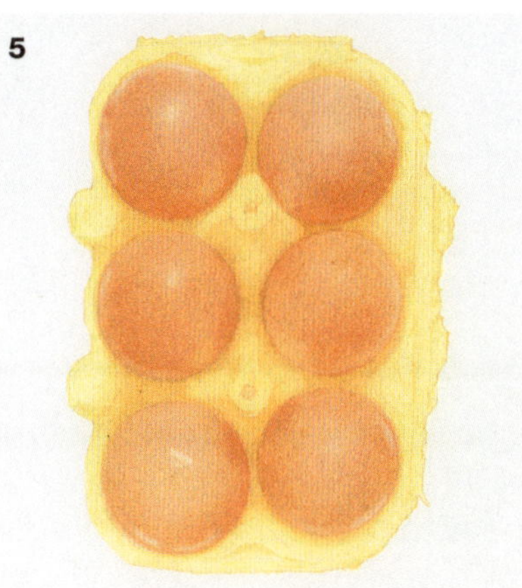

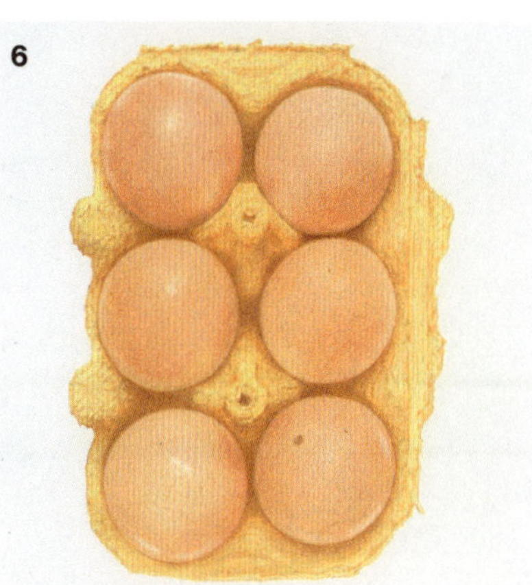

Scissors

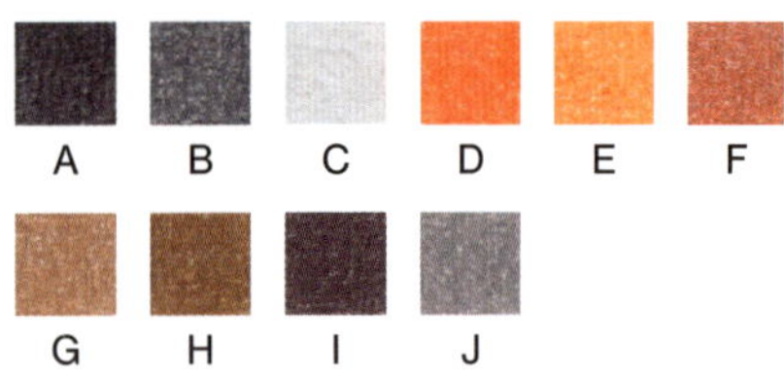

1. Select a light tone to lay down the linework. Here, mid gray (J) is used for the metal blades of the scissors and mid orange (E) for the plastic handles.

2. Use the same mid orange to shade in the background color of the plastic handles. Use light silver-gray (C) to shade in the metal blades, applying more pressure to shade in the darker reflections. Use the mid gray to shade the two sides of the pivot connection.

3. With dark orange (D), identify and shade in the darker shadows on the handles, blending carefully into the lighter background orange. Now use the mid gray (J) again to take the reflections on the blades a shade darker. Shade the sharp edge of the blade even darker by using more pressure. Use light silver-gray (C) to outline cast shadows on the surface on which the scissors sit.

4. Use pale brown (G) to add another layer of color to the handles. Focus more pressure around the darker orange zones. Use mid gray (J) with medium pressure to take the dark reflections on the blades and the pivot connection even darker.

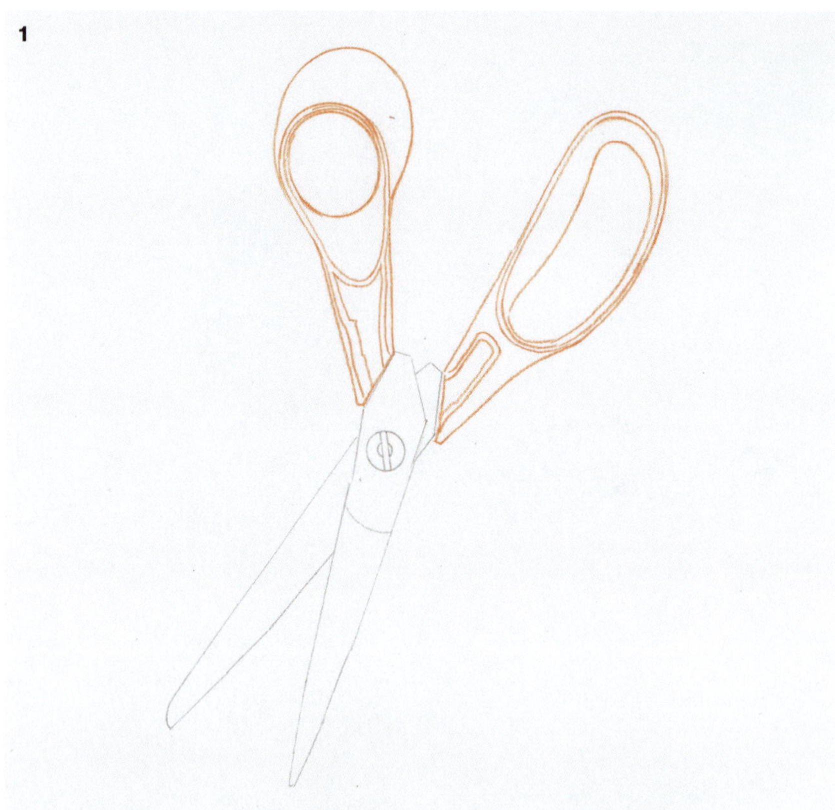

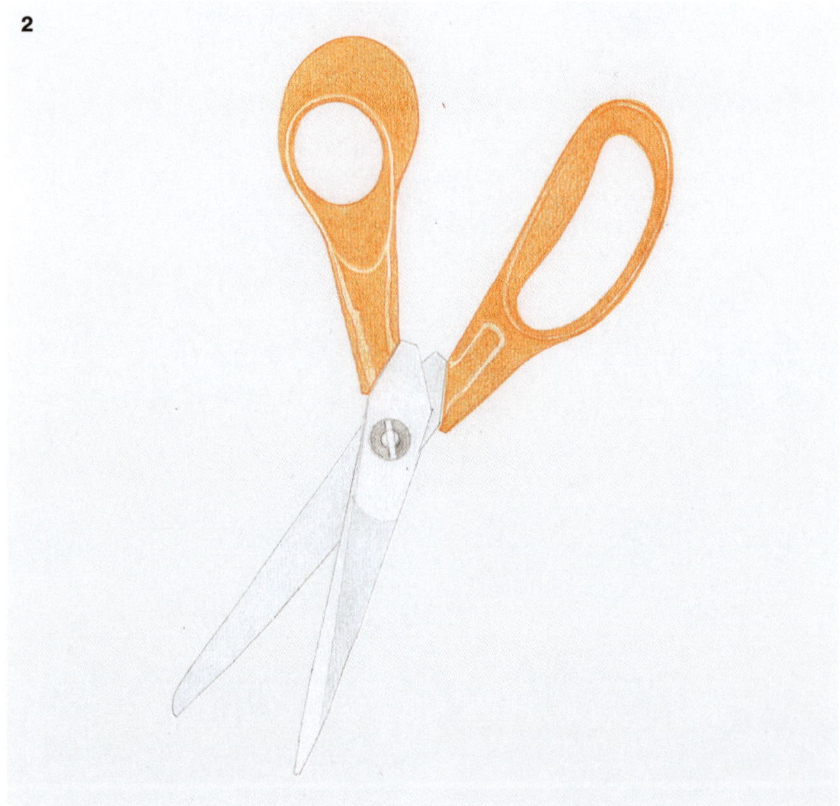

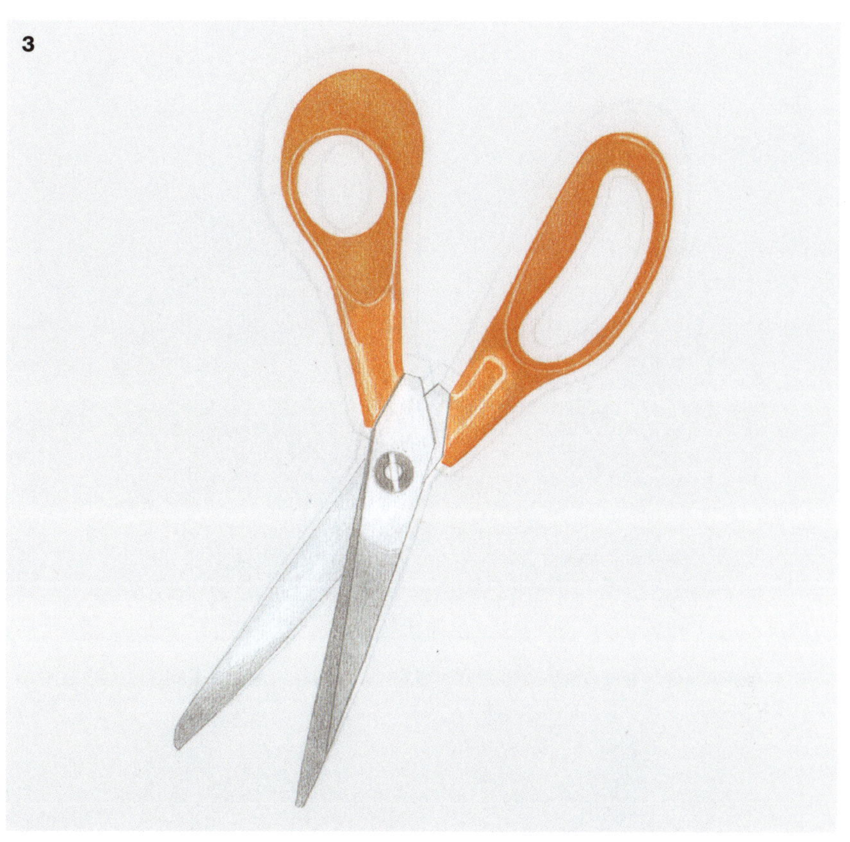

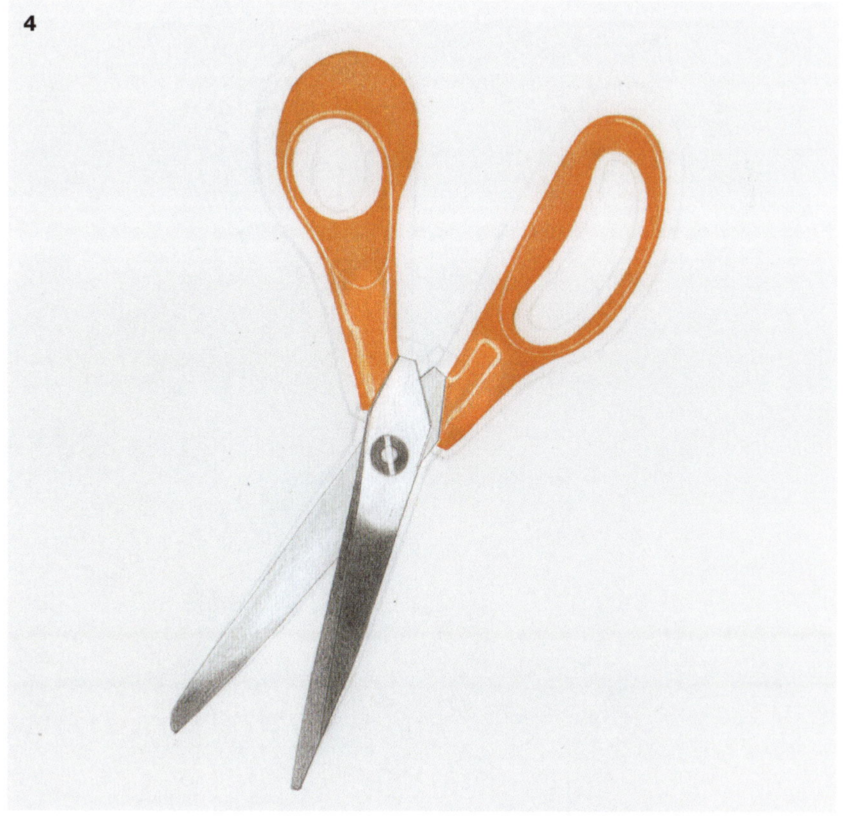

5 Use pimento red-brown (F) to add depth to the shadows on the handles. Identify and outline the curved light reflections on the inside of both handles and work around them. Use medium to heavy pressure on the shadows, blending carefully into the mid orange and pale brown base color.

6 Take the reflections on the blades and the pivot connection a shade darker using dark gray (B). Shade small random sections of the blade edge toward the end of the top blade to indicate wear and scratches.

7 Use mid brown (H) and pimento red-brown (F) with heavy pressure to take the shadows on the handles a shade darker. Continue to work around the highlights on the inside of the handles, and use a white pencil or your eraser pen to ensure these areas are defined as light orange.

8 Use light silver-gray (C) to shade in the cast shadow zone around the edges of the scissors.

9 Use dark chocolate brown (I) with medium pressure to add the final layer of color to the shadows on the handles. Work into the darkest areas and blend out, and carefully shade around the bottom edges of the handles near the blades, working up around the outline of both the handles.

10 Use mid gray (J) with light pressure to take the surface shadow around the edge of the scissors a shade darker. Where the shadows overlap add more pressure to create a defined area of even darker shadow. Use black (A) with light pressure to take the dark reflections on the blades even darker. Focus greater pressure on the blade edge and the pivot connection, and use your eraser pen to create small highlights on the round connector.

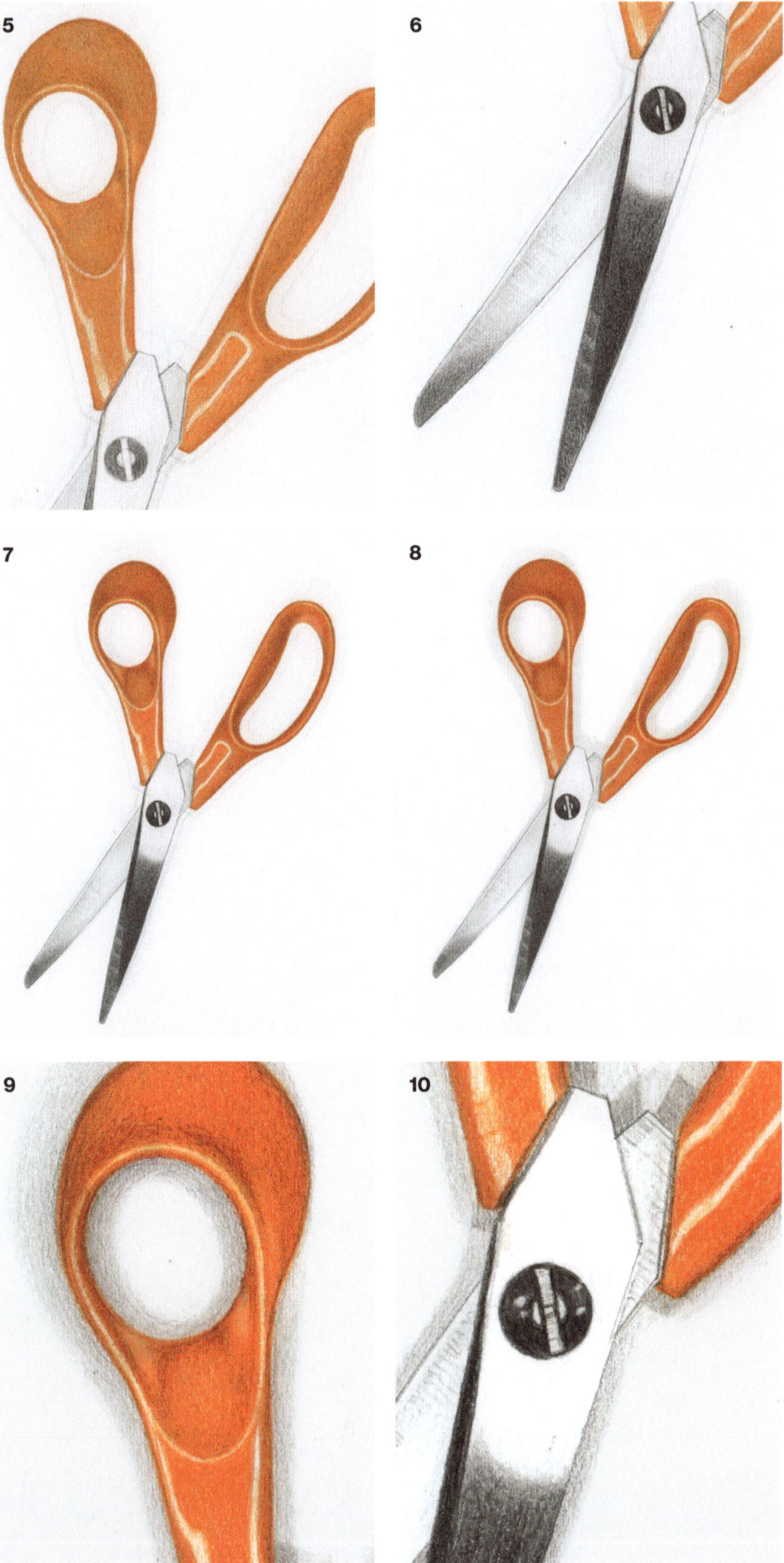

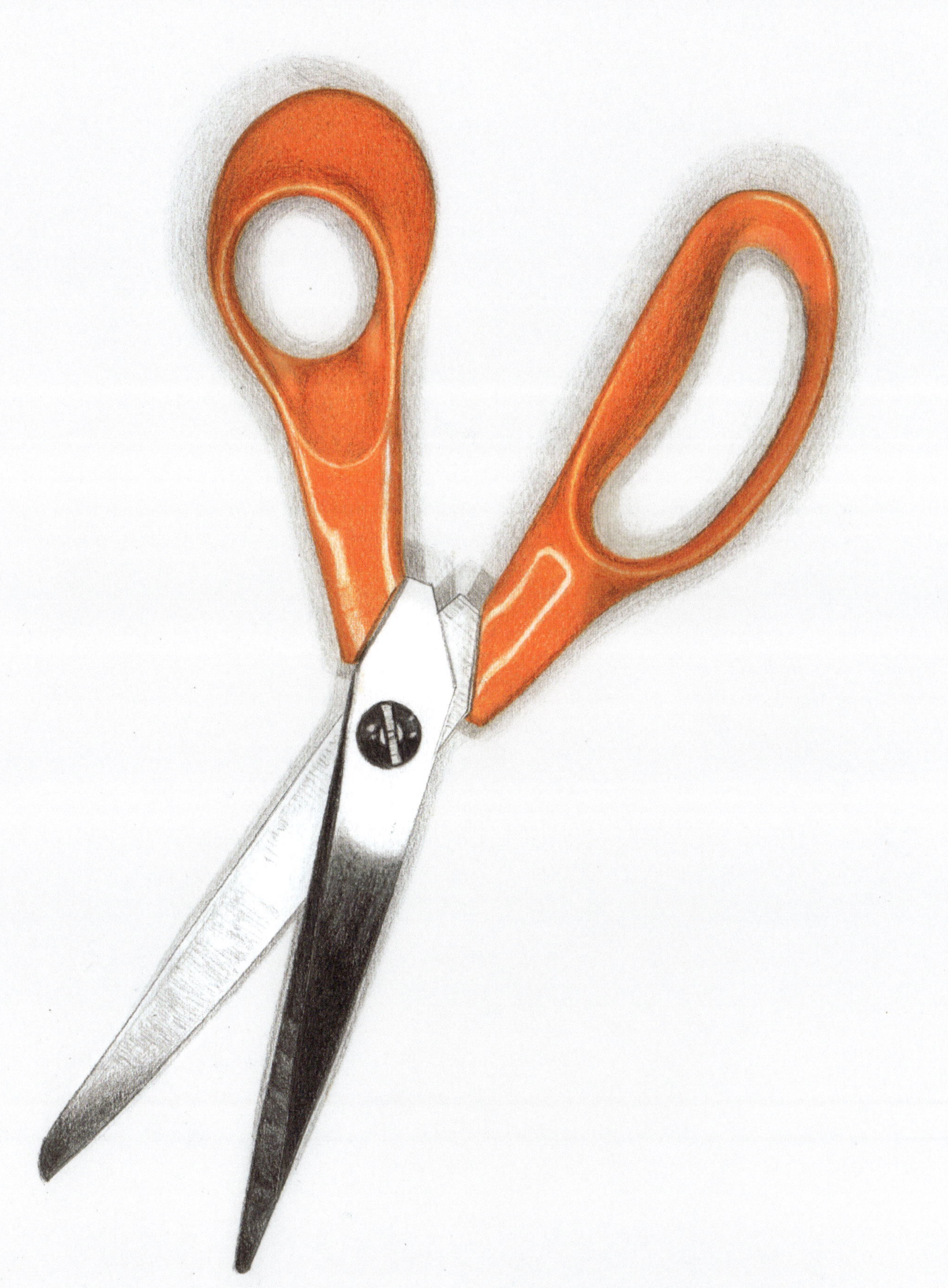

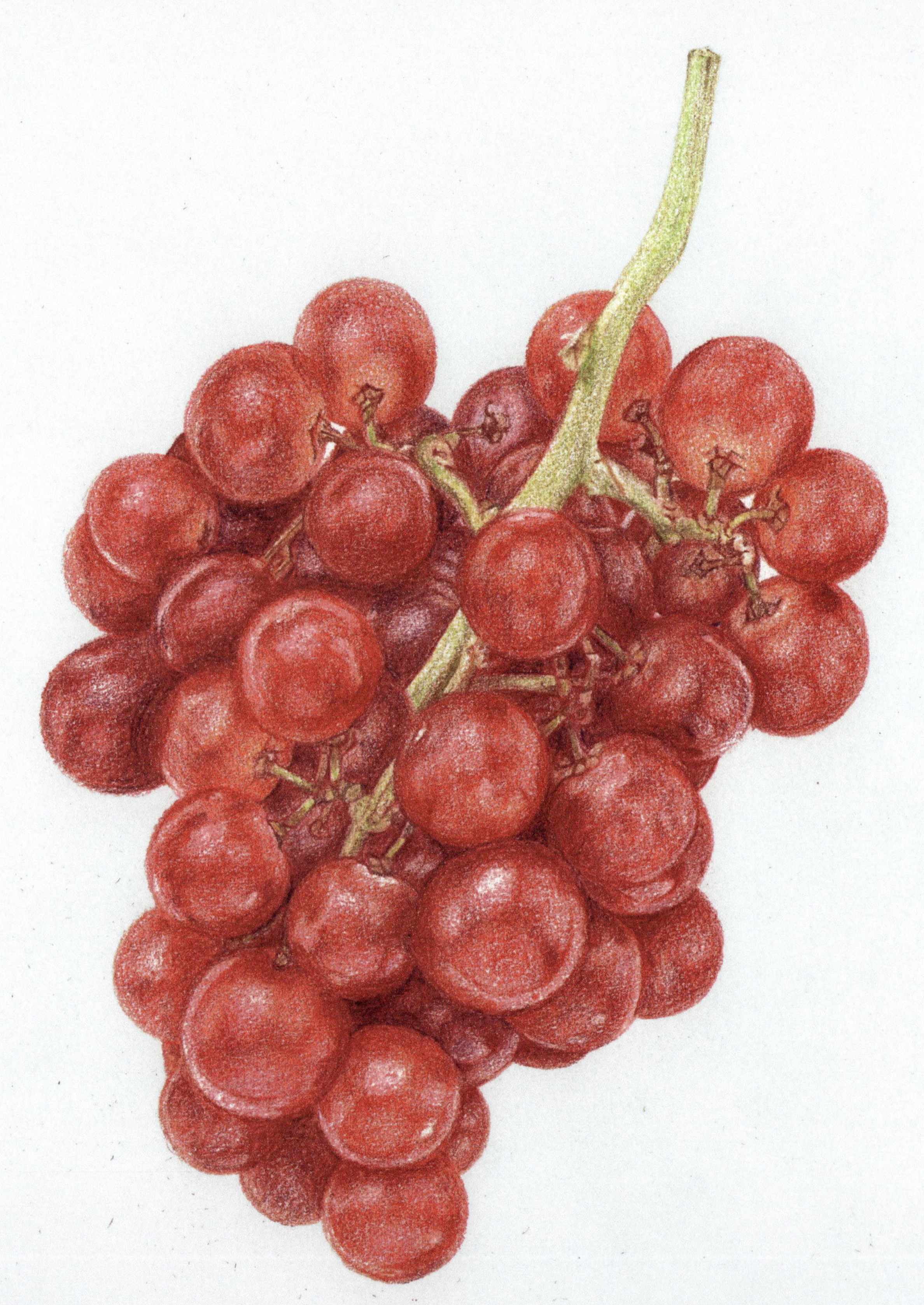

Bunch of grapes

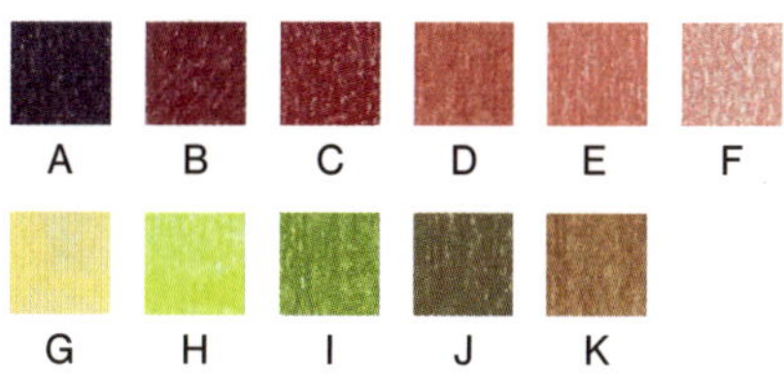

1 Use a mid-tone (K) for your linework.

2 Lay down the two dominant base colors of pale pink (F) and yellow (G), leaving highlights white. Add light green (H) to the stalks, applying pressure to emphasize shadows. Use mid pink (E) to outline smaller stalks and deep shadows.

3 Add mid pink over the light pink base, blending around the highlights to show a graduation from light to dark. Use green (I) and green-brown (J) to add shadows to the stalk and outline the smaller stalks. Use yellow (G) to give tone to the grapes.

4 Apply a layer of dark pink (D) over the mid-pink grapes, again blending around highlights to graduate from light to dark.

5 Use dark pink-purple (C) to work into the darker zones in the center of the bunch. Use mid brown (K) to further outline where the smaller stalks connect to each grape. Blend deep red-purple (B) over the grapes, graduating around the highlights and applying more pressure for a darker tone in the center of the bunch. Use dark purple (A) to add more depth to grapes in the middle.

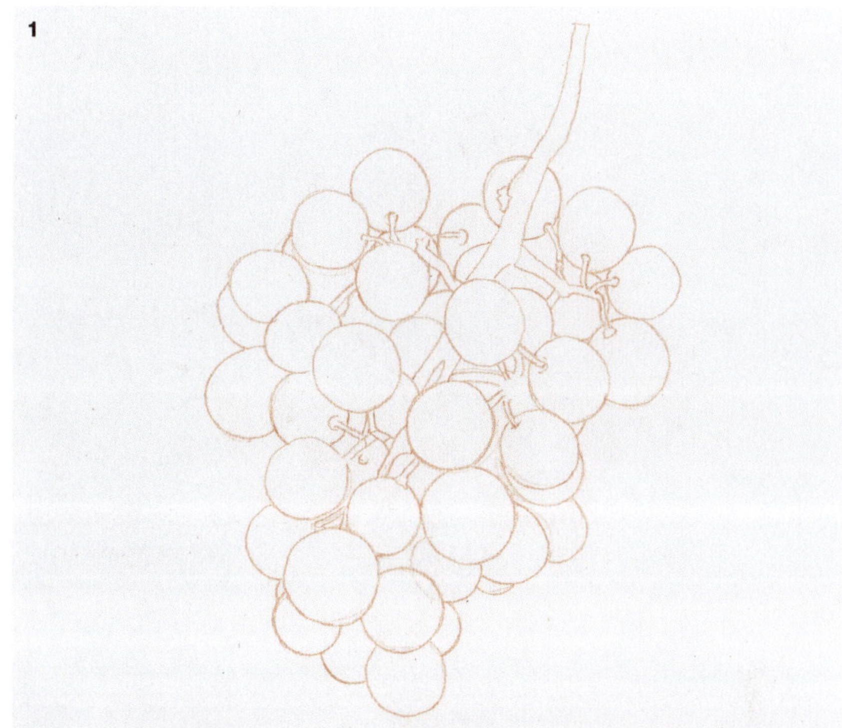

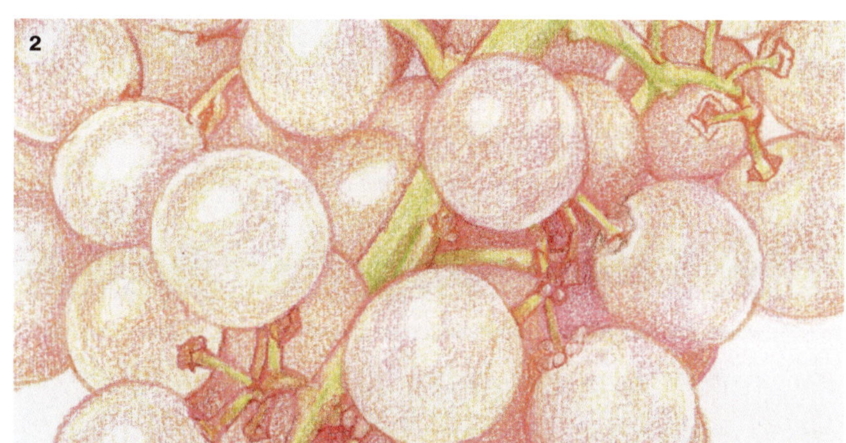

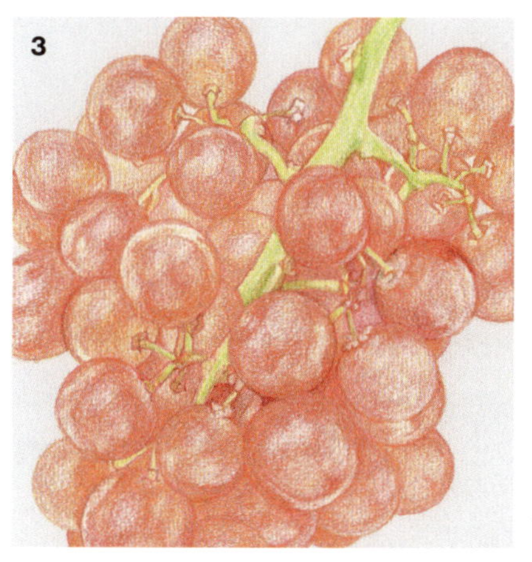

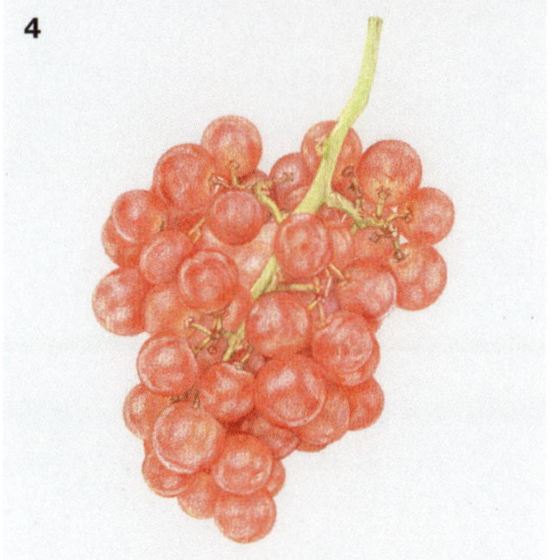

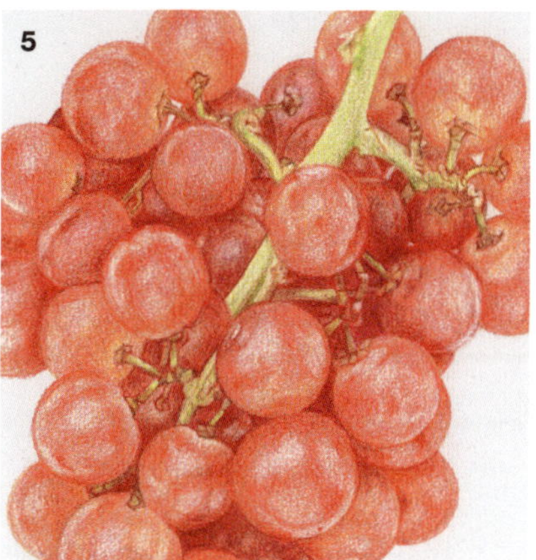

Baked beans

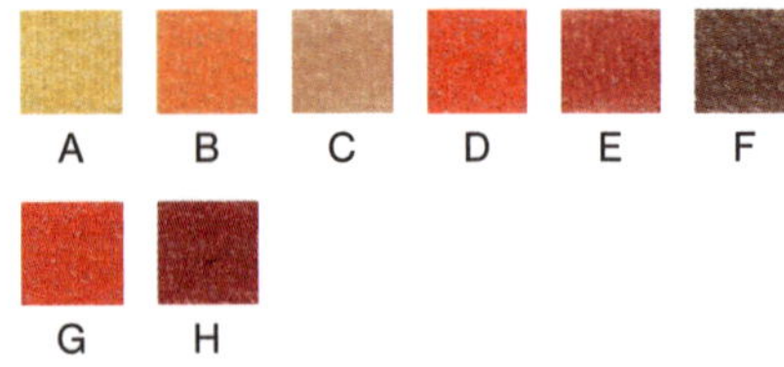

A   B   C   D   E   F

G   H

1   With light golden yellow (A), outline the beans and identify the highlight areas.

2   Shade the sauce in the same color, using heavy pressure around the beans and lightly graduating out. Use very light pressure to shade in the beans, leaving highlights white.

3   Use mid orange (B) with medium pressure to shade in the sauce, blending into the golden yellow around the liquid edge. Use pale ocher (C) with medium pressure to shade in the beans.

4   Take the sauce a shade deeper with dark orange (D), carefully blending it out to create a gradient. Use heavy pressure around the edges of each bean, and lightly add shadows and darker patches. Use pale brown (F) with light pressure to add shadow and pick out lines and cracks in the beans.

5   Bring depth to the sauce with a layer of bright red (G), applying heavy pressure around each bean and lightly shading submerged areas. With the pale brown and medium pressure, add more shadow and further define cracks and edges of highlights. Use mid pimento (E) followed by dark red-purple (H) to give more depth to the sauce, focusing on the middle. Define the edges of the highlights and use an eraser pen to enhance them.

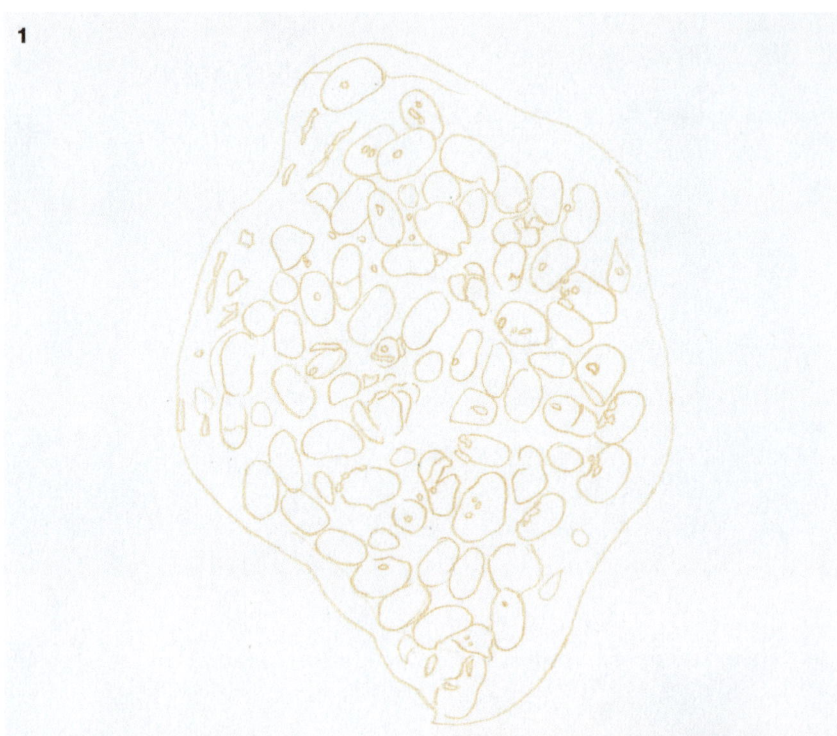

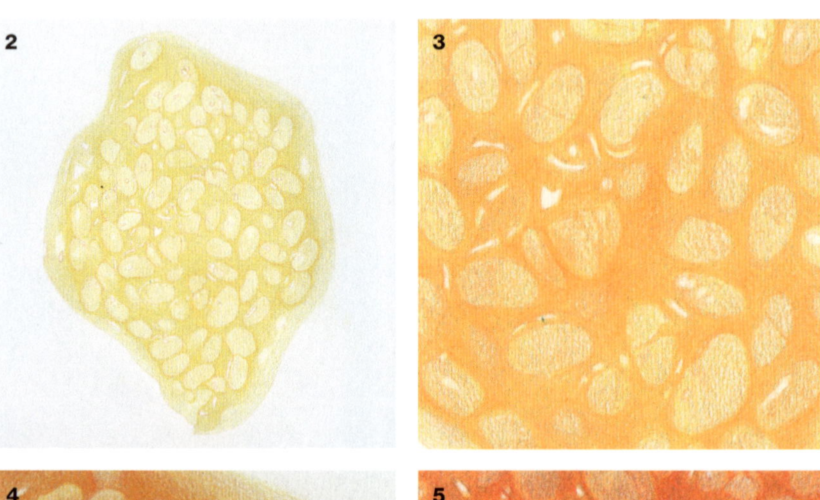

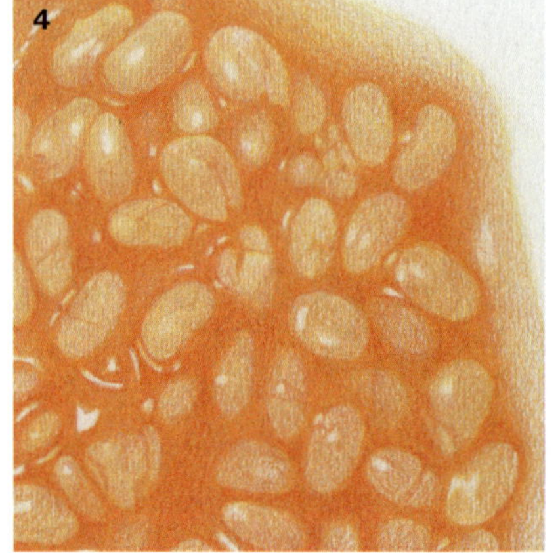

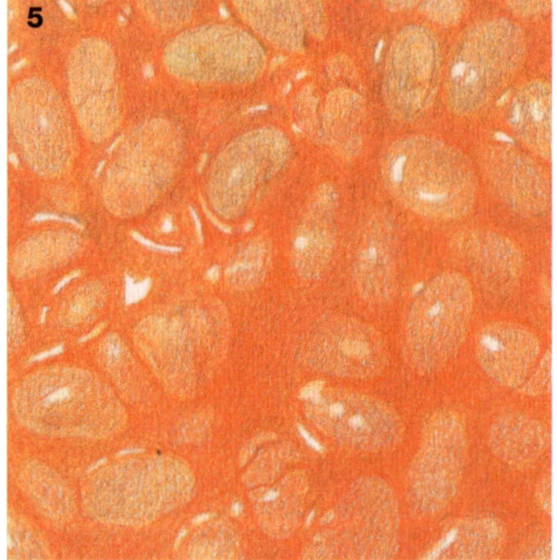

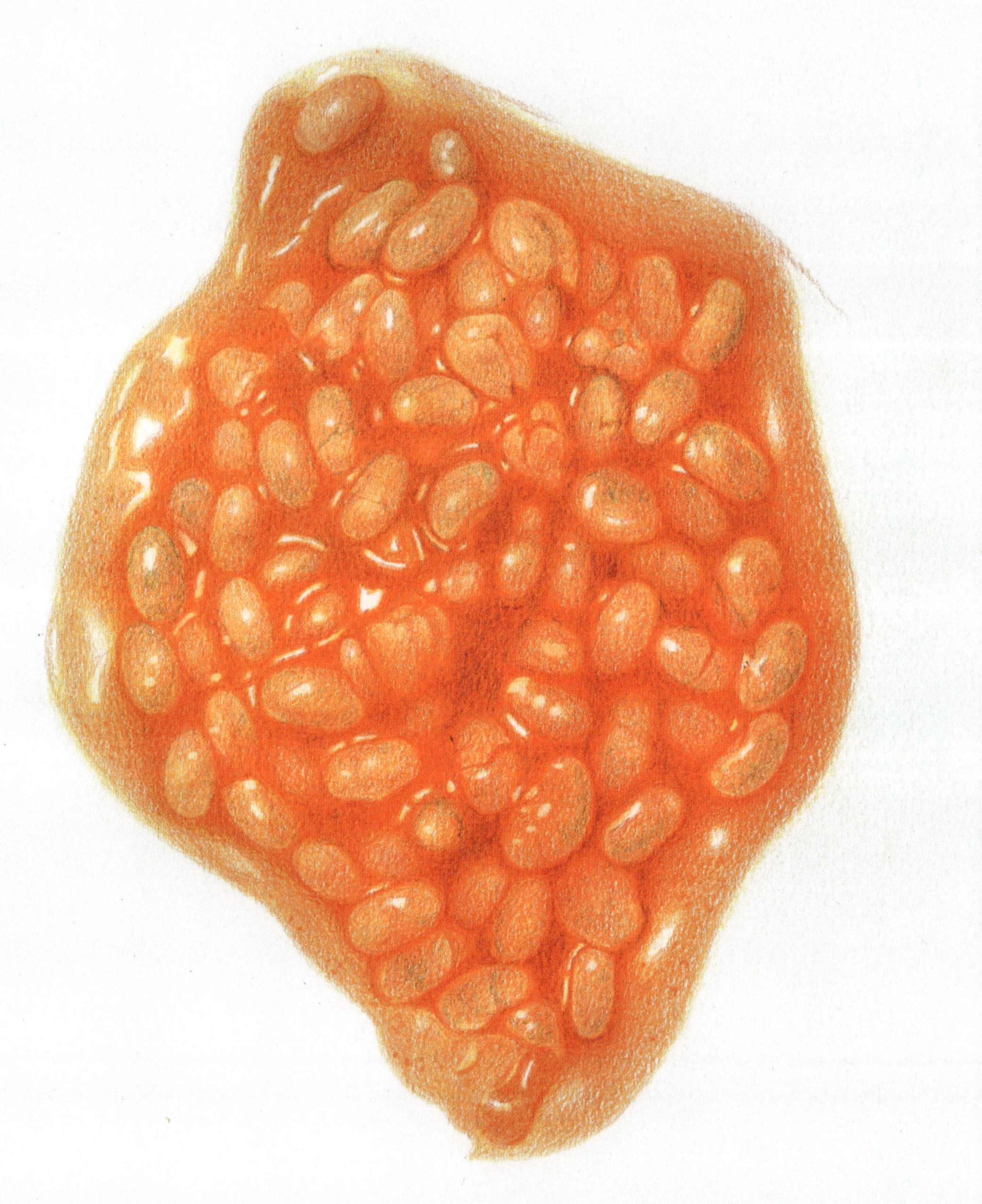

Gold bulb

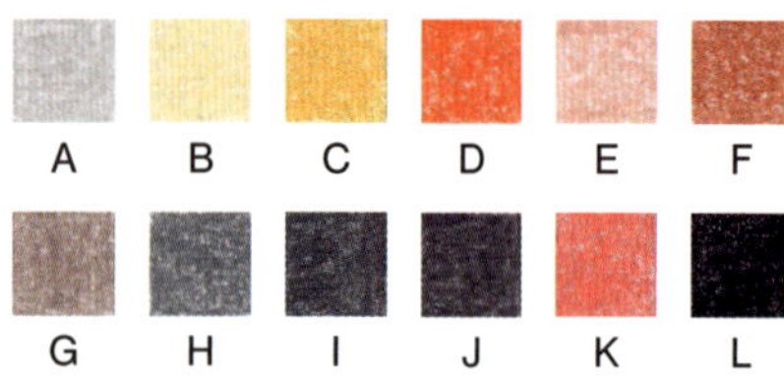

1. Select a pale gray (A) or graphite pencil, applying light pressure to set out the linework. Take care to include as much of the reflection detail as possible.

2. Use pale yellow (B) with light pressure to color the gold mirrored top, and the pale gray to shade the glass bulb, leaving the highlights white. Use mid orange (D) for the filaments. With mid gray (H), lightly shade in the reflections on the internal mirrored surface of the gold top. Lastly, use mid gray (I) to shade in the metal screwcap with light pressure.

3. Add another layer of color to the clear glass part of the bulb with warm pale gray (G). Define and shade in the internal glass stem that travels the length of the bulb, being sure to avoid the highlights. Use heavy pressure to identify the shadow at the back of the bulb where it sits on a surface. Use pale pink (E) to shade around the top of the gold mirror, applying medium pressure to blend into the yellow toward the edge of the mirror where it meets the clear glass. Use mid yellow (C) to add the darker yellow reflection, leaving the highlights pale yellow. Begin shading in the darker gray reflections of the mirror with mid gray (H).

4. Use mid orange (D) with heavy pressure to take the filaments a shade darker, and burnt ocher (F) on the top half of the filaments where they are in shadow. With mid gray (H) and dark pink (K), draw in the wires that run up the glass stem and connect to the filaments inside the bulb. Use the same mid gray to draw the dark reflections in the internal glass stem.

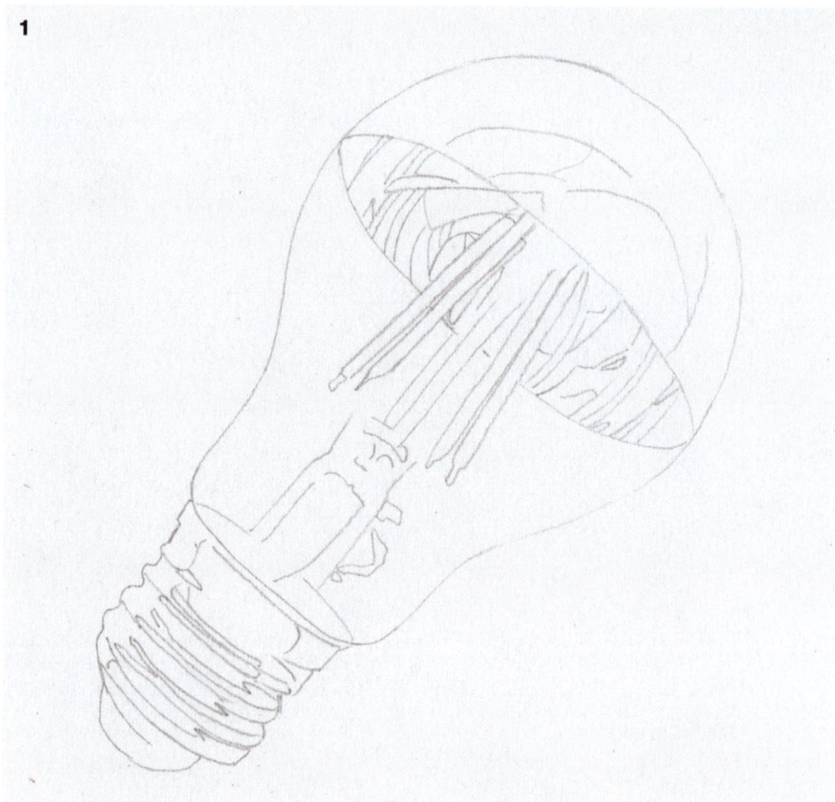

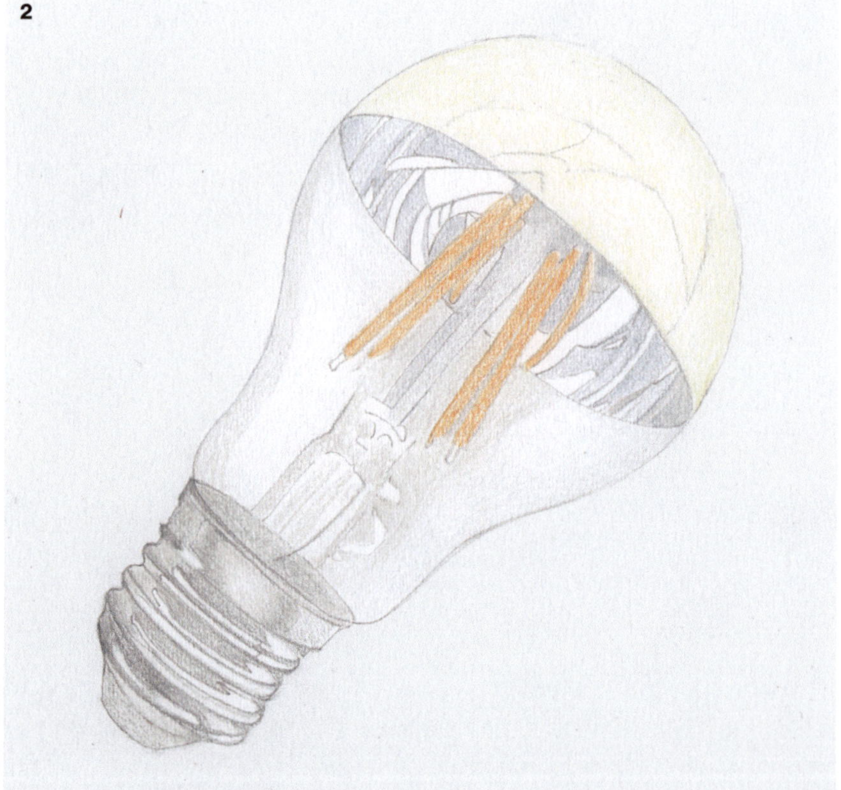

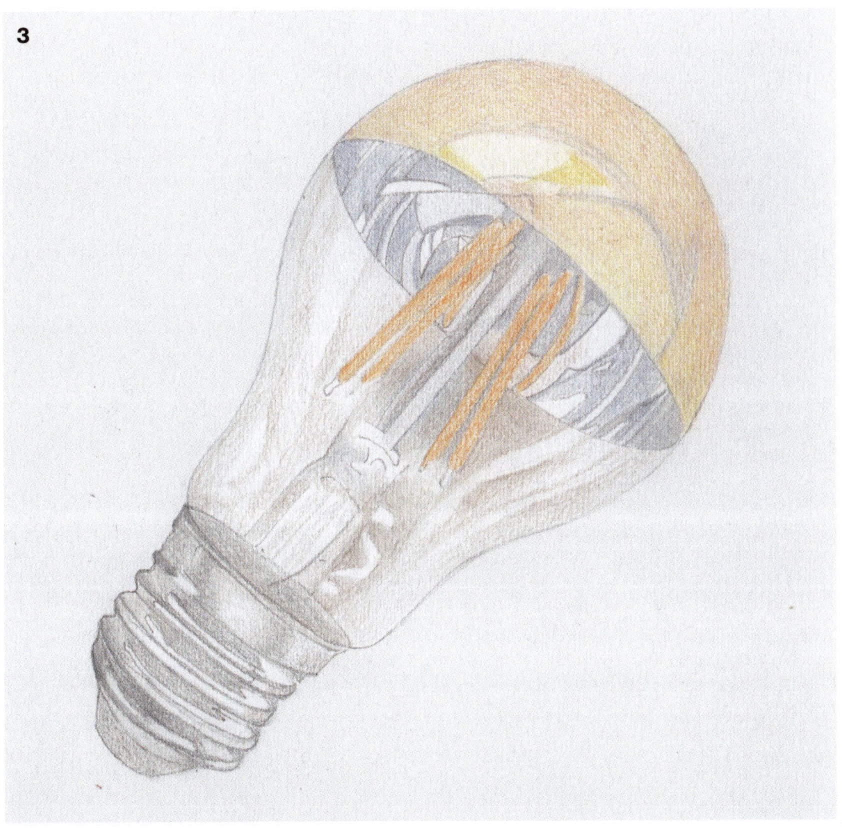

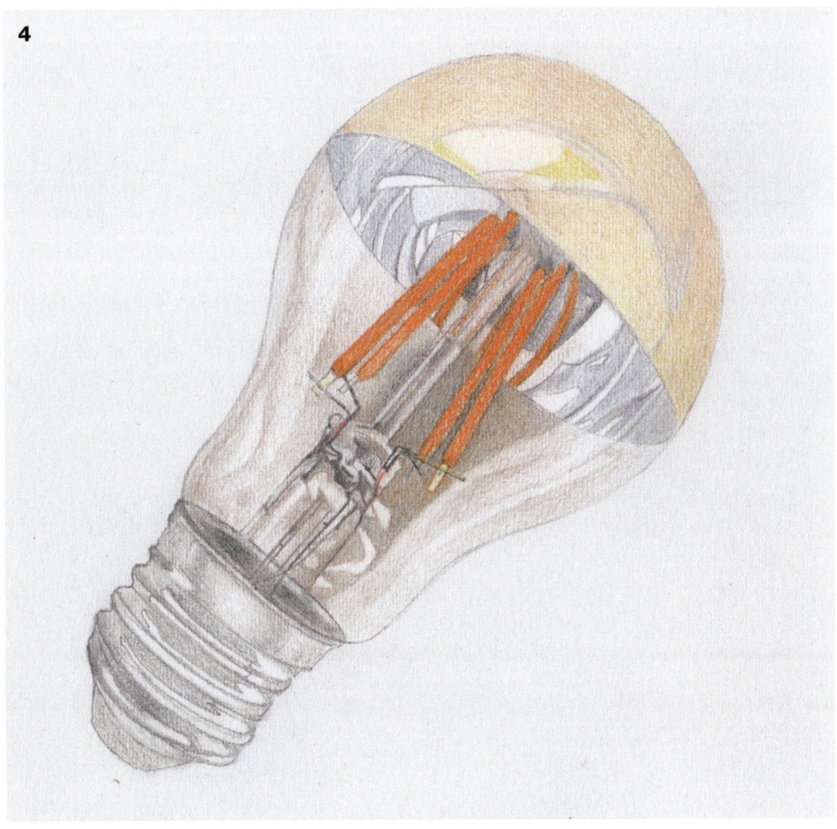

5 Use burnt ocher (F) to shade the top of the gold mirror, blending down into the yellow. Further shade in the gray reflections and pick out the line detail along the edge of the mirror in dark gray (J), leaving the yellow and pale yellow highlights alone. Use the dark gray (J) to shade in the dark reflections on the reverse of the gold mirror inside the bulb, and dark pink (K) to pick out the pink reflections.

6 With mid gray (H) and light pressure, take the reflections and shadows on the clear glass part of the bulb a shade darker. Use dark gray (J) to take the metal screwcap darker, being careful to work around the highlights. Use dark pink (K) and mid yellow (C) to lightly shade in the colorful reflections down the center of the face of the cap, and black (L) to identify the darkest shadows along the edges of the metal folds and recesses between the metal threads.

7 Use dark gray (J) to further define the wires inside the bulb, and the same dark gray to darken the reflections on the glass stem. Use mid gray (I) to draw in a bolder line defining the edge of the clear glass element of the bulb on both sides.

8 Use black (L) to color in the darkest reflections on the silver mirror on the inside of the bulb. Finally, use the mid gray (H) with light pressure to create two areas of shadow – one beneath the metal cap and one beneath the clear glass section of the bulb. The two areas should be worked up to a darker gray slowly using circular pencil strokes. Shade in a very pale gray area of shadow between the darker zones connecting them.

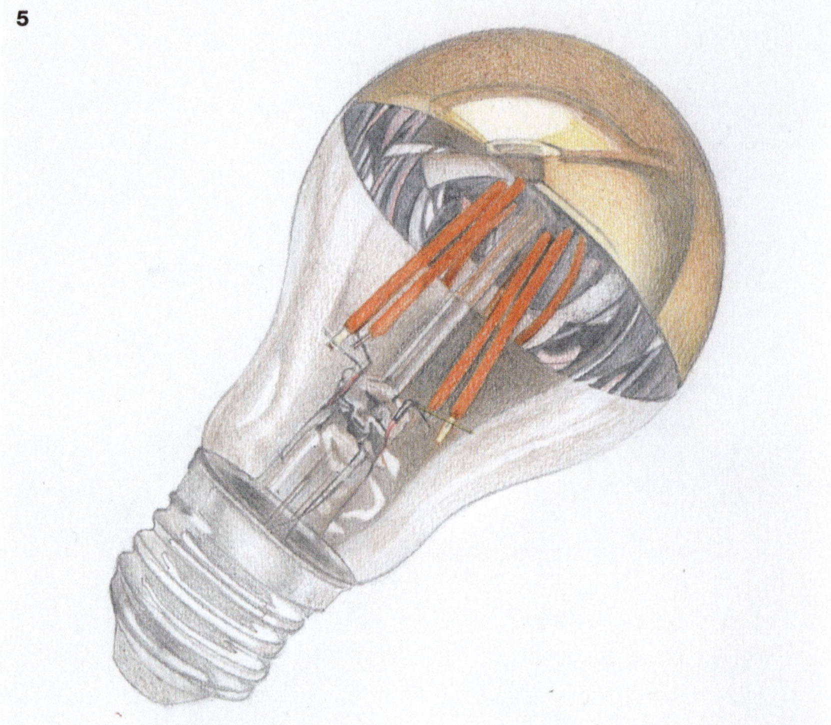

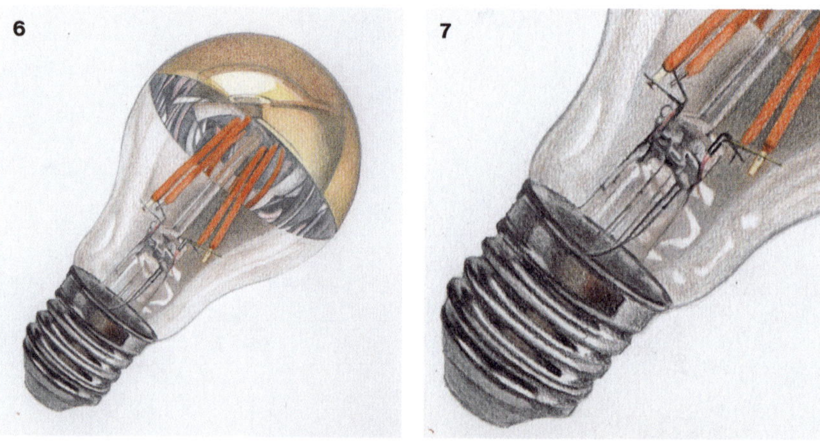

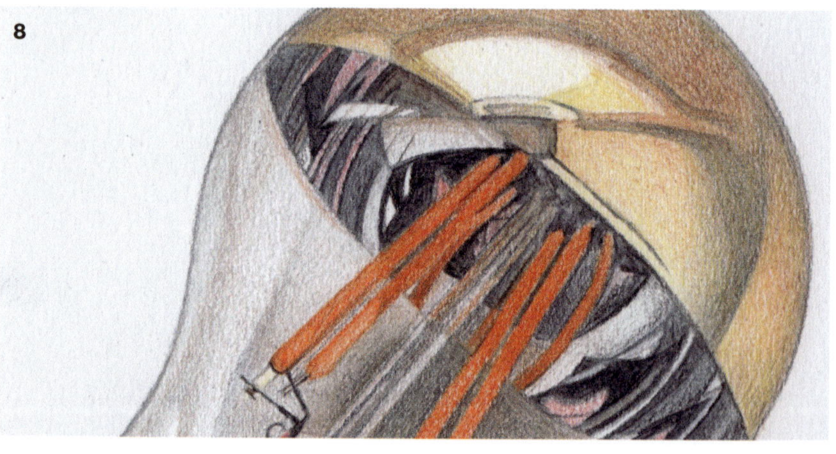

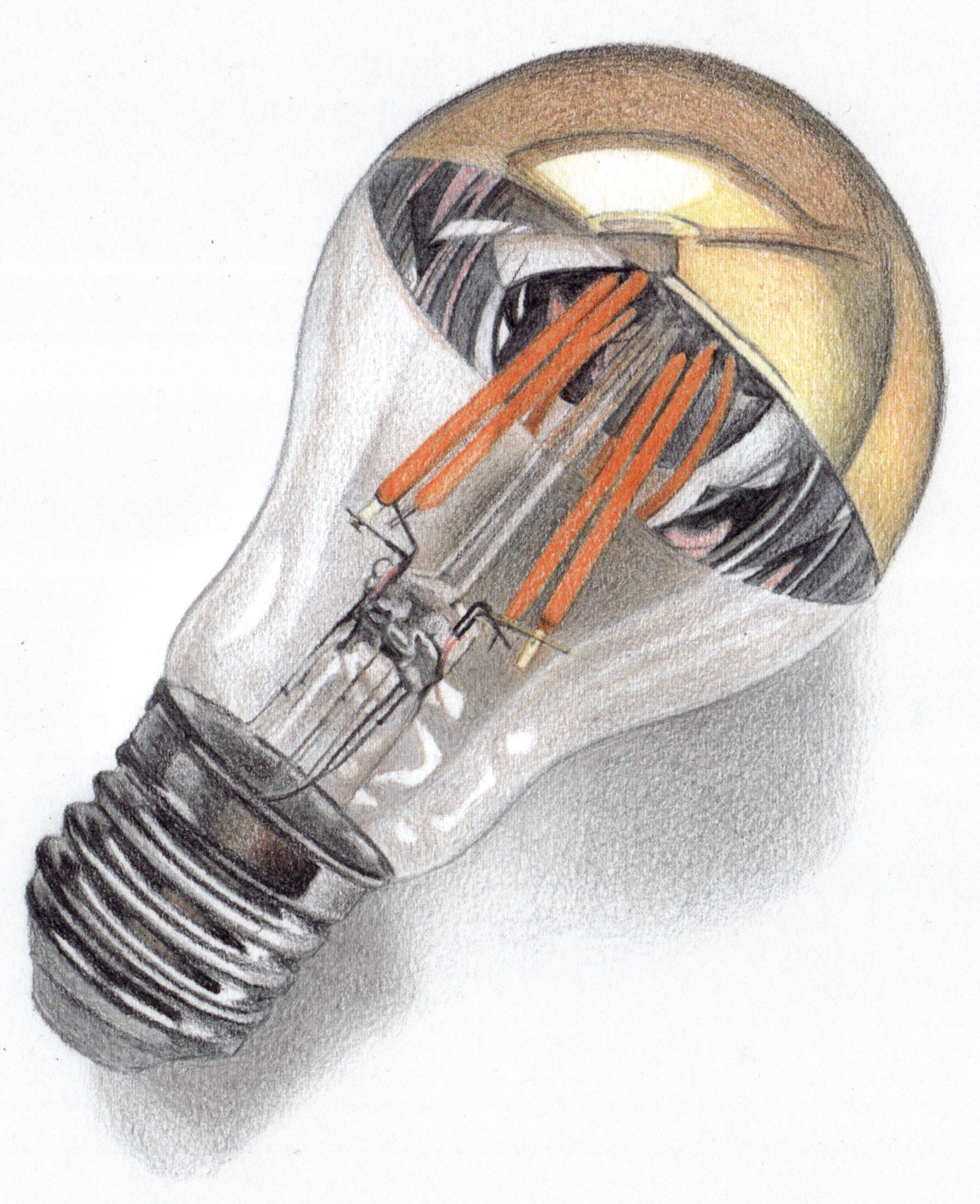

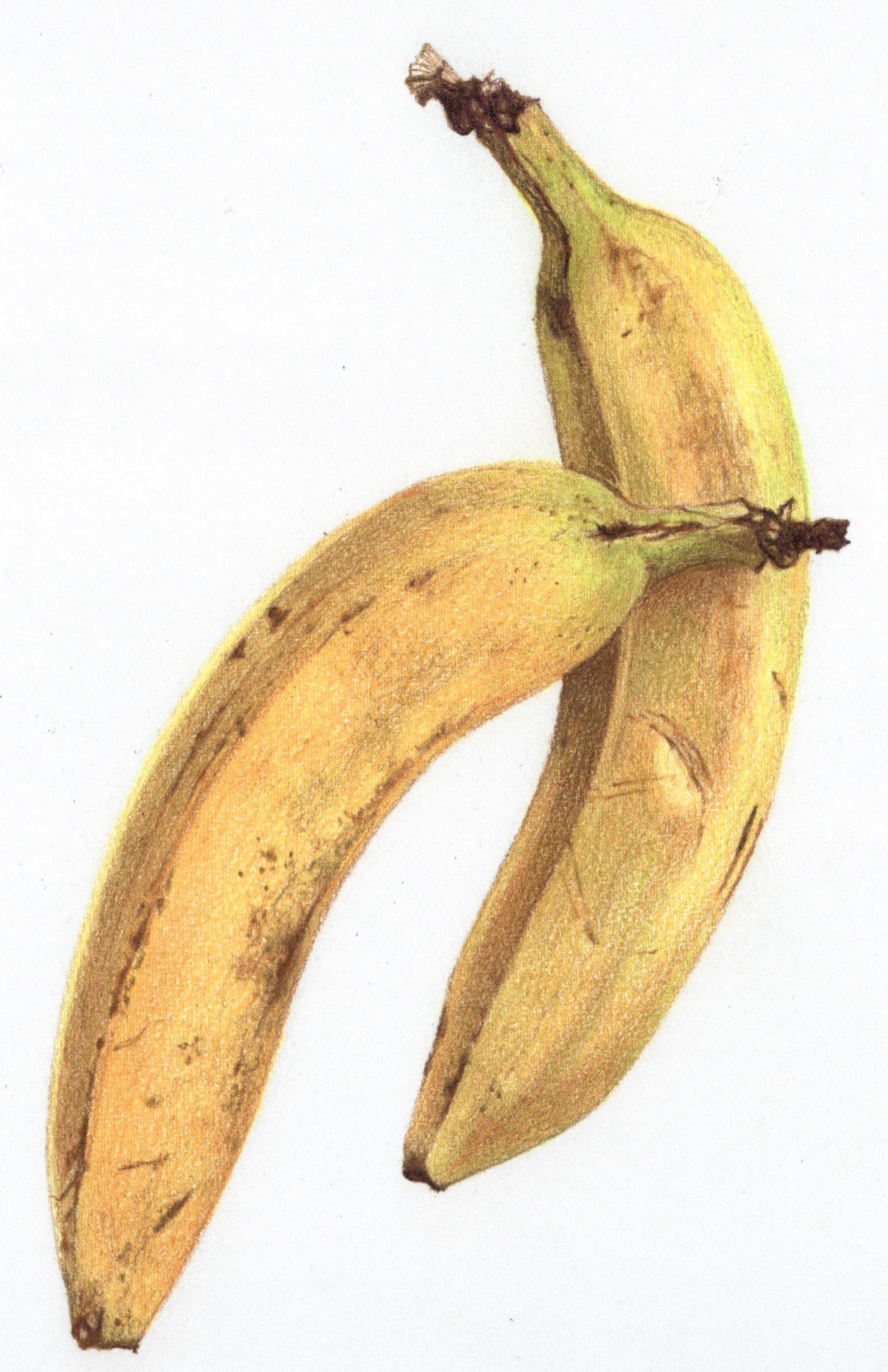

Bananas

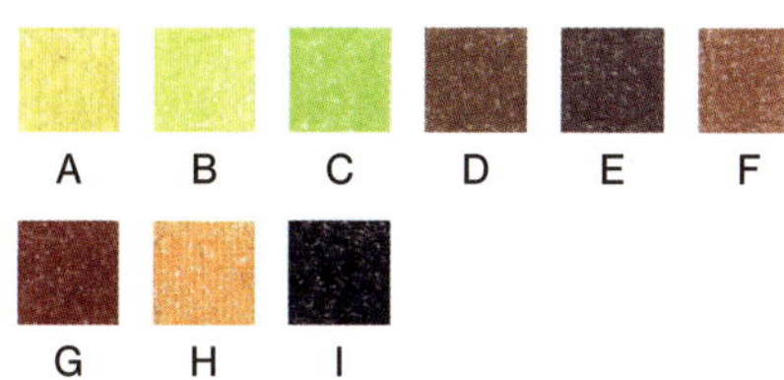

A   B   C   D   E   F

G   H   I

1 Use a pale color for the linework – yellow may be too pale, so try light brown (F).

2 Use light pressure to shade the base mid yellow (A), and heavy pressure to identify shadows. Shade the ends and edges of the banana with pale yellow-green (B).

3 Use mid brown (D) to color the tip at the base and the top of the stalks and to start adding shadow and marks to the skin.

4 With golden yellow (H) and medium pressure, make both bananas a deeper yellow. Identify the riper areas with brown ocher (G), and with mid brown (D), add more marks and spots. Using dark brown (E) and light pressure, add more depth to the shadows. Focus on the shadows created where the two bananas connect.

5 Add more color to the tip and stalk using the same dark brown with heavy pressure, and pick out the marks on the skin even more. Use deep golden yellow (H) with heavy pressure to add a final layer to both bananas, working around the marks but going over the shadows. Use lime green (C) with heavy pressure to accentuate the green around the tip and base of the bananas, and black (I) to pick out the darkest knots on the stalks.

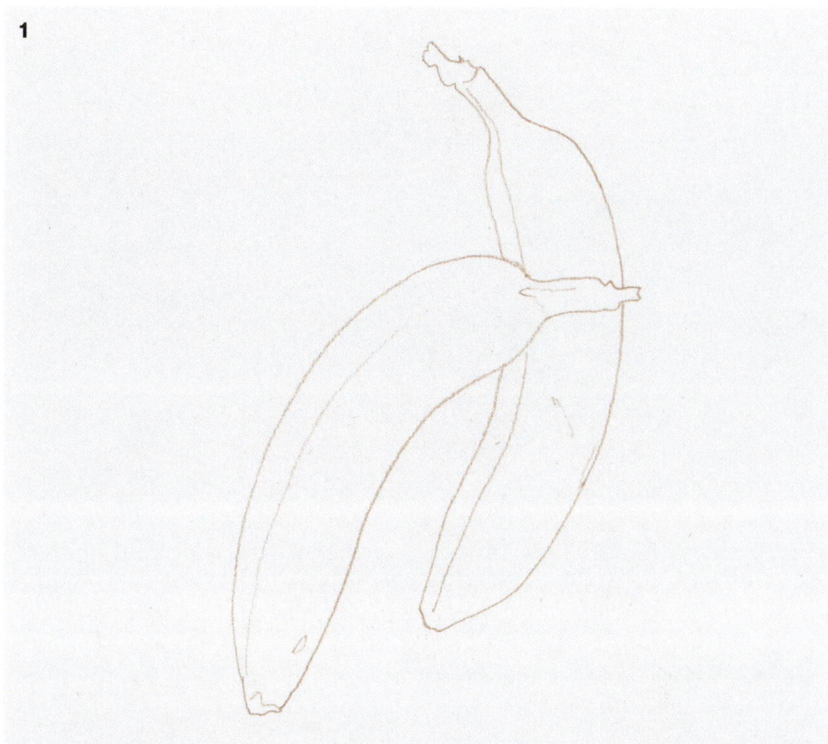

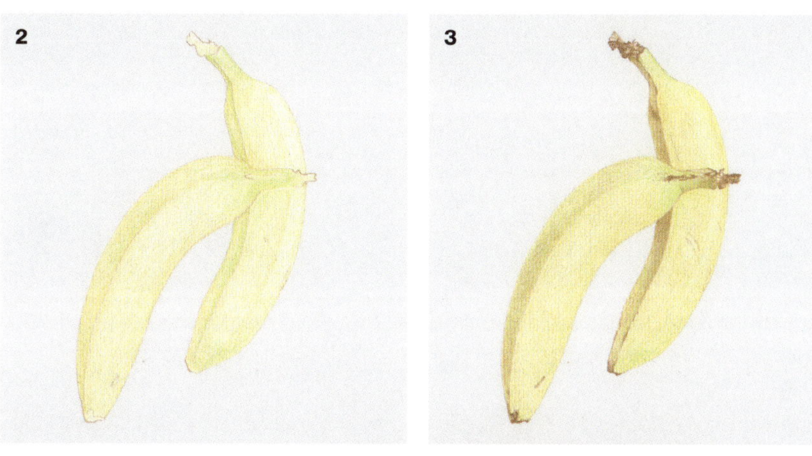

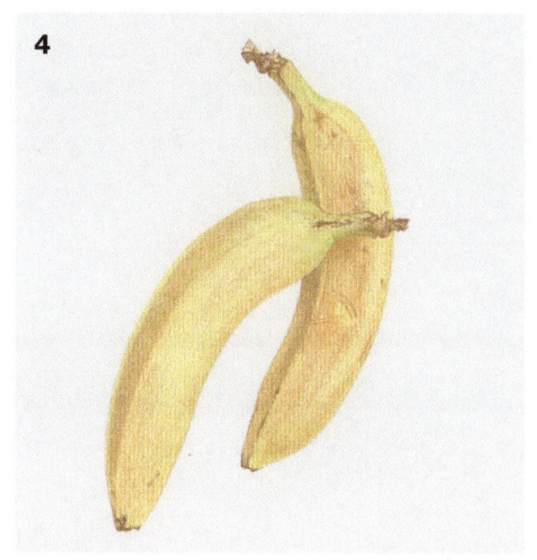

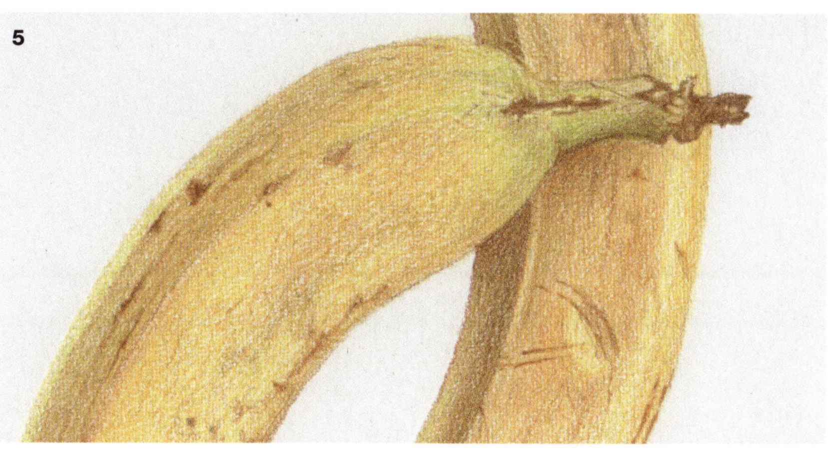

Cookie

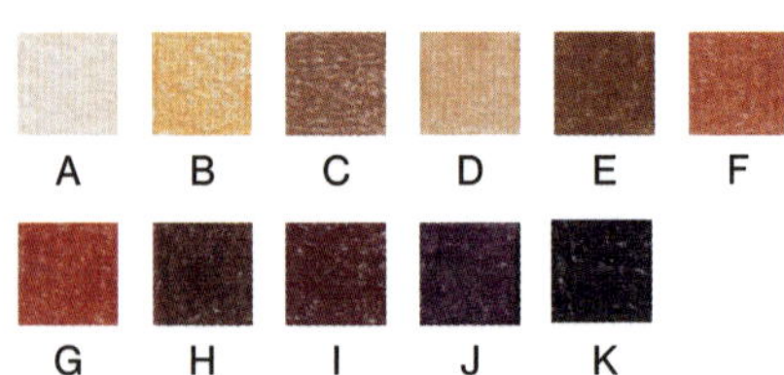

1 Select a pale orange-brown (F) to create your linework. Add as much detail as possible, defining the areas of dark chocolate and the cracks and crevices on the surface of the cookie.

2 Lay down the background color for the whole cookie in a very pale cream (A). Add a warm yellow (B) to shade around the edge of the cookie, blending a quarter of the way toward the middle. Use the same warm yellow to identify the darker zones around the center of the cookie: these warm yellow zones are going to represent the darkest baked areas.

3 Lightly use pale ocher (D) to add another layer of color and identify the salt flake shapes. Once you have done this, use a small eraser pen to remove the color from the flakes. Using both pale brown (C) and the light ocher with medium pressure, add tonal variations to the cookie's surface, working around the flakes. Shade the outer edge of the cookie with pale brown and define the small cracks across the surface. Use the pale ocher to define and shade the small ridges and bumps. With mid brown (E) and light pressure, shade in the darkest chocolate zones and add definition and shadow to the largest cracks on the surface.

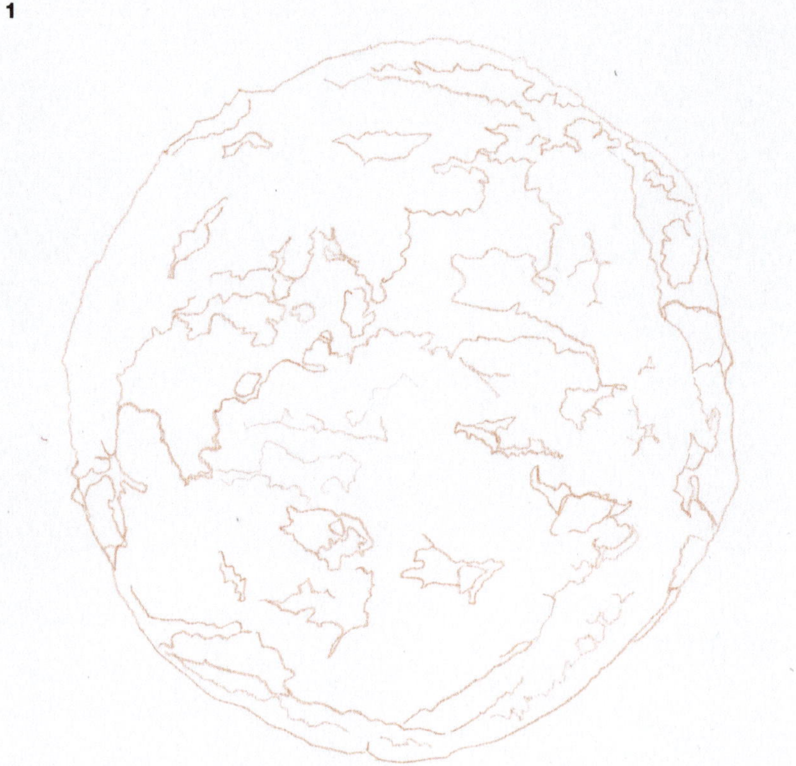

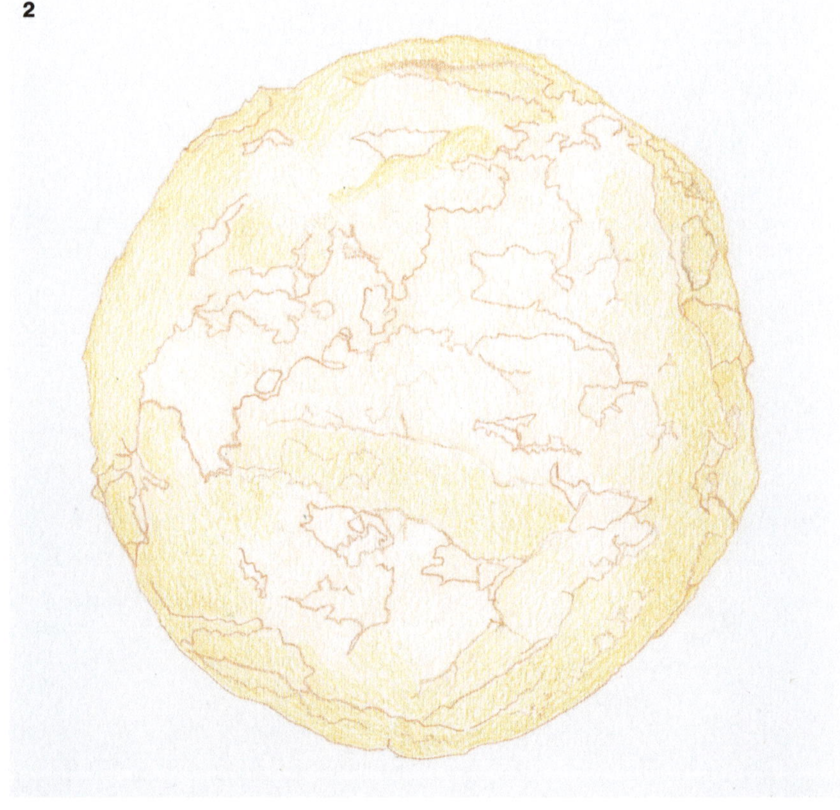

4 Bring more depth to the tonal variations using mid brown (E) with medium pressure. Use the same color to add shadow to the bumps and ridges and give more definition to the small cracks, blending around their edges. With orange-brown (F) and medium pressure give a rusty orange hue to the darker baked zones around the edge and across the surface. Carefully blend into the paler areas, using heavier pressure in the darkest spots and blending outward. Use a darker pimento red-brown (G) to bring more depth to the darker baked zones, and use medium pressure to add a deeper reddish-brown hue to the outer edge of the cookie. Use heavy pressure to create the dark cracks and crevices around the edge. Carefully work around the salt flakes using pressure to define the edges of the flakes.

3

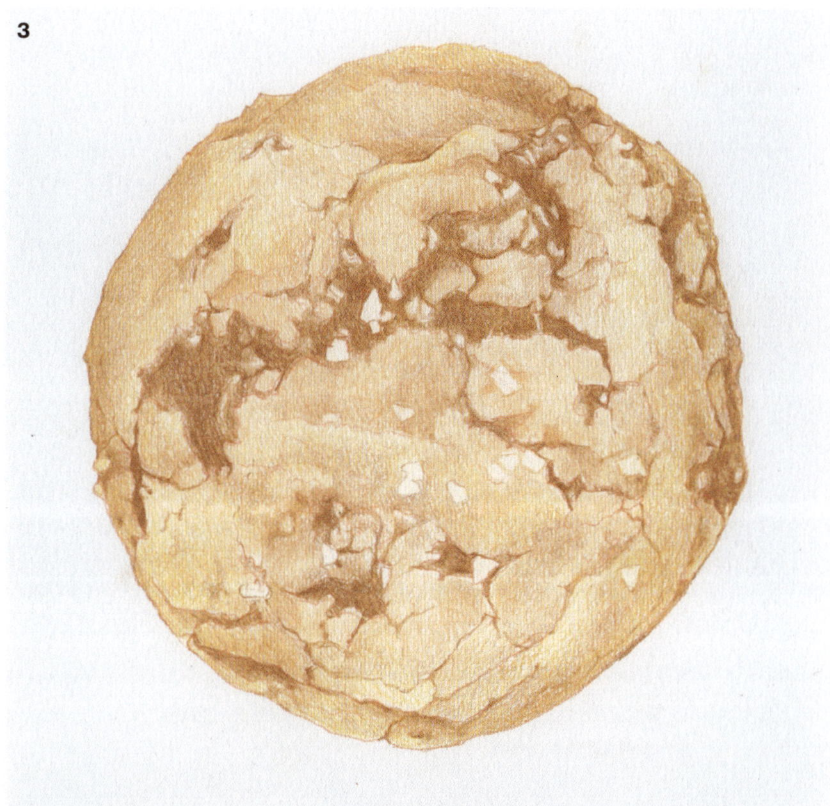

4

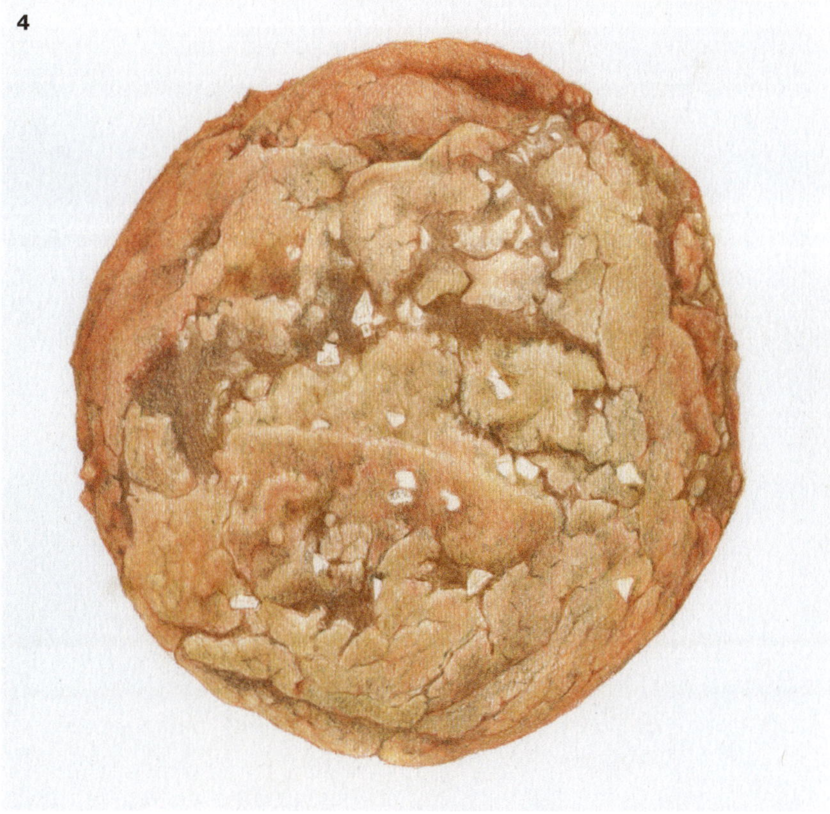

5 Use dark earth brown (H) to add another layer of color to the darker chocolate areas, giving the salt flakes harder and more defined edges. With warm yellow (B), add golden hues around the edges of the red-brown zones. Blend the yellow between these darker baked zones and the paler cookie crumb.

6 Add another layer of color to the chocolate zones with pimento red-brown (G) and medium to heavy pressure, and further define the largest cracks on the surface of the cookie.

7 Use deep burgundy red (I) to add more depth of shadow and detail to the rusty red baked zones around the edge of the cookie. Work into the cracks, crevices, and lines, and shade the very outer edge of the cookie darker, blending into the red-brown layer to create a gradient.

8 With dark purple (J) and black (K), add the final layer of color and depth to the dark chocolate zones. Use dark purple first and don't shade in the entire chocolate area, but focus on the edges where they meet the cookie crumb. Also use the dark purple to add extra definition to the largest cracks and darkest shadows across the surface of the cookie. Finally, use black to give extra depth to the dark chocolate shadows, using it sparingly and blending into the dark purple carefully.

5

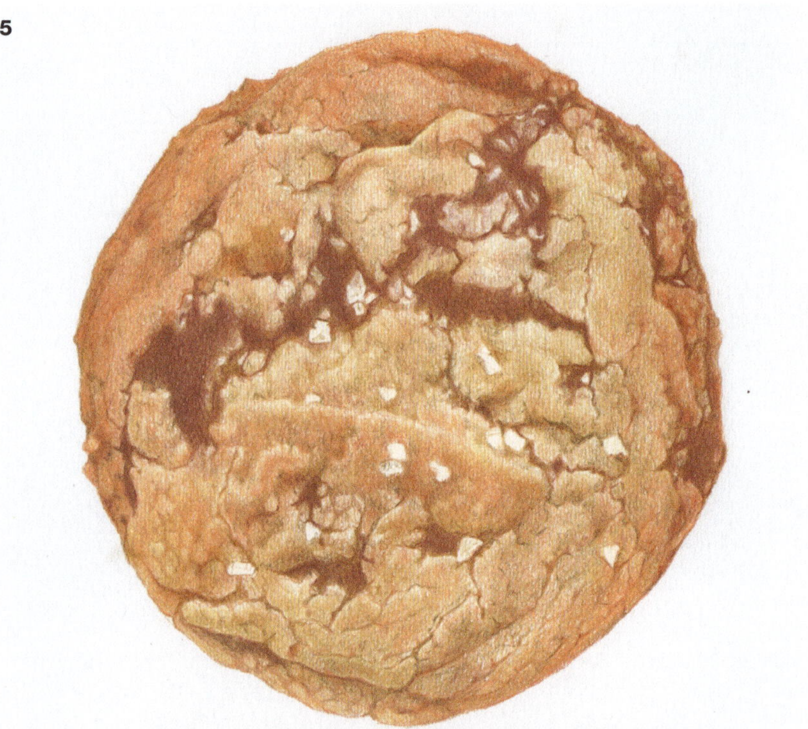

6

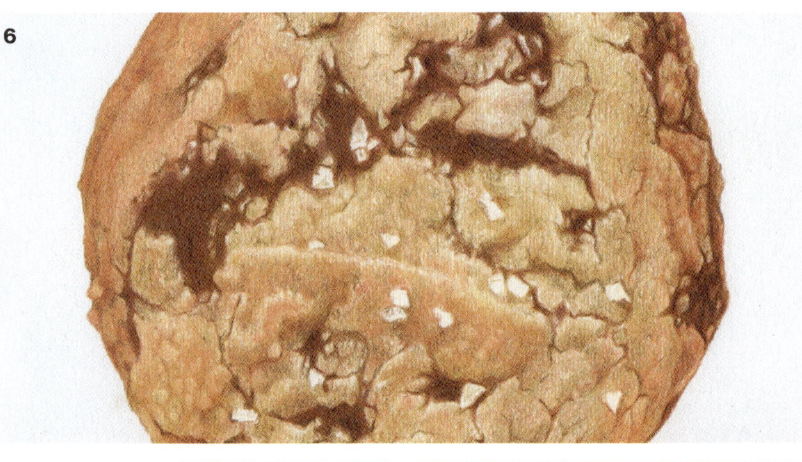

7

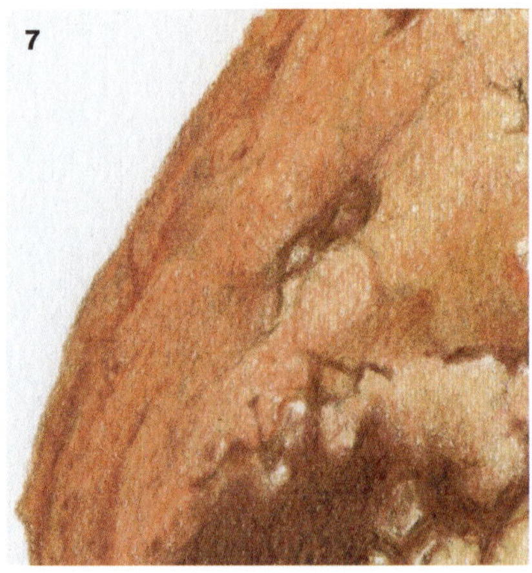

8

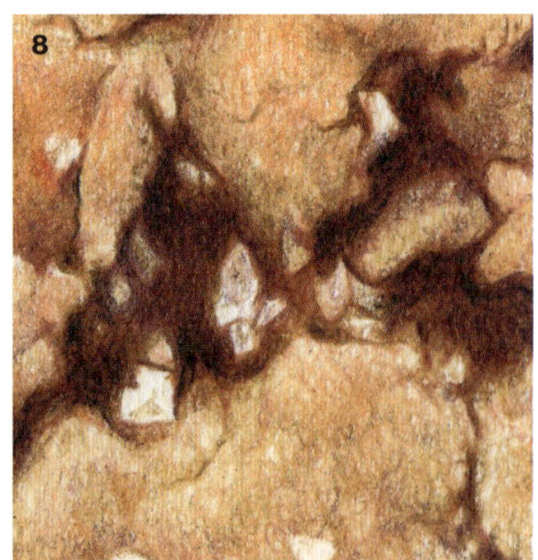

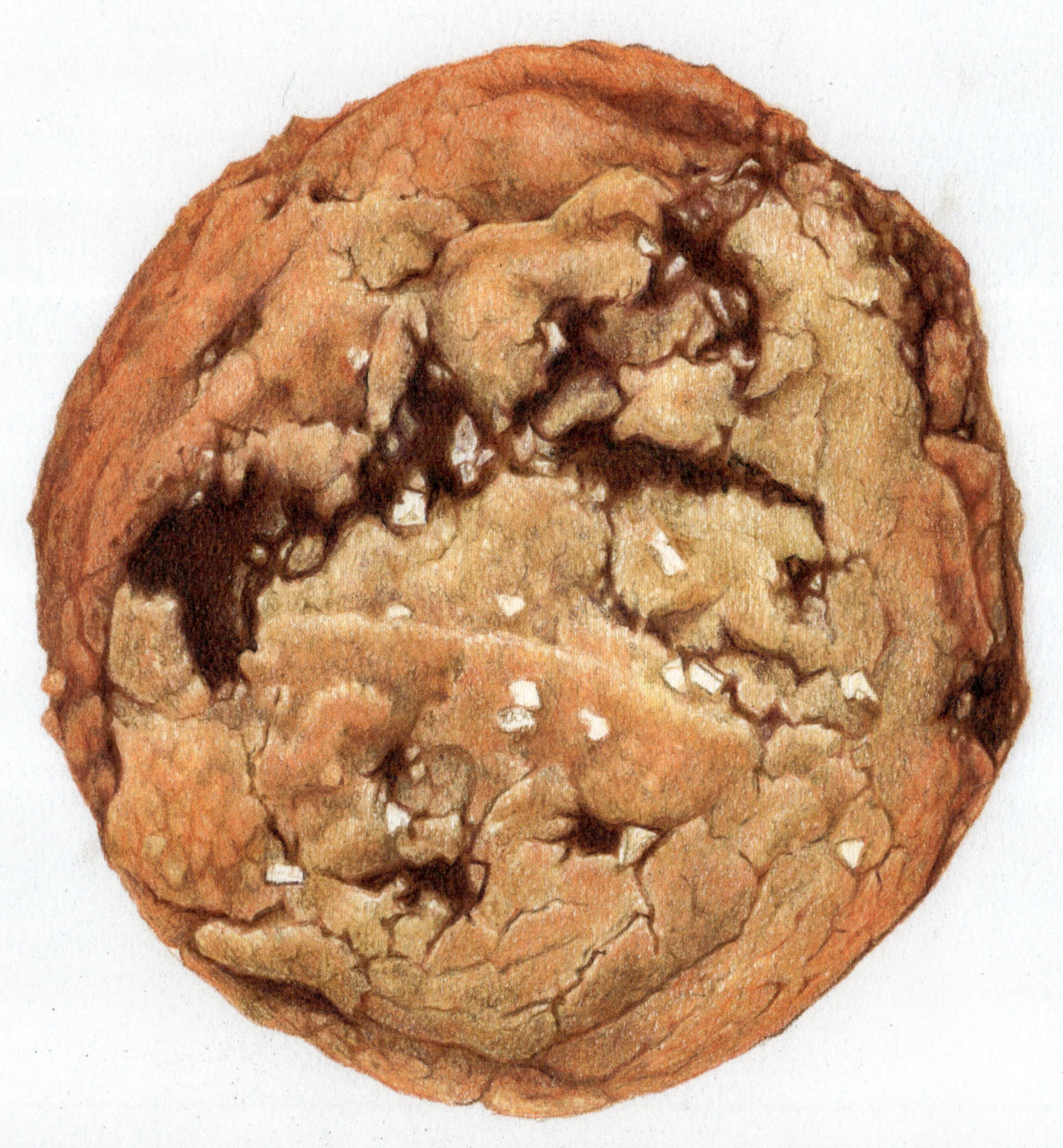

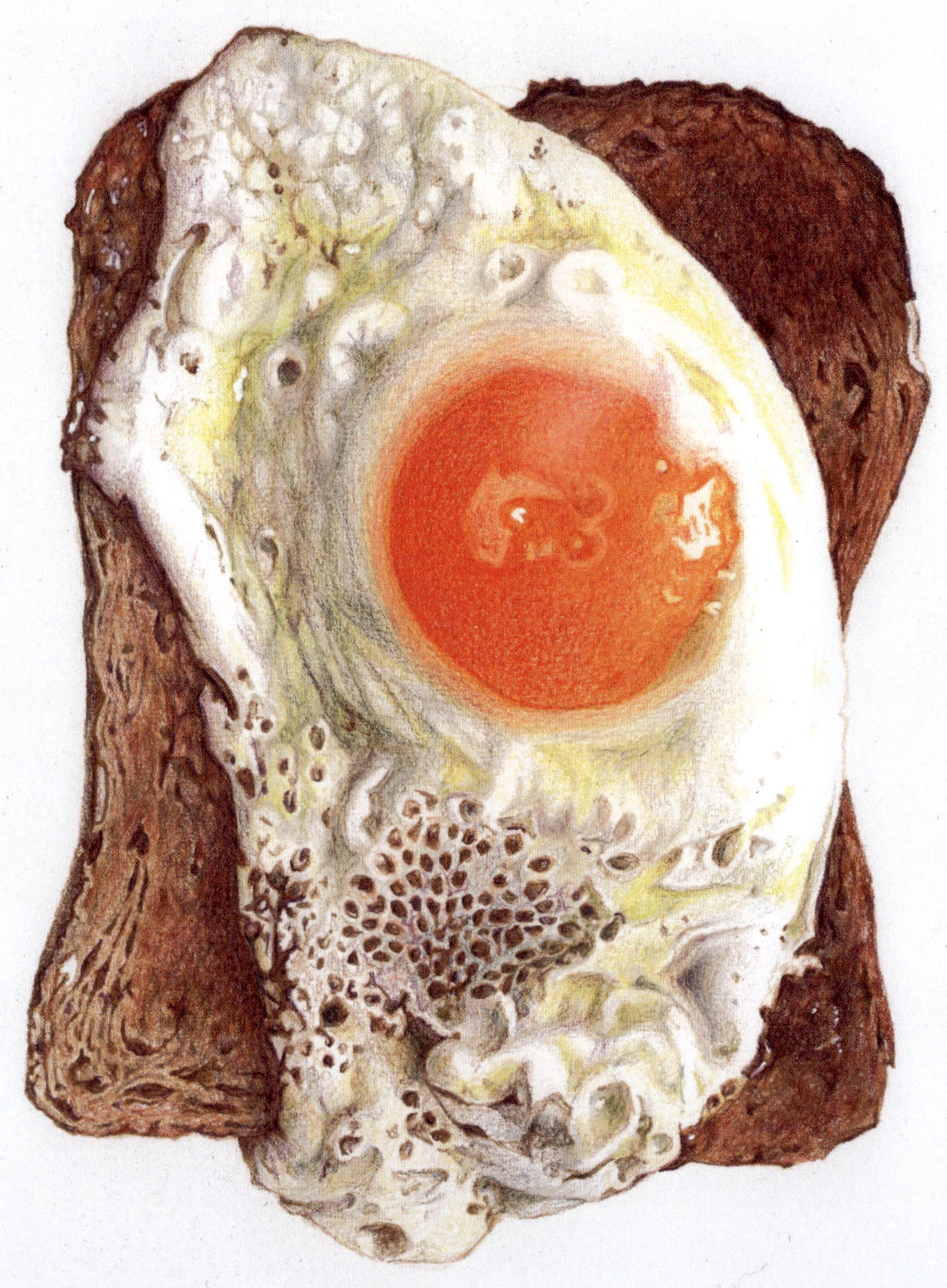

Fried egg on toast

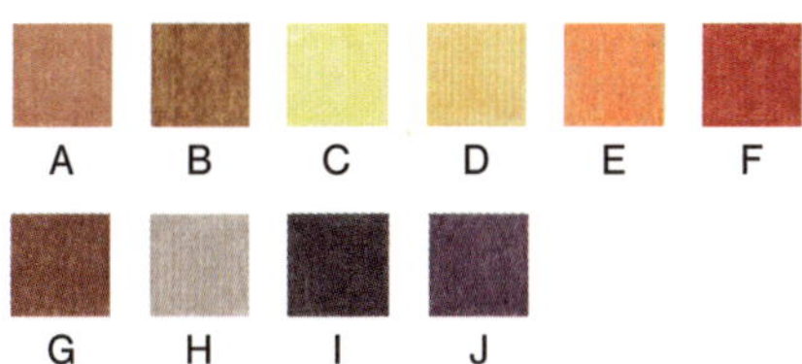

A B C D E F

G H I J

1 Select a light tone (A) for the linework.

2 Use soft brown (A) with light pressure to shade in the toast. Pick out the shadows on the egg white in gray (H), and lightly shade the yolk in mid yellow (C), leaving the highlights white.

3 Outline the crispy elements and bubbles on the egg white in mid brown (B). Lightly shade darker shadows on the egg white with the same color.

4 Use golden yellow (D) with more pressure to shade areas of yellow on the egg white. Lightly use dark brown (G) to add depth to the shadows and to pick out the darker divots and crispy edges.

5 Add a layer of orange (E) to the yolk, applying more pressure for the darker areas. Use the same orange to add an area of reflected color on the white surrounding the yolk. Lightly use blood orange (F) to give depth to the yolk.

6 Add a layer of mid brown (B) to the toast, using more pressure for the darker details, and apply dark brown (G) over darker areas. Use black-brown (I) to pick out seeds and outline the singed crust, and blackberry (J) to bring depth to the toast and definition to the crispy edge of the egg.

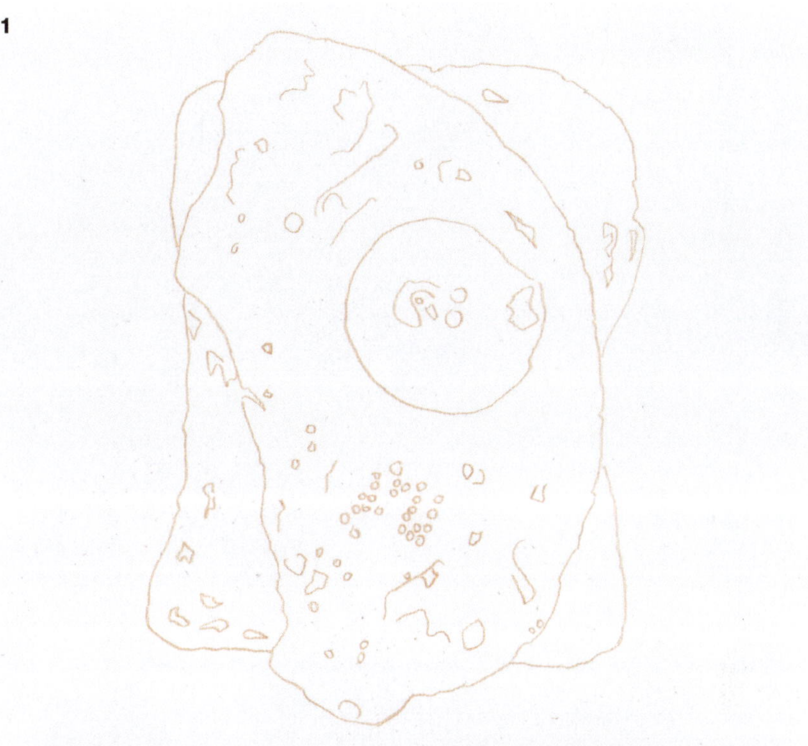

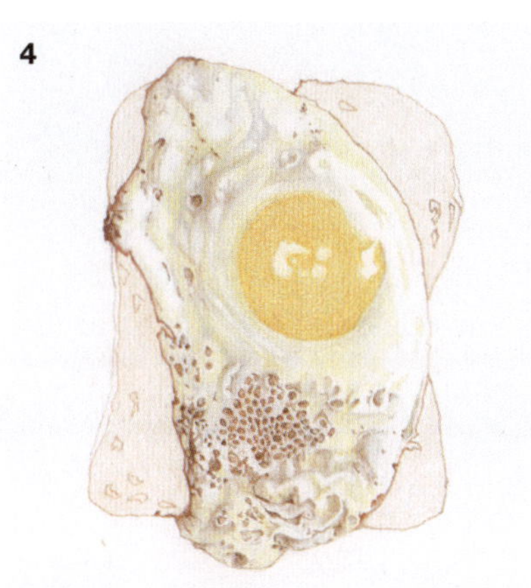

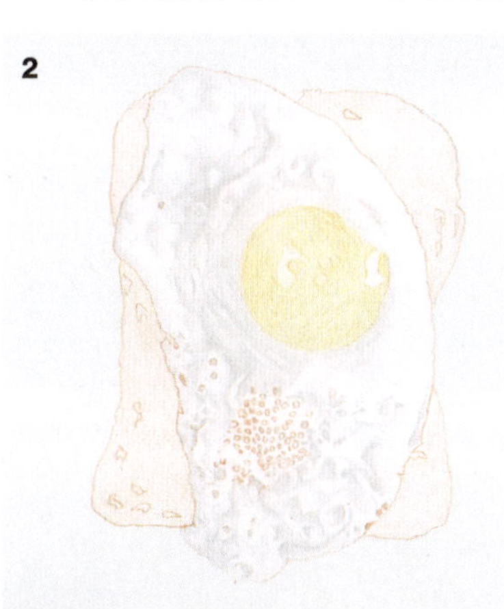

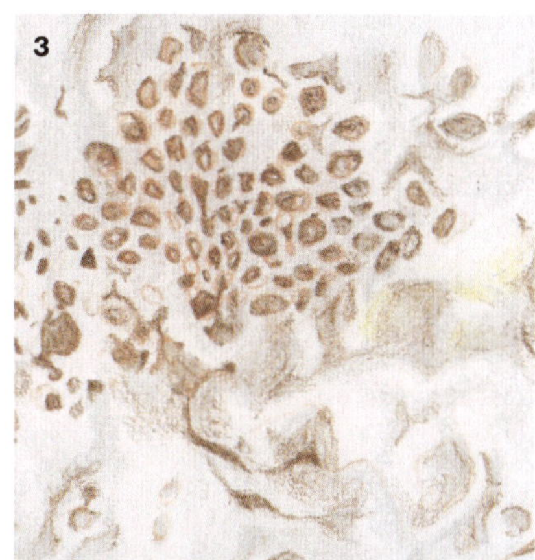

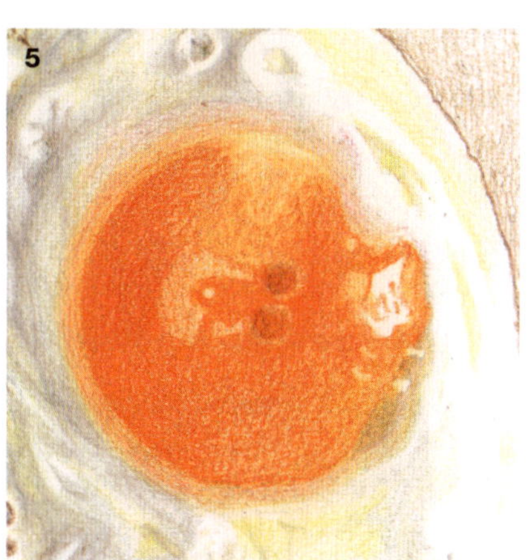

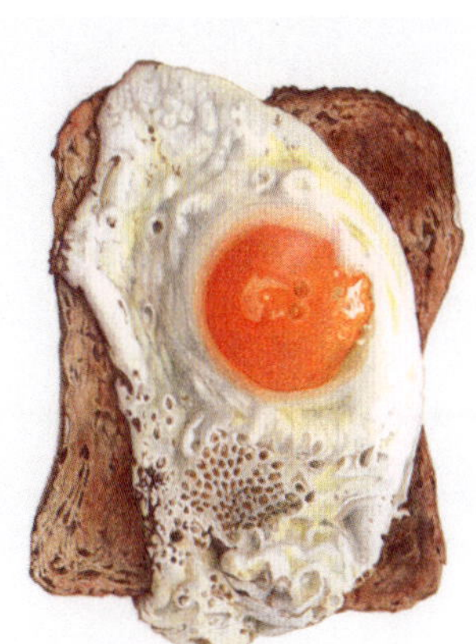

Liquorice Allsorts

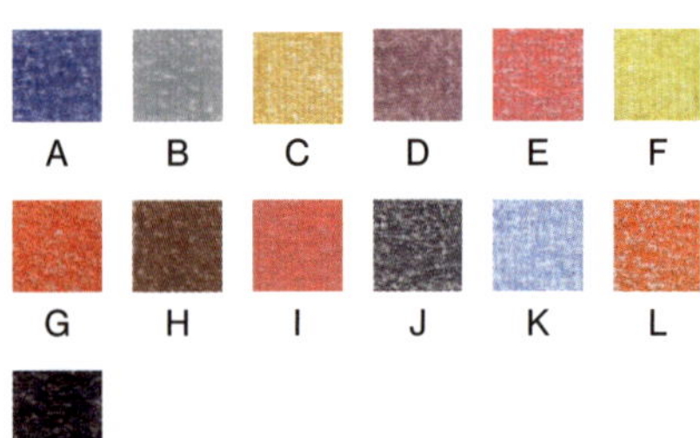

1. Select light tones for the linework. Use colors from each individual candy to outline highlights and draw on any knobbly shapes.

2. Lightly use mid pink (E), pale yellow (F), orange (L), light blue (K), mid gray (J), and black (M) to shade the background colors, leaving the highlights white.

3. Repeat the previous step with medium pressure, and use heavier pressure to identify darker areas and shadow zones.

4. Add another layer of color to all the candies, taking care to define the highlights and using heavy pressure to shade in the darker shadows. Use a darker terracotta pink (G) for the shadows and dents on the pink candies, and mid brown (H) with light pressure for the shadows on the yellow candy. Using heavy pressure, add another layer (L) to the orange candy. Enhance the shadow zones on the pink candy with pale gray-purple (D), and use a warm mid yellow (C) to add another layer to the yellow candy.

5. Use light blue-gray (B) to outline and shade in the cast shadows, using circular strokes with light pressure and applying more pressure where they overlap. Redefine the circles on the knobbly pink candy in dark pink (I) and lightly shade in random circles, leaving a few white. Do the same on the blue candy using royal blue (A). Finally, go over the licorice areas again using black (M) with heavy pressure.

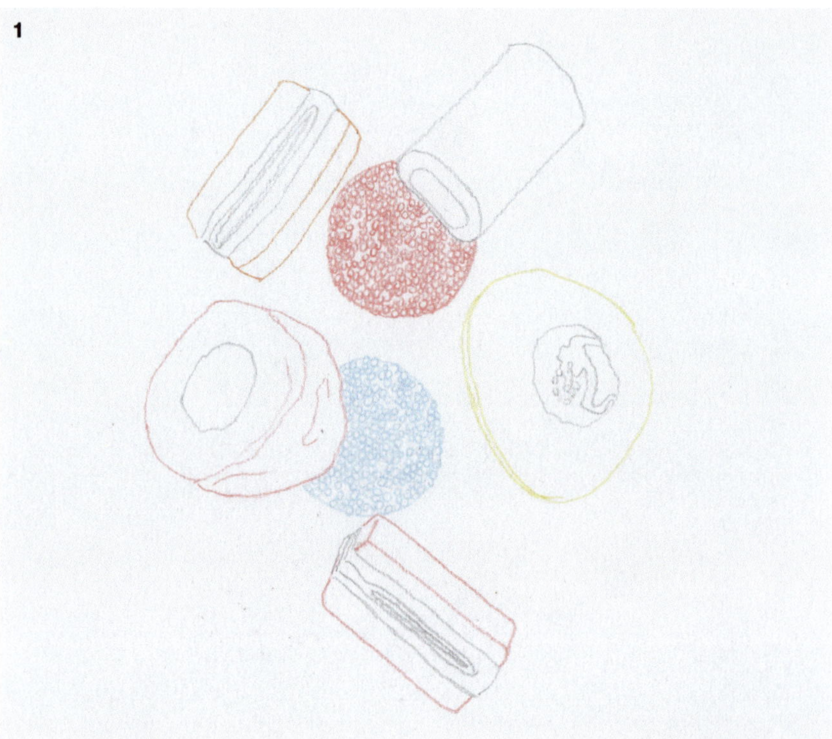

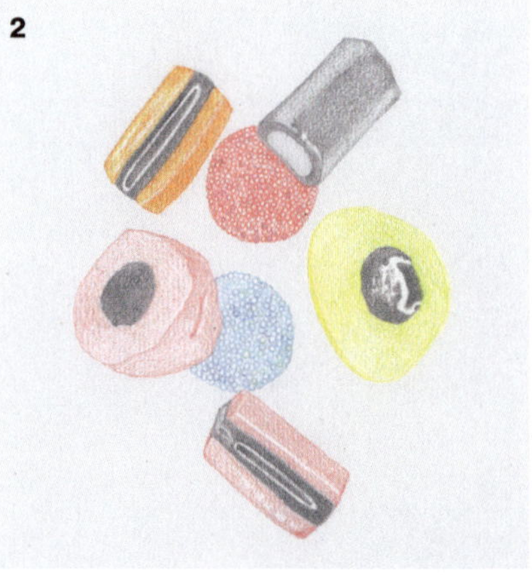

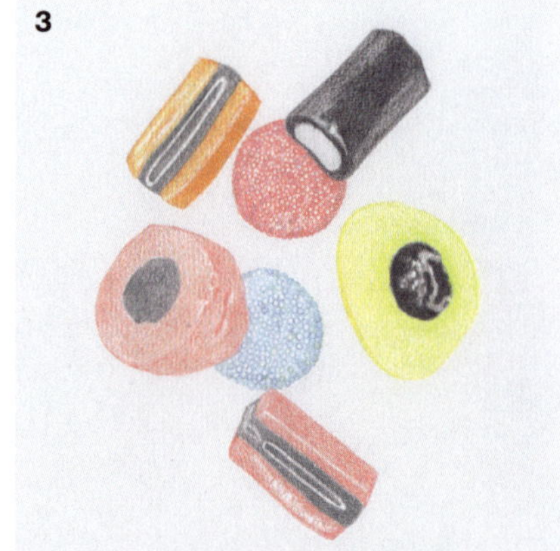

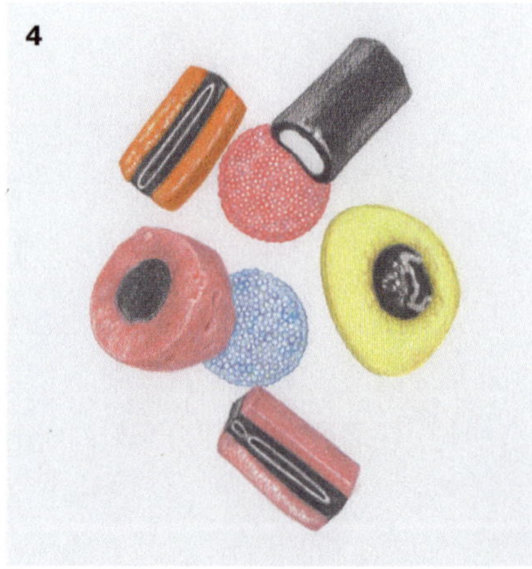

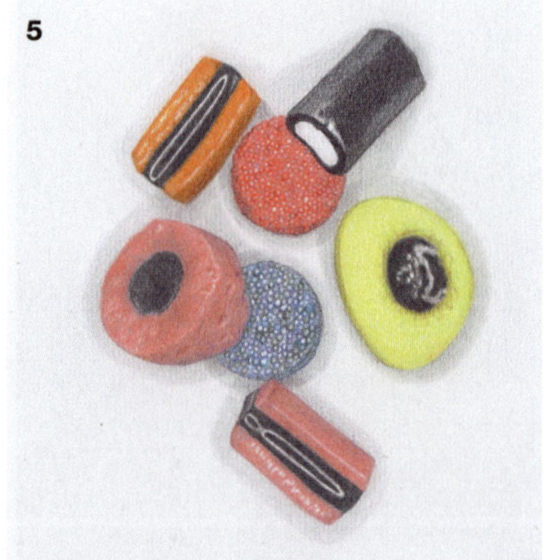

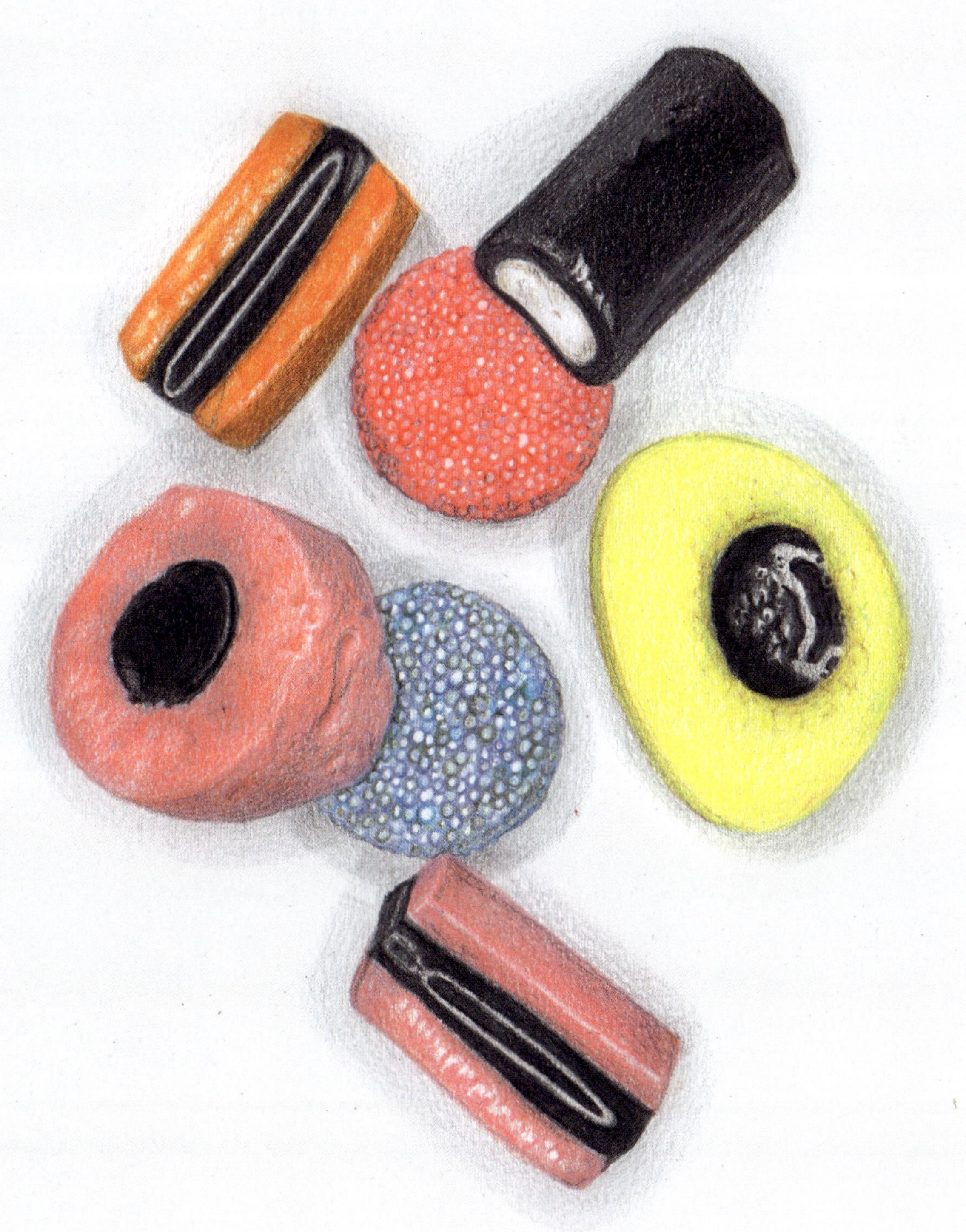

Peony

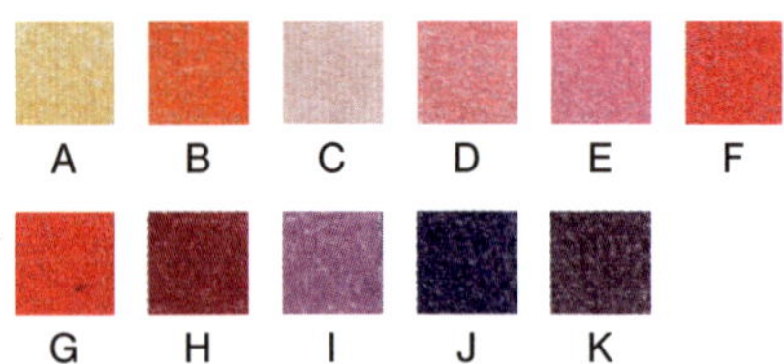

A	B	C	D	E	F
G	H	I	J	K	

1 For the linework, use mid pink (E) for the petals and mid yellow (A) to outline the central stamens. Try to include as much detail as you can for the petal work.

2 Use a very pale pink (C) to shade in the petal background layer. With the mid yellow, shade in the stamens and other central details of the flower, and use mid pink (E) for the very center.

3 Add another layer of color to the petals with blush pink (D), applying pressure to identify the areas of shadow. Use mid pink (E) to further define these areas and identify the creases and lines in the petals where needed. Use medium pressure to define the shadows cast by the overlapping petals.

4 Take all the petals a shade darker using bright pink (F), applying light pressure over the tips of the petals that are catching the light and heavier pressure over the shadow areas defined in the previous step.

1

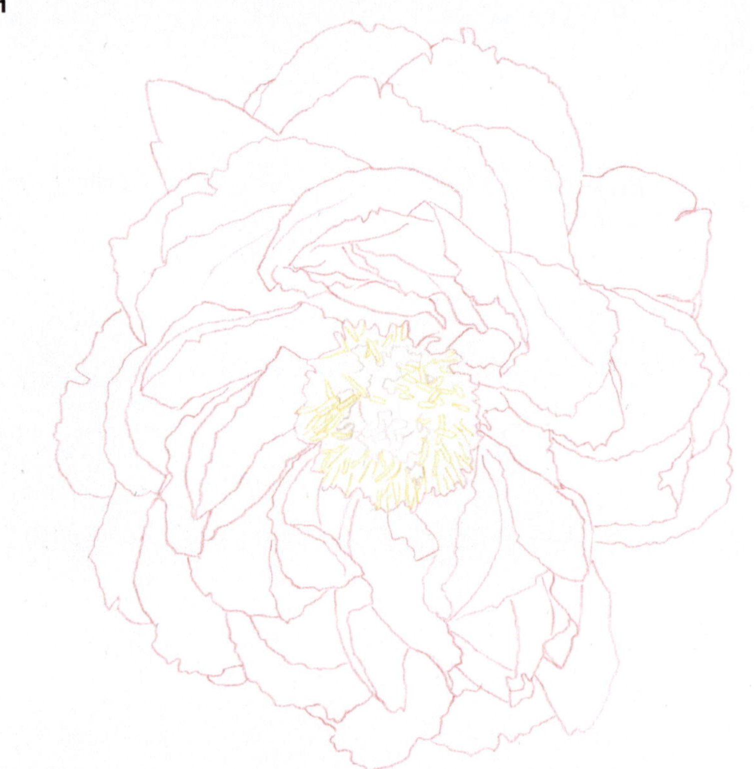

2

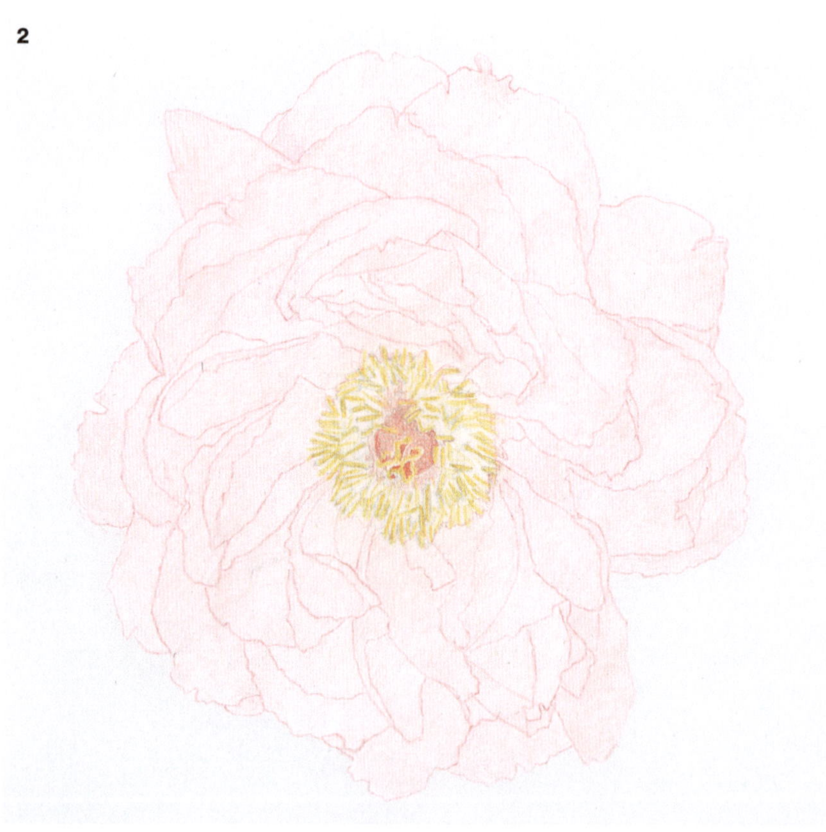

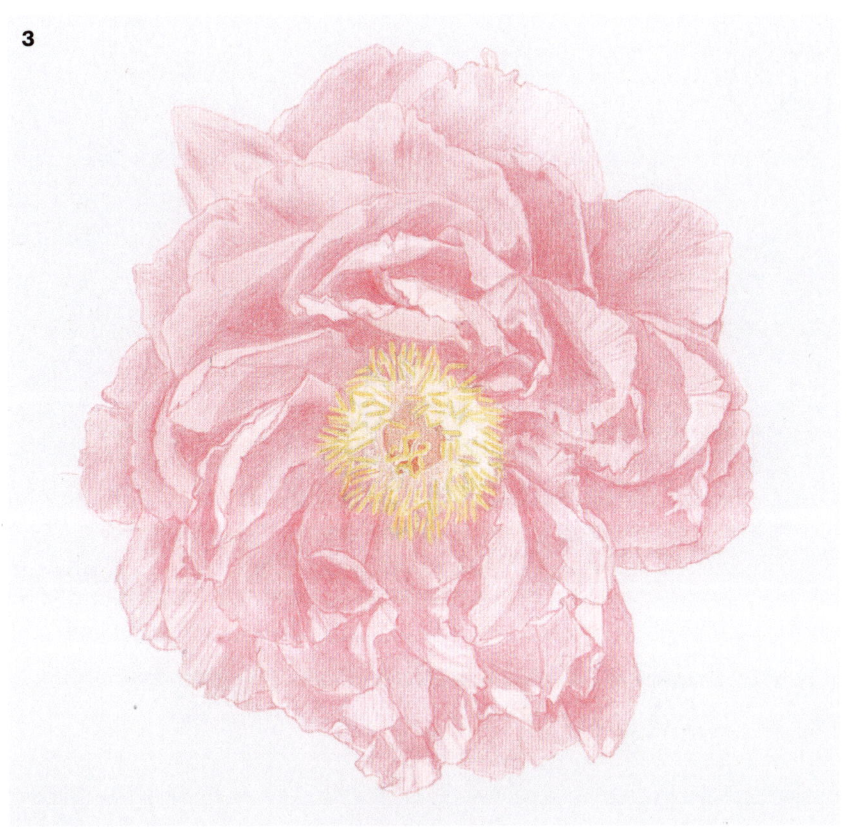

3

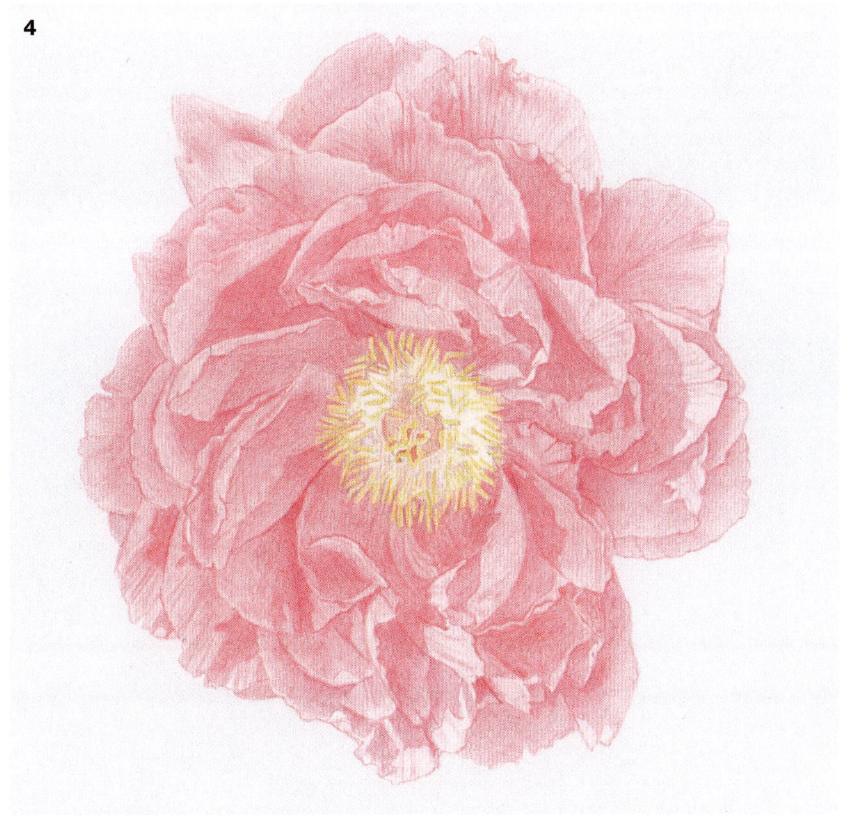

4

5 Use mid violet (I) with light to medium pressure to give more depth to the shadows. Apply heavy pressure to create darker spots at the base of the petals and where the darkest shadows are cast by the overlapping petals.

6 Carefully color around and in between the stamens in bright pink (F). Use dark cranberry red (H) to shade in the center of the flower. Apply pressure to make the outer edge darker.

7 Use mid orange (B) to darken the tips of the stamens and mid pink (E) with medium pressure to add another layer of color and depth to the petal shadows. Focus on the shadows around the center of the peony and at the base of the petals.

8 Use scarlet red (G) and mid pink with heavy pressure to add another layer of color to the darkest and medium petal shadows. Applying light pressure, shade around two thirds of the stamens on the left side with the mid pink, leaving a third in their original yellow color to indicate the sunlight catching them.

9 Use blackberry (K) and dark blue-violet (J) to add the final layer of depth to the shadows, applying medium to heavy pressure around the stamens and the clusters of overlapping petals. The aim is not to go over all the areas in shadow with these final dark colors, but to use them to emphasize the deepest shadows at the base of and between the petals. Use more pressure in the darkest zones and blend toward the lighter zones with less pressure, creating a consistent gradient from deep blue/purple to dark pink.

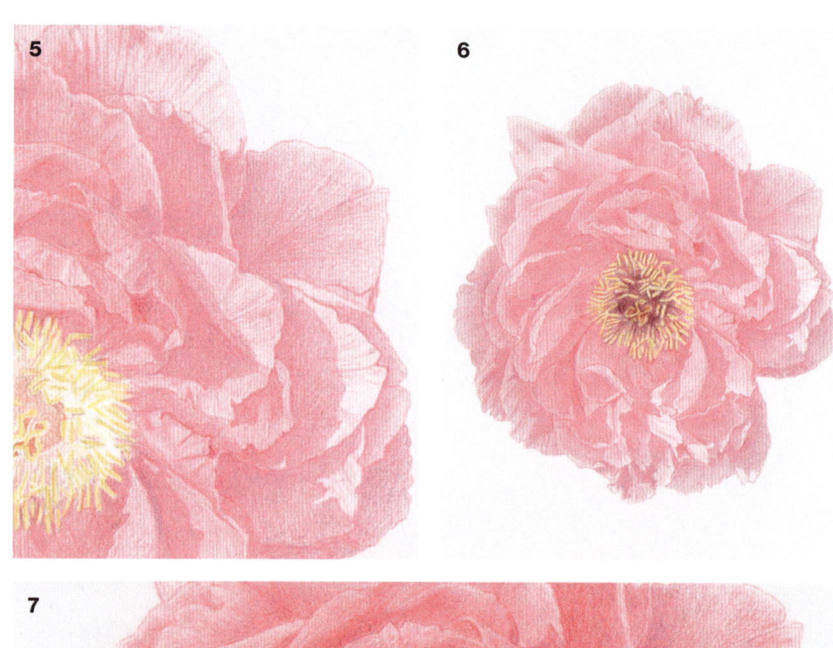

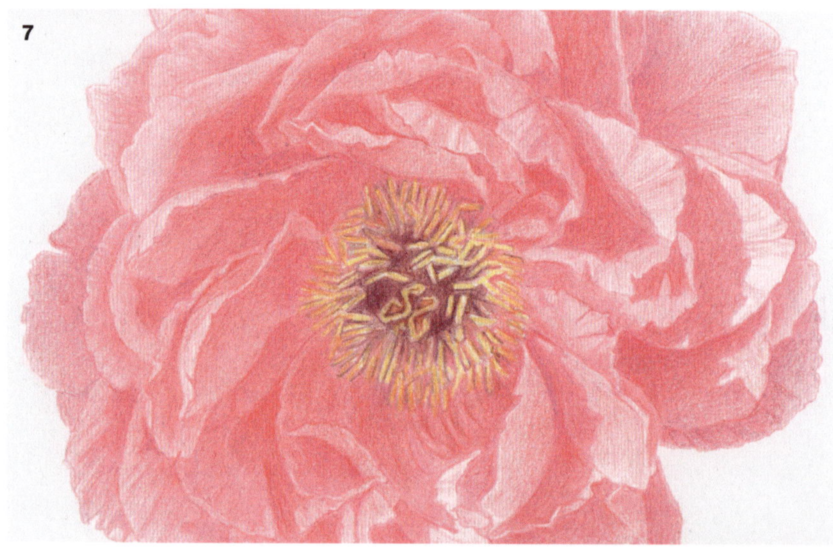

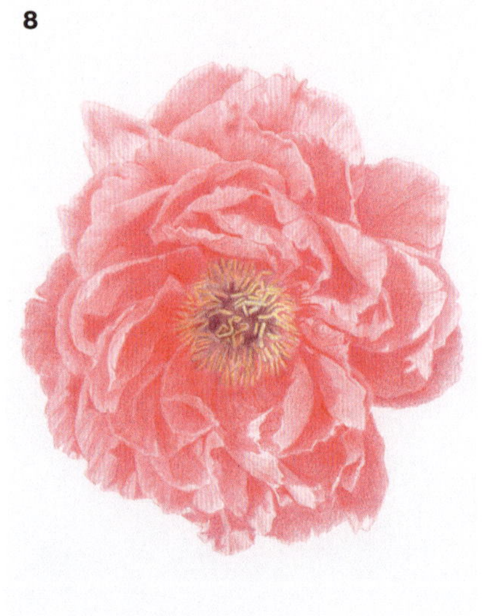

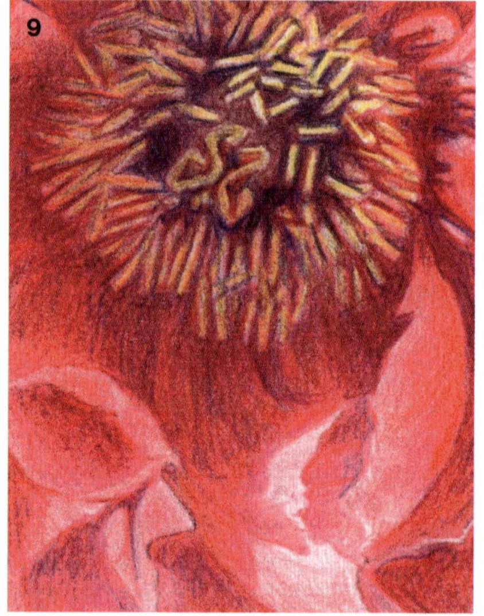

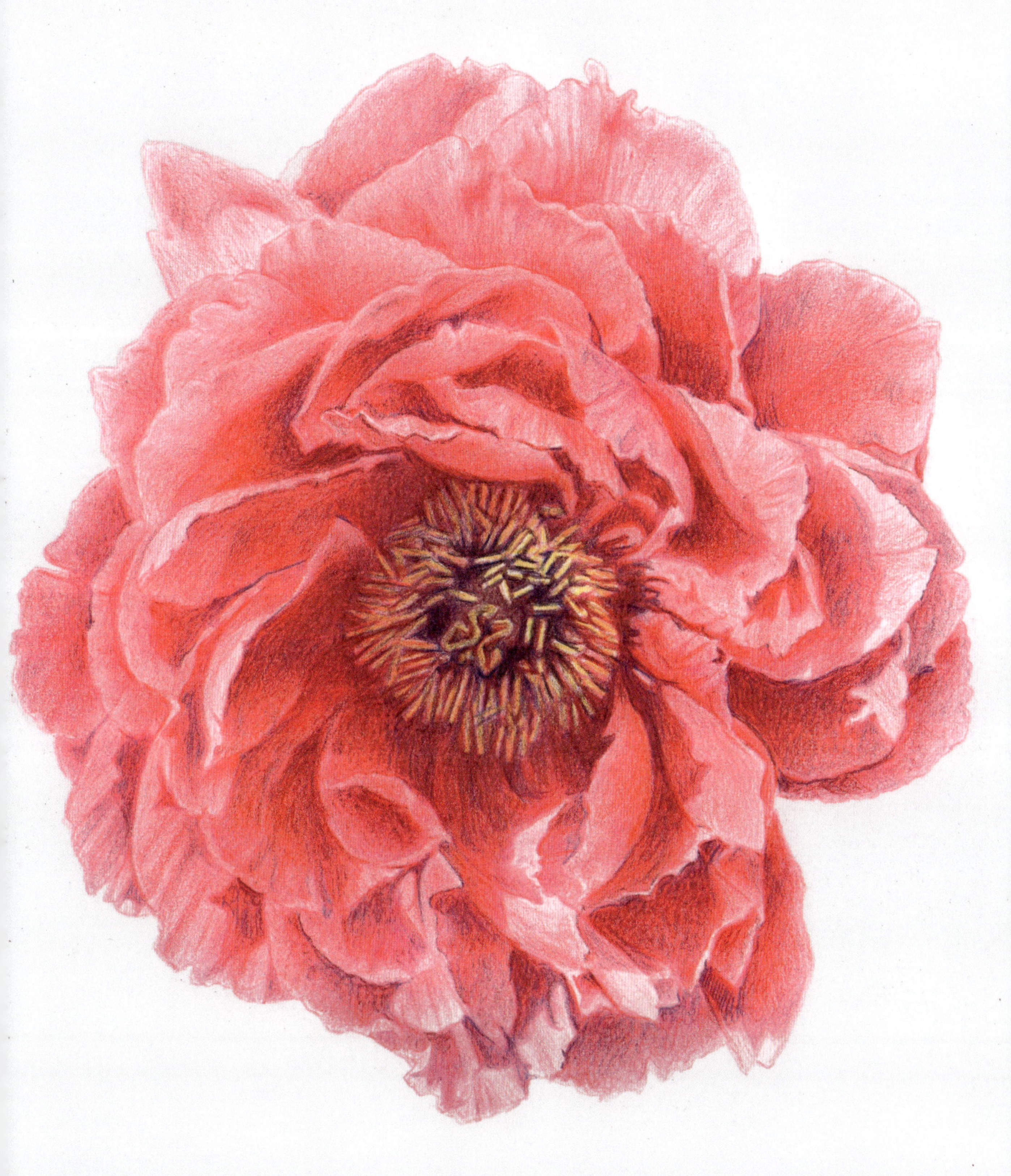

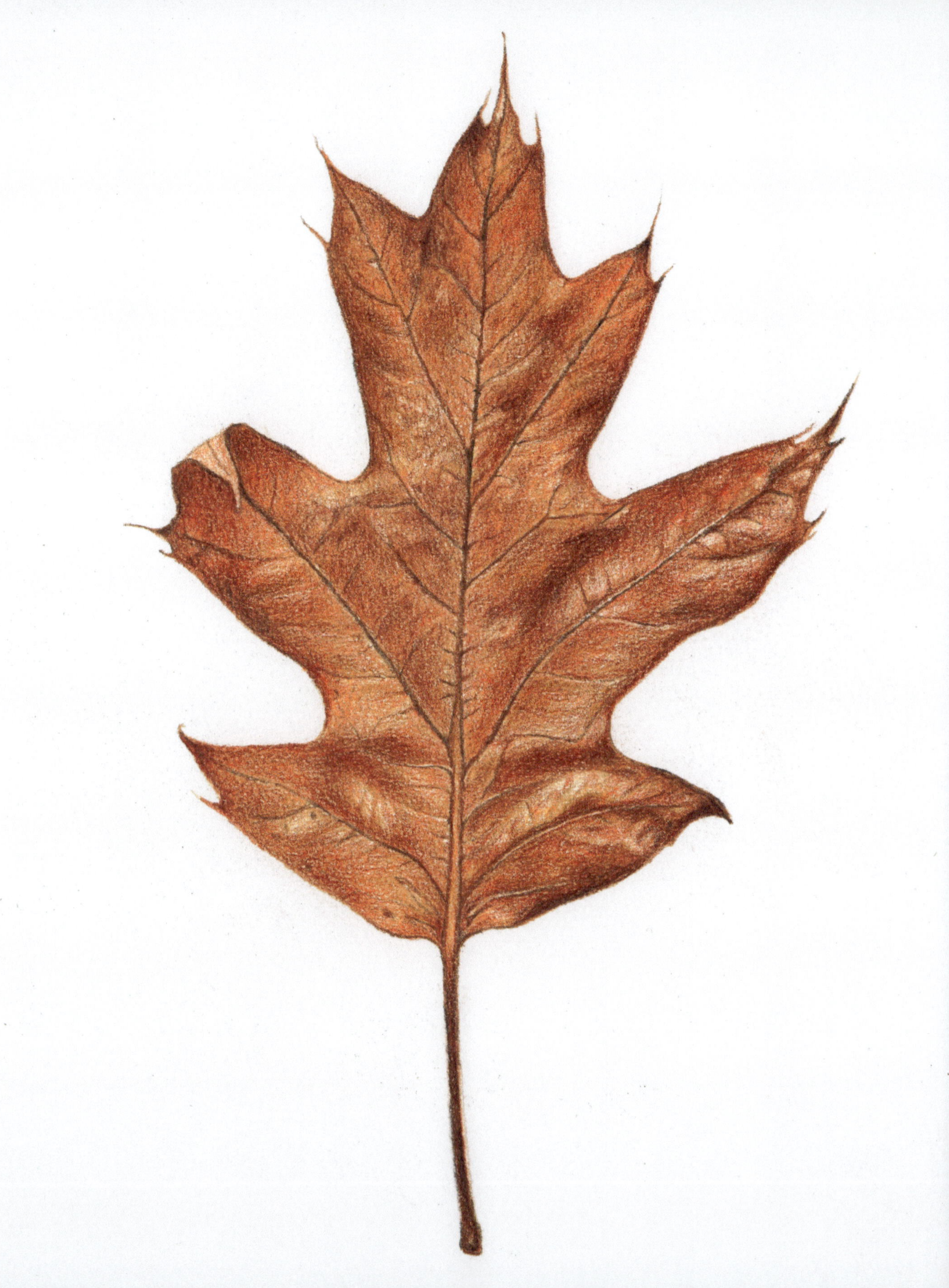

Autumn leaf

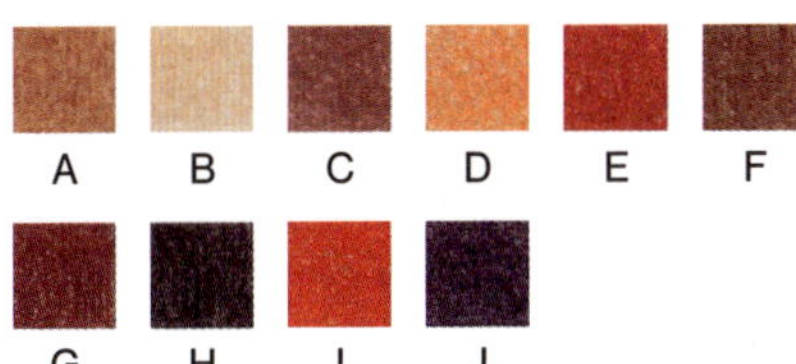

A B C D E F
G H I J

1 Use a light tone (A) for the linework, indicating the main vein lines.

2 Shade the entire leaf and stem in warm peach (B). Use light sienna brown (A) to identify the smaller veins and stem and shade in the darker zones. Use less pressure over the highlights.

3 Using mid ocher (C), add warmth to the darker zones and more definition to the veins and stem. Add warmth to the highlights with dark yellow-orange (D), using light pressure. Use pimento red (E) to take the entire leaf and stem a shade darker, applying more pressure on the darker zones and less around the highlights. Shade around the edge of the whole leaf in mid brown (F).

4 Use dark terracotta (G) to take the entire leaf a shade darker, focusing pressure on the edges of the leaf and the stem. Define the veins and sharpen the edges of the tips of the leaf with dark brown (H).

5 Use rusty red (I) to add warmth to the medium shadows and around the edges of dark shadows. Use pimento (E) to give an opaque finish across the rest of the leaf, and blackberry (J) with light pressure to further define the darkest areas.

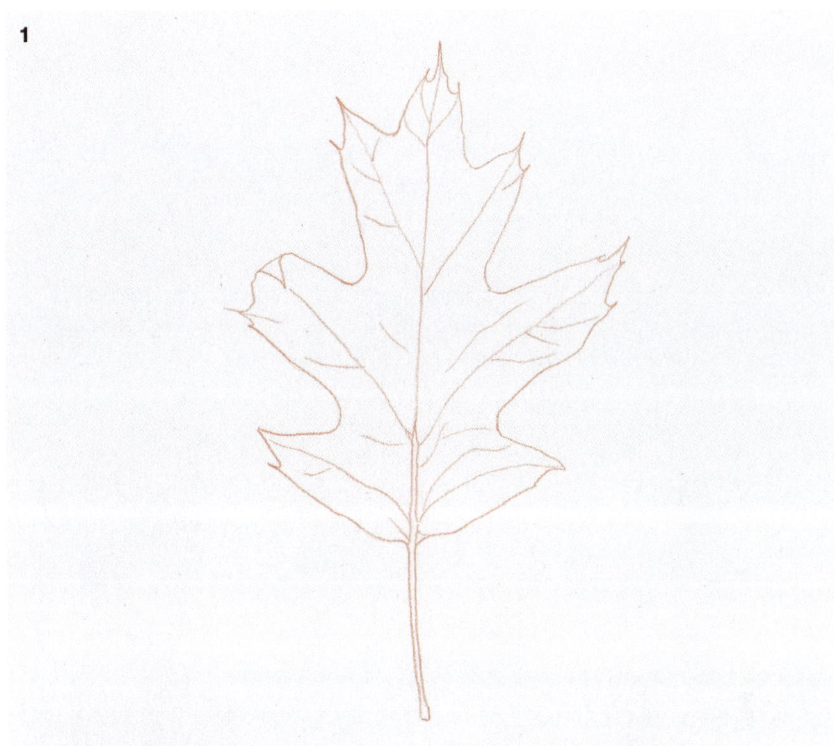

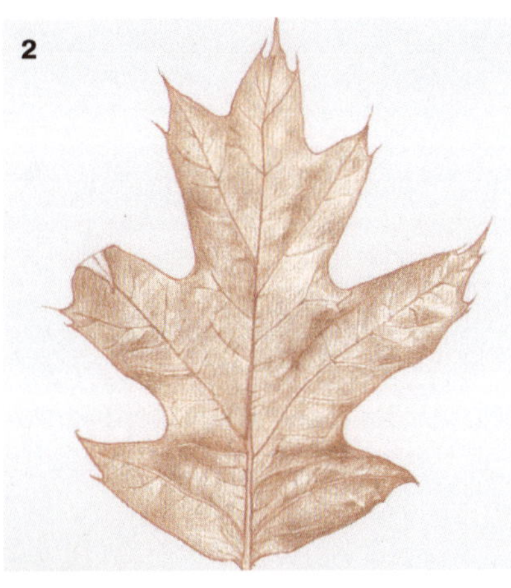

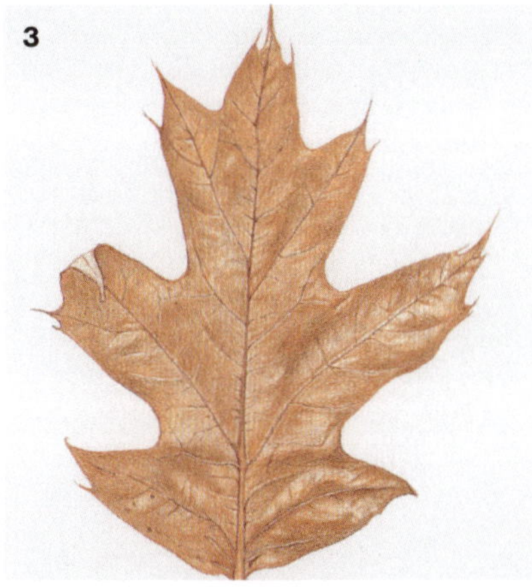

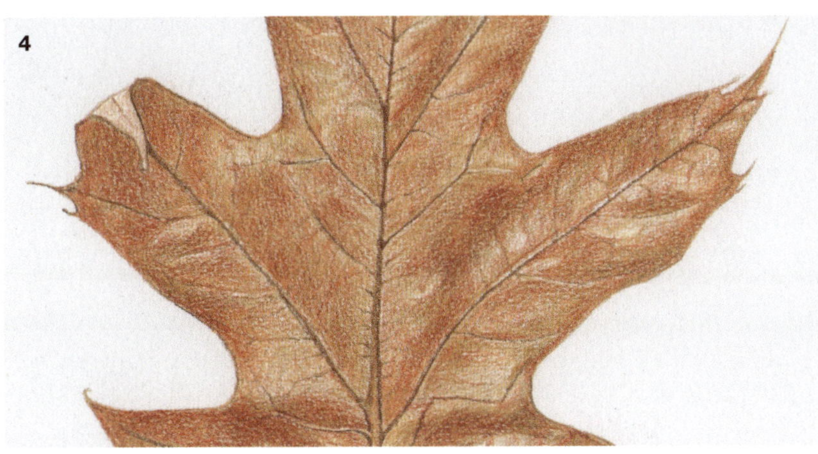

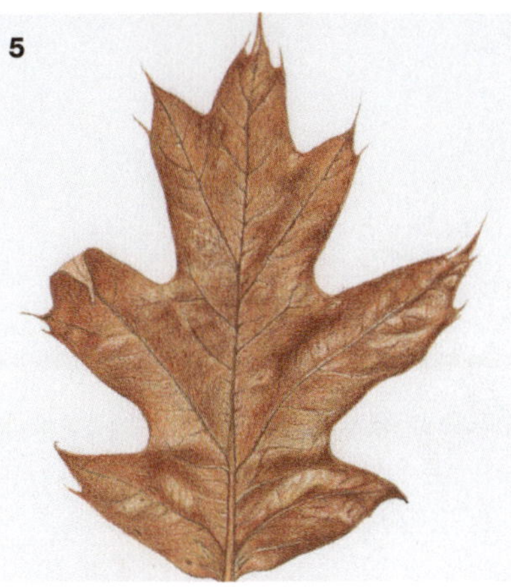

Steel jar

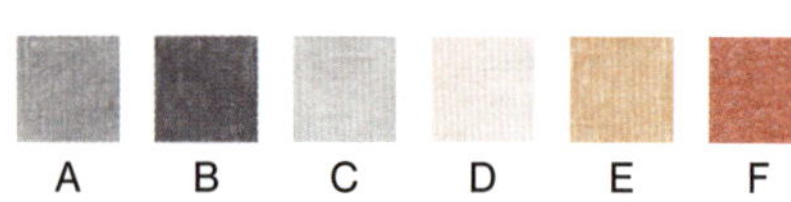

A   B   C   D   E   F

1 Lightly sketch the linework (A). Guidelines should show sections of color across the reflective surface as well as its shape.

2 Lay down a pale gray (C) base layer for the pot and mid gray (A) for the metal band around the lid. Leave the main highlight area free of color.

3 Use the pale gray to pressure shade over the base layer of the pot, leaving the smaller highlight areas white. Pick out and shade in the dark areas in mid gray (A).

4 Shade the lid in pale gray, and use mid gray to pick out the darker details. Lightly use a pale flesh tone (D) to shade in the lid's semi-transparent rubber seal.

5 Pressure shade over the mid-gray areas, taking them a shade darker, applying more pressure to the darkest areas. Add reflections of pale terracotta (F) on top of the pale gray, and a pale ocher (E) layer on the lid's seal, pressure shading over the top with mid gray (A).

6 Use mid gray to take the whole metal base a shade darker, working around the highlights. Increase the terracotta reflections, pressure blending into the dark gray. Use charcoal gray (B) for the final layer of shadow and detail, going over the dark gray reflections and accent details on the lid.

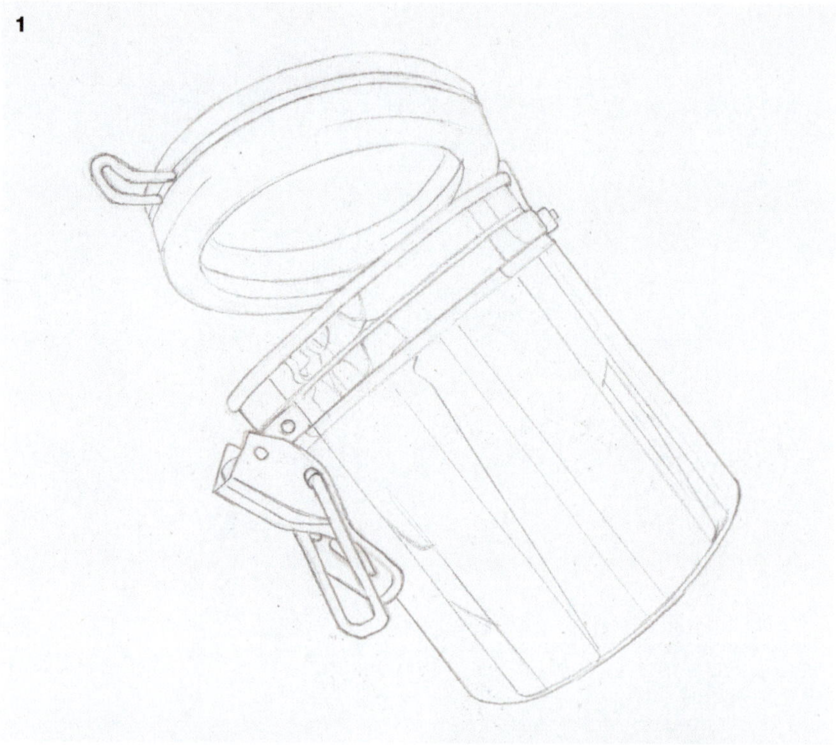

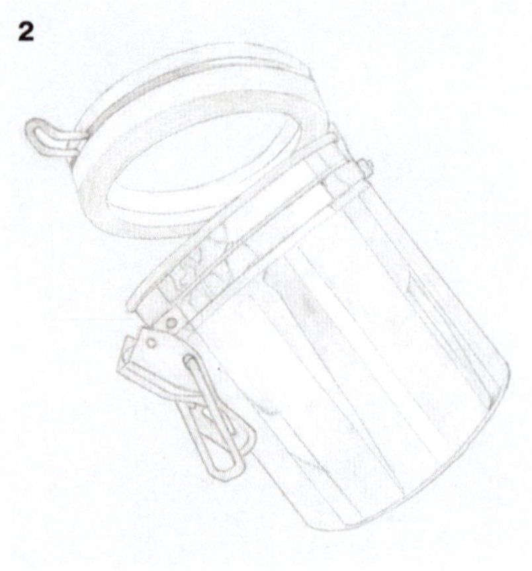

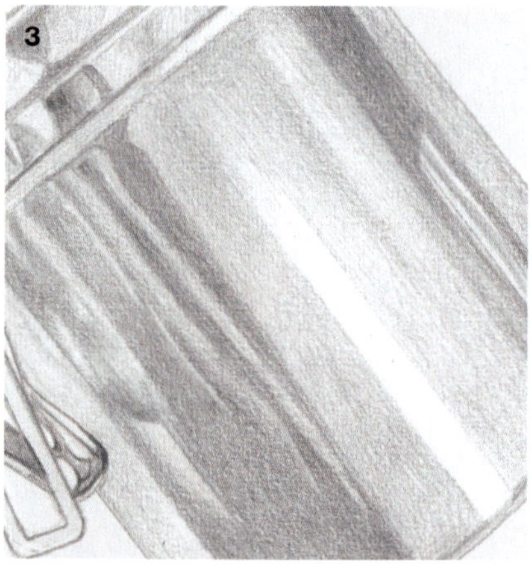

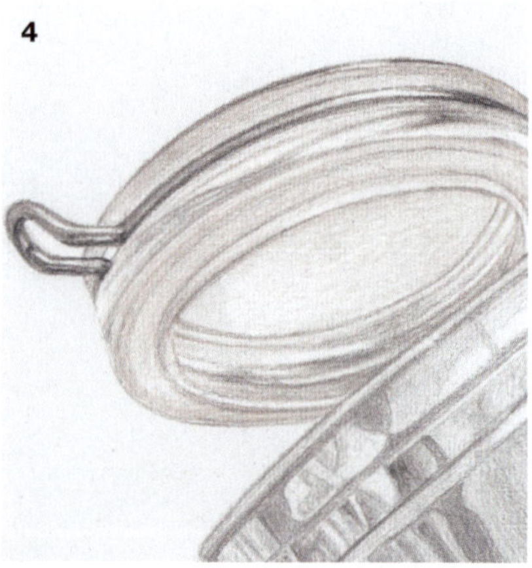

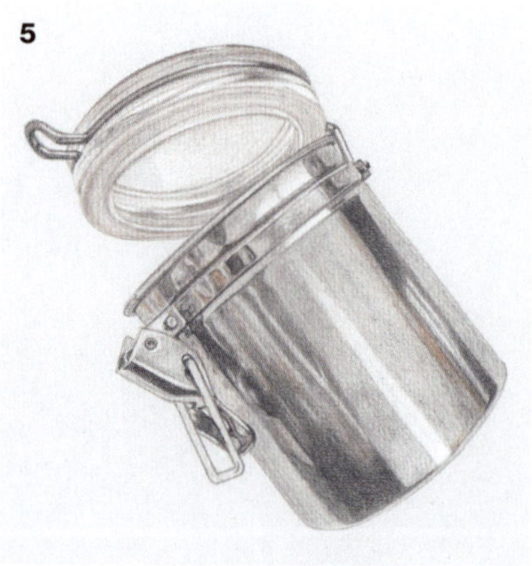

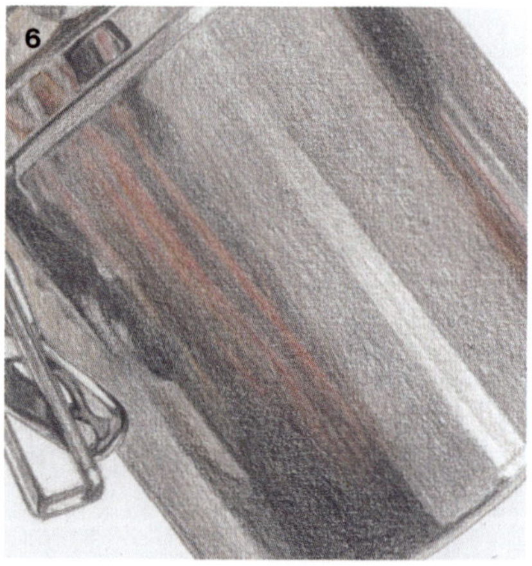

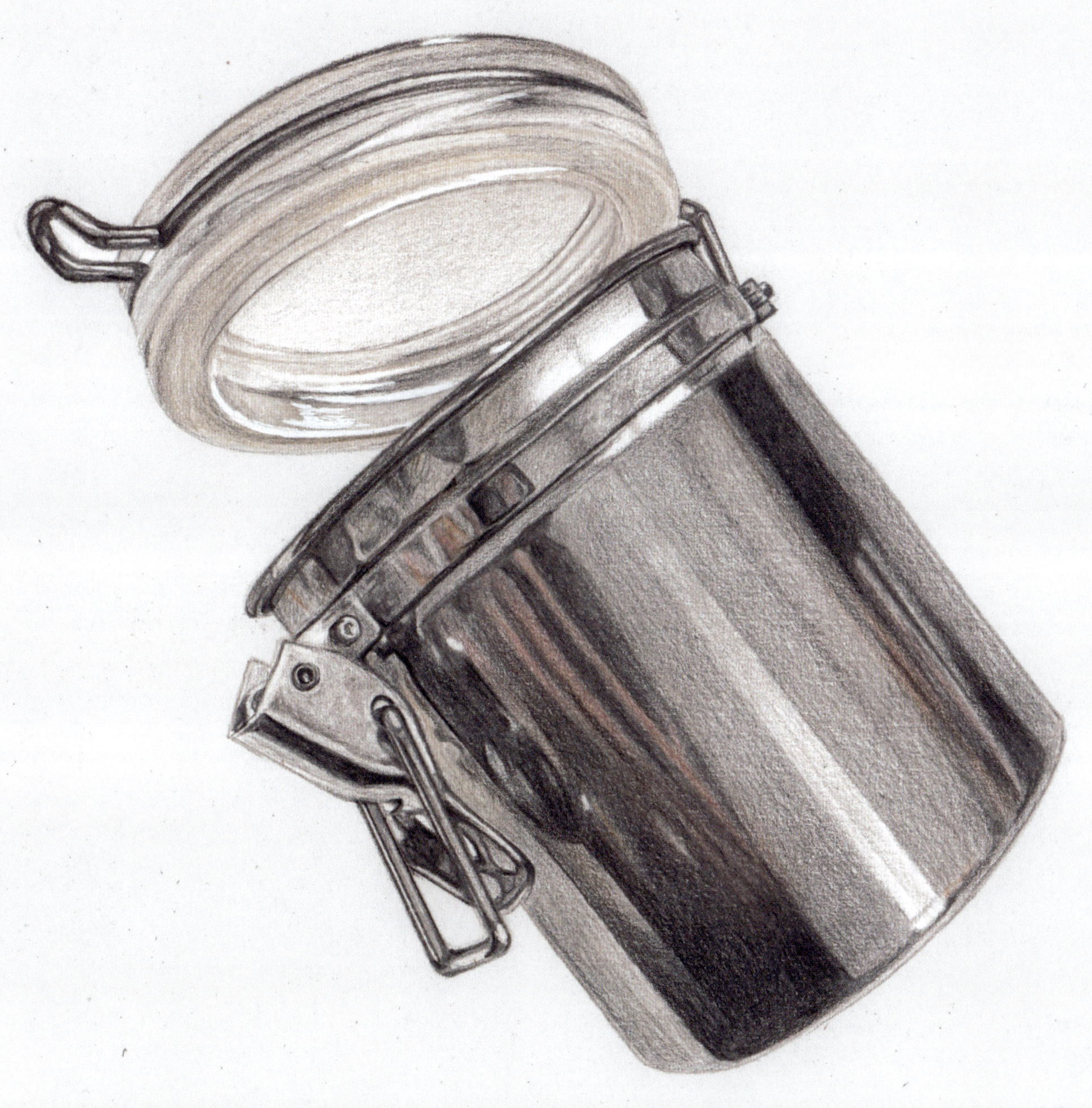

Resources

Artists are always encouraged to check out their local art stores in person to experience the look and feel of tools and materials. When choosing paper it is crucial to be able to feel the weight and see the grain in order to decide what's best for your project. Similarly, colors of pencils can appear different when you are viewing them on a screen, and you can often try out testers in-store. Staff can also be a great source of advice and help. The following key brands and major retailers are recommended, so check them out online, and look out for them in your local area.

Pencil brands
Derwent Art: derwentart.com
– Derwent Lightfast
– Derwent Coloursoft

Blick Studio: dickblick.com
– Artists' Colored Pencils and Sets

Caran d'Ache: carandache.com
– Caran d'Ache Luminance

Faber-Castell: faber-castell.com
– Faber-Castell Polychromos

Paper brands
Daler-Rowney: daler-rowney.com
Strathmore Artist Papers: strathmoreartist.com
Canson: en.canson.com

Art equipment suppliers
Artist & Craftsman Supply: artistcraftsman.com
Blick Art Materials: dickblick.com
Jerry's Artarama: jerrysartarama.com
Michaels: michaels.com